Ian McKellen

IAN McKELLEN

Joy Leslie Gibson

WEIDENFELD AND NICOLSON · LONDON

To My Mother

Published in Great Britain by
George Weidenfeld & Nicolson Limited
91 Clapham High Street
London SW4 7TA

This paperback edition published by
George Weidenfeld & Nicolson Limited 1990

ISBN 0 297 81056 1

Printed in Great Britain by
The Guernsey Press Co. Ltd, C.I.

Contents

Illustration Acknowledgments

The photographs in this book are reproduced by kind permission of the following:

Bolton School 1; *Central Productions Ltd* 6 above; *Joe Cocks* 3 below; *Donald Cooper* 4, 5, 6 below; *East Anglian Daily Times & Associated Papers* 2 above; *John Haynes* 7 below; *Stuart Morris* 8; *Prospect Productions Ltd* 2 below; *Syndication International* 7 above; *Weidenfeld Archive* 3 above.

Acknowledgments

I would like to thank the following for permission to quote from their books: John Barton, Trevor Nunn, Susan Hill, Sir Harold Hobson (and also for an encouraging letter), Sir Peter Hall and John Goodwin and their publishers Hamish Hamilton, Gerald Jacobs, and Chatto and Windus for permission to quote from *The Common Pursuit* by F. R. Leavis. The following newspapers have also given me permission to quote from them: *The Times* Group, The *Telegraph* Group, The *Guardian*, *The Financial Times*, The *Express* Group, The *Observer*, The *Independent*, The *New Statesman*, The *Coventry Evening Telegraph*, The *Bolton Evening News* (and my thanks to Leslie Gent, the editor for information), The *Stratford Herald*, The *East Anglian Times* Group, The *Watford Observer* and *Drama Magazine*. And to Emrys Bryson of The *Nottingham Post*, a very special thank you.

The following theatre archivists and PROs have been very helpful in delving into their archives for me: I am most grateful to The Belgrade Theatre (and for a super day with them), The Cambridge Theatre Company, The Forum Theatre, Billingham, The Palace Theatre, Watford, The Royal Court Theatre, The Hampstead Theatre, The Liverpool Playhouse, The Crucible Theatre, Sheffield, The Yvonne Arnaud Theatre, Guildford, The Playhouse, Nottingham and The Chichester Festival Theatre, The Royal Shakespeare Theatre, Sue Hyman, and also The National Theatre.

To the Bursar of St Catharine's College, James Wright, my thanks: To John Andrews and Dr Richard Bainbridge, thank you for information about McKellen's career as an undergraduate. To Mrs Dorothy Cooper of Bolton School, my grateful thanks for finding me notices and photographs of McKellen's performances at school, and to Mesnes School, formerly Wigan Grammar School, my thanks. To Mrs E. Parkinson, thank you for an informative letter and also to Iris Murdoch for writing.

To *The South Bank Show* and Capital Radio – thank you for allowing me to quote from scripts. And, as always, my gratitude to the Records Department at *Spotlight*.

To the Theatre Museum of the Victoria and Albert Museum, to the British Council, the librarians of North London Polytechnic, St Pancras, Kensington and Richmond, thank you. To Dr Levi Fox and his assistants at the Shakespeare Centre my gratitude is immense for their help and their beautifully kept cuttings books.

Above all my thanks have to go to the people who let me interview them: Bill Beresford, Robert Chetwyn, Elspeth Cochrane, Martin Connor, Richard Cottrell, Robert Eddison, Ronald Eyre, Clare Fox, Jill Fraser, Philip Grout, Sara Kestelman, Eddie Kulukundis, Jack Lynn (whose encyclopaedic knowledge of the theatre solved not a few problems), William MacDonald, Margery Mason, Trevor Peacock, Bob Peck, Tim Pigott-Smith, Toby Robertson, Clive Swift, Donald Torkell, Bridget Turner, Jennifer Tudor, Duncan Weldon and Irene Worth.

To David Roberts my editor at Weidenfeld and Nicolson – well, what can I say? David asked me to write this book on my birthday February 1985 – it was the best birthday present I had! So thank you, a big thank you. I hope you enjoy the book, it comes with my love and gratitude to you all.

Prologue

Winter 1977. Eddie Kulukundis and I are driving away from the National Film Theatre. We have just seen three films, one after another. My birthday treat. But I don't like films and the last one, a Western, was very boring. I am tired and fed up and I want to go straight home to Richmond. Eddie wants to eat. The atmosphere in the car is decidedly edgy. We stop at some traffic lights and a moped draws up alongside. The driver, helmeted, looks sinister. He taps on the window. 'Don't, don't,' I say, scared, as Eddie winds it down. 'Hello, Eddie.' It's a voice I recognize. 'Why it's McKellen,' says Eddie. Seeing me in the car, McKellen leans forward, gives me his beautiful smile and says, 'Hello'.

He and Eddie exchange a few sentences, the lights change and McKellen zooms off into the darkness. But the atmosphere in the car has altered. We have been touched by charisma.

'Being a great actor is nothing to do with being in an obscure place in an obscure town with your mates.'

> Dinsdale Landen in an interview
> with the author, 1978.

'... the first instinct of any actor, however great, is to be noble, upright, and charming to the audience.'

> Sir Peter Hall: *Diaries*

'The tragic experience, however it is to be defined, is certainly not anything that encourages, or permits, an indulgence in the dramatization of one's nobly-suffering self.'

> F. R. Leavis: *The Common Pursuit*

'I suppose you think acting is an art, don't you? It isn't even an art, it's just entertainment at its highest and prostitution at its lowest ... All you want to do is get your face in front of the public and yell, "Get me get me get me." '

Margaret Drabble: *The Garrick Year*

'In some ways he is a very private person.'

Tim Pigott-Smith in an interview
with the author, 1985.

I
Boyhood

There is one fact that everyone knows about Wigan: it has a pier. A lot of people also think that it is the birthplace of one of our most charismatic actors, Ian McKellen, for he is often called the 'Actor from Wigan'. But they are wrong, for Ian Murray McKellen was born in Burnley, Lancashire, on 25 May 1939. His father was Denis Murray McKellen, a borough engineer whose wife was Margery Sutcliffe. There was already a sister for Ian called Jean. But it was not long before the family moved to Wigan and it was there that Ian attended the Methodist School.[1]

The family used to go to church and Ian's maternal grandfather was a non-conformist minister, while the McKellen grandfather was a lay preacher who had a compelling presence and made 'large gestures from the shoulder like an actor'.[2] It was at a carol service that McKellen made his first public appearance, reading the Nativity story. The school also had a team which used to recite in non-conformist churches and McKellen was a member of it.[3]

The family was not rich, but circumstances were much above average. They lived in a four-bedroomed semi which was between the grim middle of the town and the green belt suburbs, in a road called Parson's Walk.[4] His father, 'a lovely man',[5] was a Socialist and both parents voted Labour, but the family were firmly middle-class, his father earning around £1,000 in 1949,[6] this at a time when the average wage for a male manual worker was around £7.10s.

It was war-time and the industrial north was busily producing arms, steel and coal. It was a fairly prosperous time for Lancashire but schoolboys and schoolgirls, unless they were directly enduring air-raids or evacuation, and neither seemed to touch the young McKellen, were pre-occupied as always with examinations, schoolwork, hobbies and their immediate surroundings. Everyone spoke in the flat tones of the region and traces of Lancashire can still be found in McKellen's voice today, adding a distinctive quality to it, though he is not an actor who is good at accents, nor can he successfully disguise his beautifully inflected voice. Although none of the family was a professional actor there was a great interest in the theatre; cinemas were visited and so was the local rep run by Frank H. Fortescue, an extraordinary man who kept theatre alive in the provinces. There was the library and on summer Sundays there was a brass band in the park and cricket, that game that makes all Englishmen equal, and McKellen scored for the second eleven local team. He went to Sunday School and in 1944 the family had some evacuees billeted on them.[8] Of course, the usual privations were felt: food rationing, few sweets, shortage of clothes, but the family was hospitable. After the war they entertained a German soldier for Christmas, and other German friends from before the war came to see his father. Then there were visiting actors who came on tour and the fair, whose skilful and cheerful hands captivated McKellen, as did the man who sold patent medicines, charms, sweets and all sorts of things in the market. McKellen identified this as street theatre from an early age, and thus set one of the patterns discernible in his work; the relation between a classic text and today's preoccupations, a theme that was to be intensified at Cambridge. McKellen was bright at school and passed to go to Wigan Grammar School, also in Parson's Walk, but he was there for less than a year when his father was appointed Borough Engineer of Bolton and McKellen was transferred to Bolton School in July 1951.[9] If chance shapes our destinies, then this was one which determined the direction of McKellen's career.

Bolton School was, and is, one of those good old-fashioned grammar schools which used to abound in this country. There is a school crest, and although academic standards are high the boys are encouraged to pursue interests outside the curriculum. There are Scouts and a number of societies – Literary, and Debating, Geographical, Railway – which are under the supervision of a master but run by the boys. In McKellen's days there was a great interest in acting and there was a Sixth Form Camp to Stratford-upon-Avon each year.

But soon after the family had moved to Bolton, when Ian was thirteen, his mother died.[10] It was deep and tragic experience for him. His father married again and Ian had a good relationship with Gladys, his step-mother.[11] He was generally liked at school. Mrs E. Parkinson writes, 'I worked as a waitress in the boys' dining-room and I served him his dinner many times when he was on one of my tables. On one occasion he showed me a photo of a girl he was friendly with at that time. He was always a likeable lad.'[12]

Later on McKellen was to say that at Bolton School it was achievement that was regarded as estimable, but that it didn't matter at what. To be a Queen's Scout, captain of a team or to play a leading part in a play was considered of equal prestige. And besides excellence the school encouraged leadership and self-sufficiency. McKellen took advantage of this situation and became one of the leading actors in the school.[13]

'I don't remember him before he was fourteen,' Donald Torkell told me,[14] 'but then I was two or three years older than he was and so wouldn't have had much to do with him. But he was probably in the Middle School play before then. The Seniors generally did a Shakespeare play every year and the Middle School also did plays.'

'I watched him on quite a few occasions,' writes Mrs Parkinson, 'as we used to be allowed in to see the school plays. I remember seeing him in *Julius Caesar* and he was a good actor even then.'[15] Indeed he was – or at least the school magazine thought so.

In 1953 he played Margaret in *Friar Bacon and Friar Bungay*; three years later he progressed to Prince Hal and the following year Henry v. One boy said to another, 'Well, what did you think of it?' to receive the reply, 'better than last year', and indeed so the reviewer thought, too. Commenting on Ian's performance in the school magazine, he wrote:

There was, of course, an outstanding performance. Prince Hal and I. M. McKellen seem to have matured together, *pari passu*. In the part of Henry, McKellen amply fulfilled our expectations. His conviction and poise, timing, modulation, gesture and demeanour were rarely at fault. If the pointing of some lines appeared rather odd, let me not cavil: his originality was like a breath of fresh air. Youthfully, majestic, he always dominated the stage.[16]

The notice already seemed to bear many of the hall-marks of a McKellen performance today.

But this, of course, was not the first time that McKellen had appeared on the boards. He showed Kenneth Easthough of the *Daily Mirror*[17] a scrap-book in which *My First World Premier* was noted – it was a play by two schoolmasters in which he had appeared in 1952 as a girl called Rosie Meadows! However, his parts were now very serious for the next year he appeared as the Father Provincial in that difficult play *The Strong Are Lonely* by Fritz Hochwalder. Again the School Magazine was laudatory:

A heavy burden of responsibility fell on I. M. McKellen, who played the part of Alfonso Fernandez, Father Provincial of the Jesuits: his almost continuous presence on the stage emphasized the essential unity of the action, and he tackled an extremely difficult role with an astonishing degree of maturity. For a young man to play the part of an old one is in itself not an easy assignment;

and McKellen gave a thoughtful and rounded performance, complete in every gesture and movement. He was particularly good in the scene where he pleaded with Lorenzo Querini, the emissary of the Father General, and outstanding in his ability to convey eventual despair. The purely material reasons given by the two Indians, Candia and Naguaca, for their desire to be baptized implied the complete failure of the Jesuit mission. Alfonso Fernandez's moment of bitter realization, the philosophical climax of the play, was most memorable. McKellen was less convincing in his deathbed scene and sounded less sincere – appearance no doubt belying reality, but after all, in the theatre they are not the same thing.[18]

And acting in the school play was not the only acting that McKellen did. Two of the masters, one of them the Latin Master, George Sawtell, took over an old house near the school and turned it into a small theatre, called the Hopefield Miniature Theatre where the stage-struck boys used to go during lunch breaks and in the evenings and holidays, acting, writing and directing plays, building scenery and making props.[19] It became something like a weekly rep company. He also acted with the Bolton Little Theatre in the junior group and later with the seniors in *Twelfth Night*.[20]

It was at Bolton School, too, that he learnt to speak without his Lancastrian accent. As he said in the *Sunday Times Magazine*, 19 January 1986, 'A starting point for anyone born and brought up in South Lancashire and acts ... is what to do with the accent which God and the environment and your parents have landed you with. I can well remember one of my parents boasting on my behalf to a friend that, "Ian had two accents: one that he used at school and one that he used at home, and I remember thinking how clever Ian was to be able to sound differently in different situations."

'I didn't have my accent "taken out", which is how one friend in Bolton put it. He's had his accent "taken out" as if it were some useless thing like an appendix.'

But I. M. McKellen was not giving all his time to acting, he played an active part in two school societies. In 1957 he was Secretary of the Geographical Society and notices of the Society's activities appeared in the school magazine, *The Boltonian*, under the initials I.M.M. Another society in which he was evidently a leading light was the Literary and Debating Society and again he held the office of Secretary. The reports, also appearing under the initials I.M.M., and presumably McKellen's, are amusing in a schoolboy way. On one occasion he wrote:

'The following week, four maiden speakers – J. Potter and M. Greenhalgh, J.E.M. Owen and D.H. Lowe – competently introduced the motion "That this House is more interested in the past than the future". The most notable feature of the debate was the array of quotations on display. The proposer of the motion treated us to an extract from *Henry IV* (the part was unspecified); the fourth speaker then quoted, with a charming nonchalance, Burke, the New Testament and an unnamed Latin author; whilst the Secretary, never to be outshone, added Marlowe to the list.'[21]

McKellen was also prominent in the annual joint debate with the Girls' Division (School) on the motion, 'This House considers that the emancipation of women has led to the enslavement of men'. Together with Susan Parry, McKellen 'violently opposed' the motion and 'although unfairly accused of irrelevance' the opposing pair 'successfully seized the motion by 129 votes to seven, with twelve abstainers'.[22]

In 1958, McKellen showed his increasing involvement with serious theatre by giving a paper on Samuel Beckett. According to the school magazine, 'He described Beckett's writings and their features with the chief emphasis on the plays *Waiting for Godot, All That Fall* and *Endgame*. The speaker distinguished the graduations of pessimism in the plays, praising the perception of the oppressiveness of daily life – "Nothing happens, nobody comes, nobody goes" – but condemning the cynicism behind Beckett's facile pessimism, his mockery of prayer, or the idea of virtue. The growth of pessimism in each successive work was shown, and the view expressed that for Beckett the tragedy of existence is not death, but life. The greater the despair, the less becomes the dignity of man. The intensity of human relationships in Beckett's works was emphasized, such as Gogo and Didi in *Godot,* the Rooneys in *All That Fall* and Hamm and Clov in *Endgame*. McKellen held everyone's attention with his treatment of the plays and his compelling selection of quotations. His obvious interest in his subject undoubtedly stimulated his audience into a desire to know more about this remarkable Irish–French playwright.'[23]

The following meeting was given over to a reading of a reading. The play being *Malvolio,* a sequel to *Twelfth Night* by Stephen Williams, in which McKellen played the eponymous hero, now a keeper of an apothecary's shop.[24]

But school was not the only place where McKellen was enjoying plays. He used to go to the Grand Theatre in Bolton where his father knew the owner. He would watch, often from the wings, music-hall performers of the calibre of Jewel and Warris, Suzette Tarri and Jimmy James.[25,26] 'There, silent and ignored among the dust, I marvelled as the comics and magicians, the chorus girls and the acrobats, disguised their grinding hard work as glamour on stage. Their sweat shone like stardust, I despaired only that I should ever know enough to shine like them,' he was to write years later.[27] He would also go to the local rep and, of course, there was the annual School Camp to Stratford each year.

In 1956, the first year that he was a sixth former, McKellen wrote in *The Boltonian*:

To contradict the guide-books, disillusion the Americans, and state the obvious, every wall in Stratford-upon-Avon is not half-timbered, nor is every roof thatched. The people there have modern lives to live and earnings to gain. Thus the large cattle market meets weekly, attracting farmers from the neighbouring slopes of the smooth Cotswolds. The gas works and the general hospital stand as huge Victorian sentinels of the tiny railway station. A cinema and fish-and-chip shop (bar or saloon) are nearby. The latest addition to these giant anachronisms is an 'American Coffee Bar' for the Stratford townsfolk (returning, possibly, their compliment of 'English Tea-rooms' for the American visitors!).

It was in this colourful establishment that some Bolton Schoolboys were to be seen and heard on the wetter days of one week last July. They were members of the annual Stratford Camp for Sixth Formers, sited as usual in a grassy meadow bordering the Avon.

This year the camp of about twenty boys was led by Mr W. E. Brown and Mr A. Birch. The four plays we were to see at the Shakespeare Memorial Theatre were *Hamlet, Othello, The Merchant of Venice* and *Love's Labour's Lost*. Whilst few were entirely satisfied with these productions we are all grateful to the organizers of the camp for allowing us the opportunity of seeing them. Our thanks are also extended to Sergeant Best, who cooked the meals.

Much, indeed too much, has been written about Stratford. Some have referred to 'the Shrine'; sentimentalists to the 'Heart of England'; and (most amusing of all) that American, Calvin Hoffman, has talked of 'enemy territory'! To the Bolton School campers who annually take advantage of its hospitality, Stratford has become a synonym for enjoyment. After the stickiness of the examination room comes the fresh air; 'green papers' become the green leaves of the Warwickshire countryside; and, more important, the Shakespeare of set books comes alive in the mouths of the actors of the Memorial Theatre.[28]

The following year, though, the report was much more succinct:

The annual Senior Stratford Camp was held this year two months later than usual. The party of twenty-seven, led by Mr Sawtell and Mr Greene, was thus able to see performances of all the Memorial Theatre's repertoire: *The Tempest, As You Like It, Julius Caesar, King John* and *Cymbeline*. Sergeant Best cooked most expertly.[29]

It was not, of course, McKellen's first experience of seeing Shake-speare. Lancashire was particularly lucky in theatre productions. Indeed, Burnley had been the headquarters of the Old Vic Touring Company during the War, and the Stratford Company also used to tour there. 'I saw marvellous touring companies when I was young – they came to Manchester and Liverpool, both within easy distance from Bolton. There were productions that were coming and going from the West End. I saw an awful lot of theatre ...'[30]

He remembers seeing Sir John Gielgud as King Lear, and because a woman in front of him giggled at the mad scene, the young McKellen hit her hat.[31] He saw Olivier's fabled 1955 season: *Twelfth Night*, with Olivier as Malvolio; the renowned and much acclaimed *Macbeth*[32]; Peggy Ashcroft as Imogen and Rosalind; later on Peter O'Toole as Shylock, and Paul Robeson's third Othello 'blundering and bellowing like a wounded elephant'.[33] And he met the stars, too. In 1957 he approached Alec Clunes, who was playing Caliban in *The Tempest,* for his autograph and was interested to note that the actor shrugged off McKellen's praise with a profanity about his hot rubber suit! He was thrilled when Peggy Ashcroft walked by the queue for tickets and he saw her Imogen at both the matinée and evening performances on 4 August 1957, a tribute that he was also to pay the production of *Coriolanus.* What charmed him about Ashcroft's performance, was the youthfulness, the warmth and generosity which she portrayed. In fact, he says that the emotion on perceiving her great acting was akin to falling in love. He noted how her voice soared, yet was perfectly controlled, the way she stood, the way her hands moved. And measured by her skill he felt the inadequacy of his own stumbling efforts.

The boys, mostly standing at the back of the theatre, were not, however, allowed to watch the plays without making some critical appraisal of both play and acting. Indeed, the camp fire, with the excellent food provided by the school janitor, Sergeant Best (so cour-teously thanked in the school magazine), was surrounded by boys making judgements and assessments, and not much escaped the sharp eyes of McKellen.

He writes of the exciting moments that have remained in his memory: of the flirtatious Alan Badel who, as Berowne, seductively threw a rose into the audience after his soliloquy – a romantic but narcissistic gesture, of Max Adrian as Feste with his habitual air of cynicism which was somehow ingratiating as he appealed to the audience by flinging out his arms at the end of *Twelfth Night;* he loved the flamboyance of Olivier and the danger of that tremendous fall from the archway at the end, when Olivier hung upside-down, held – but only just – by another actor holding on to his ankles. Olivier again, this time as Macbeth, hands behind him, earnestly plotting with the murderers but in a brisk way. And the magic of Gielgud's noble Prospero, the civilized High Renaissance Prince, restored to power, his blue costume filling the stage with a magical, translucent glow.[34]

These are interesting memories, ones which reflect many of the qualities which are found in McKellen's own acting, the extravagant danger of his playing: the memorable gestures – the over-flowing, flamboyant range of his acting which somehow is always ingratiating, yet at the same time you feel that the charm could be cynically thrown away. The words we use to praise are often indicative of those qualities which we also possess.

One thing, though, he did find disconcerting, as indeed all young people do, and that was how much older the actors were than the characters they were playing! But actors are chameleons, and as Edith Evans used to say, 'I think myself beautiful', so if they are any good at all, actors can think themselves, as indeed McKellen does, into any age, any type of looks, any period that they wish.

Stratford proved an education in other ways as well, for the boys were allowed to bike over the surrounding countryside and visit places that were renowned for their beauty and historic charm. They watched the company play a sort of game of cricket, too, Peggy Ashcroft refusing to acknowledge that she had been caught: Glen Byam Shaw, the director, fielding from a deck chair, Alec Clunes batting left-handed. The scorer of the local cricket team must have been amused![35]

All this time, McKellen was learning to assess and judge, to work out how an effect had been made: what exactly was exciting, what had failed to excite. And how the show was directed, and why. When he returned again to Bolton the local repertory were assessed with his new-found knowledge and McKellen would mark his programme each week assessing the capabilities of the cast, giving them marks out of ten.[36]

Though he was so wrapped up in the theatre other things were not suffering. He became Head Boy of the School, and doubtless this experience helped him to develop the qualities that made him such an outstanding leader of companies later on. 'People always used to ask me what I wanted to be when I grew up ... I said an actor and they always laughed. I laughed with them because I never thought of it as a serious ambition.'[37] He may be sincere in saying that but there is a curious quality in McKellen, that of not always knowing what he is capable of, of denying that the next difficult step is the one he really

wants to make, and is capable of making. He publicly hangs back, and
many times in his life he has expressed a contentment with what he has,
only to reach out later and take something he has always denied wanting.
It is a caution that seems to underlie his life, or perhaps just the disguising
of what he really wants under a diffident exterior. He can be disarmingly
modest and so, perhaps, it was modesty that made him laugh when he
was introduced as, 'This is Ian, he wants to be an actor'. About this
time, when he was seventeen, he appeared in a Granada TV programme
Youth Wants to Know as one of a group of young people asking
questions of Randolph Churchill.[38]

He did think of other occupations – he wondered about being a
journalist. During his schooldays he contributed to the *Bolton Evening
News*. Alas, the lineage books for that time are no longer available so
it has been impossible to trace the contributions that McKellen made
to 'Topics of the Day' but he claims 'they were about things like the
leaves coming out on the common and in the park, that sort of thing,'
and he remembers that it brought him in 7s 6d a time. He was sufficiently
interested in writing (and, indeed, today he writes in a way to make
most journalists turn green with envy) that he asked the then Editor of
the *Bolton Evening News*, Frank Singleton, whether he could be a
journalist. 'He told me that he got as many requests for jobs in a week
that he could fill in a year, so I realized that journalism wasn't that easy
to get into.'[39]

The other career he considered was being a chef. He is very interested
in food. 'He is a wonderful cook, a really wonderful one,' says actress
Sara Kestelman. 'He makes *the* most wonderful desserts, really mouth-
watering. And he is a great licker of plates, indeed he believes that
plates *ought* to be licked.'[40] He remembers, too, with evident enjoyment his mother's Parkin and the fact that she used to bake twice a
week, and that in the war, when sweets were scarce his father used to
bring home Horlicks tablets from the ARP post.[41] Academically he
was doing well, too. He won an exhibition at St Catharine's College,
Cambridge (which is also Sir Peter Hall's old college, though he
preceded McKellen by about nine years) to read English, and thought
vaguely about teaching[42] – yet another career possibility. Bolton School
had, though, done well by McKellen. It had instilled in him a love
of good acting; a chance to try out what he had imbibed from seeing
it on the stage, and he had appeared in many plays and in leading parts;
it had given him also a good academic background. He acknowledges
his debts to it, and particularly to George Sawtell, the Latin Master
who was also responsible for drama in the school. The school

had shaped the boy, and Cambridge was to work her magic, as it so often does, on these beginnings. For Cambridge was alive with drama.

2
Cambridge

In 1958 Cambridge had returned to herself again. During the war she had been host to London University: afterwards she had been filled with mature men, returned from the wars, and then men had come up after doing National Service, wiser and more experienced than the young pre-war undergraduates. But the McKellen generation were all coming directly from school, and were aiming at having fun as well as working. It is now a legendary generation, all set to win the glittering prizes, which most of them have now attained. And McKellen has added to that legend. The way he got into St Catharine's is, indeed, itself one of the Cambridge legends. He was being interviewed by Brigadier Henn, himself a Yeats scholar and a theatre-lover, who would ask candidates to read some poetry to him, believing that this showed a young man's sensitivity to words. He asked McKellen to read something.[1] Leaping on to a chair, McKellen recited, 'Once more unto the breach dear friends' from the *Henry v* he had just played at Bolton School. The Brigadier must have been impressed for McKellen became an Exhibitioner.[2]

Also up at that time were Corin Redgrave; Derek Jacobi, already famous for he had given a remarkable performance in Marlowe's *Edward II* directed by Toby Robertson, himself a Cambridge man; Clive Swift, another leading Cambridge actor; and Margaret Drabble, brilliant both as a scholar and an actress. Eleanor Bron was to follow, as was Trevor Nunn, and director Richard Cottrell was acting, directing and writing plays. David Frost was pontificating, Joe Melia, John Bird and Peter Cook were writing sketches for revues and light entertainments. There were many drama societies – the prestigious Marlowe Society, the ADC (the Amateur Dramatic Club, which had its own little theatre), the Cambridge Mummers, The Fletcher Society, the Dryden Society – as well as college dramatic societies and, of course, Footlights.

However, the more serious actors did not concern themselves with Footlights, 'Footlights does revue. There were many other outlets for an actor,' McKellen says, 'I would love to have been part of Footlights, but it was all *so* professional. Peter Cook had two revues on in London when he was an undergraduate. David Frost was already working as an interviewer for Anglia Television.'[3]

'We never stopped acting,' says Clive Swift. 'Very few of us ever did much work, though we had no idea that we would really take it up professionally. I didn't at least, though I don't know about Ian. He was always rather quiet about himself. But we had the greatest fun. It was all centred on ADC with the Marlowe play each year, of course.'[4]

Eleanor Bron thought it all a bit too much. In *My Cambridge* she writes, 'I did not even bother to audition for the ADC because I found the ambiance over-intense and self-conscious, and joined the Mummers ... which was not quite so serious, and less exclusive, with a membership drawn, to its advantage, from Town as well as Gown ... It was clear that very many of these [actors and directors] would become professionals because they were so good at it and so dedicated.'[5]

'But we really had no idea that we would be professionals,' emphasizes Swift, 'except perhaps for Corin Redgrave, I certainly didn't. But because of not working, and acting so much, one was really left with nothing else to do! In my case, in 1960 I was offered a contract with the RSC and thought I might as well take it.'[6]

But it was not all just undergraduate fun – Eleanor Bron was right, the ADC was very professional, and there were three older men who greatly influenced them, and who might justly claim to have cultivated and influenced the whole of English Theatre through the young men and women who came under their tutelage in their Cambridge years. They are George Rylands, John Barton and F. R. Leavis, whose seminars McKellen attended.[7]

George Rylands, a Fellow of King's College, has devoted much of his life to teaching young would-be actors the clear speaking of Shakespeare's lines. An excellent actor himself, he passionately believes in the spoken word and that Shakespeare should, or rather can only, be realized in performance. It was he who taught McKellen to respect the written word and the sound of it. He is also a notable director, and among his most prestigious achievements during the late fifties and early sixties, has been the recording of all Shakespeare's plays on disc. Looking through the prospectus one sees a mingling of names – dons like George Rylands, Donald Beves and Dr Richard Bainbridge, the present Secretary of the Marlowe Society: professional actors like Robert Eddison, and the 'stars' of the undergraduate actors. Derek Jacobi playing half-a-dozen leads, Corin Redgrave, also prominent, Clive Swift and Ian McKellen playing Lysander in *A Midsummer Night's Dream* and First Gentleman in *The Winter's Tale*.

The second influence was F. R. Leavis, that extraordinary teacher to whom so many Cambridge actors and directors, writers and teachers owe so much. In his *Diaries*, Sir Peter Hall quotes from a piece about himself which first appeared in *Time*:

By the time he finished Cambridge, Hall had already directed several plays and, perhaps more significant, had studied English under F. R. Leavis. Even though Leavis hated theatre, he made a lasting impact on Hall with his scrupulous examination of a text, particularly for its ironies and ambiguities and the sense that a work of art should be placed in a social context ... Hall clearly believes that to immerse an audience unforgettably in a play, the cast and director must locate and pinpoint the vital element that T. S. Eliot once called 'the present moment of the past'.[8]

Hall later claims:

... I never actually met him, but I went to his lectures. They were the inspiration of my Cambridge years. He somehow inculcated a feeling that art was to do with better standards of life and better behaviour. The paradox is that all we students pretended we sped to his lectures to imbibe his humanism. In fact, we were enjoying his character assassinations. Strange that a great moralist could be so destructive about creative artists.

All the textual seriousness at the basis of Trevor's [Nunn] work and mine comes from Leavis, and there is a vast band of us. Comical to think that Leavis hated the theatre and never went to it. He has had more influence on the contemporary theatre than any other critic.[9]

Leavis's own attitude to Shakespeare can be summed up by a passage he wrote in *The Common Pursuit*. These lectures were published in 1952: written a few years before McKellen went up:

We know that poetic drama is something more than drama in verse, and that consideration of the drama cannot be separated from consideration of the poetry. We are aware of subtle varieties of possibility under the head of convention, and we know we must keep a vigilant eye open for the development of theme by imagery and symbolism, and for the bearing of all these on the way we are to take character, action and plot. Shakespeare's methods are so subtle, flexible and varied that we must be on our guard against approaching any play with inappropriate preconceptions as to what we have in front of us. By assuming that the organization is of a given kind we may incapacitate ourselves for seeing what it actually is, and so miss, or misread, the significance.'[10]

It is interesting to compare this paragraph with comments made by McKellen in an RSC Workshop Programme presented by London Weekend Television as a *South Bank Show* on 16 December 1979. 'If this workshop's done anything, I hope it's scotched the, in my view, wrong belief that Shakespeare's verse is music and all you have to do is find out the tune and everything will be all right. Rather, I believe that if you look after the sense the sounds will look after themselves ... You have to think and have analysed in rehearsal totally so that your imagination, being fed by the concrete metaphors, concrete images and pictures, can then be fed through into the body, into gesture, into timbre of voice, into eyelids, into every part of the actor's make-up, so that it does seem – as Trevor [Nunn] has just said, that he is making it up as he goes along, although the actor, of course, knows that he isn't.'[11]

Those words seem to express much of what we find amazing in a McKellen performance, the surprise of hearing even a well-known text rendered in a completely original way. Of course, every actor and director working together gives a different interpretation of a text, but McKellen's seem to have some extra authority, some extra scrupulousness, which can come only from a trained mind, a textually trained mind, working on a work of art, to produce another. He himself has written that Cambridge taught him a respect for a text. That respect and searching of a text is something that he has transferred into rehearsing and playing a part; that and the playwright should have the first and foremost place in the theatre.[12] What Leavis gave to his students was, in the words of John Andrew, Senior Tutor at St Catharine's, 'a commitment to the intellectual and moral bias of the text'.[13]

The third man who was the most influential of all was John Barton. 'He Eminence Gris'd us all,' says Swift. 'He directed many plays during our time there and his advice on what parts we should play was always right. He would tell us not to play certain parts but to try for others.'[14]

Trevor Nunn has written a wonderful description of the man who was to become a trusted and valued colleague as a Director of the Royal Shakespeare Company:

The young man with the Renaissance face was John Barton. I had heard of him, of course, but there on the stage of the Arts Theatre, Cambridge, directing a battle scene for a Marlowe Society production, was the man himself, with tapered trousers and bulky cardigan, giving him a seventeenth-century silhouette confirmed by a noble beard, high forehead, an expression in the eyes both haught and hawk and rich brown crinkled hair. He was Essex or Raleigh – dashing, formidable and in bursts of energy, like a whirlwind. My mental picture of my first sighting of John Barton betrays something of the impressionable eighteen-year-old student I was, and something of the need eighteen-year-old students have for legends, and larger than life heroes and enemies. In 1959 John was a Cambridge legend; he had directed countless university productions to professionally high standards, he had become a young and romantic don as the Lay Dean of Kings; with the Elizabethan Theatre Company he had pioneered small-cast, touring Shakespeare productions; and he had been invited to become a founder director of the Royal Shakespeare Company in Stratford-upon-Avon. None of that of course contributed much to the legend – no it was the fact that he chewed razor blades for fun, that he knew every line of the First Folio by heart, that he spoke Chaucer's English, that he was a brilliant and extremely dangerous sword fighter, that he was hilariously absent-minded, obsessed with cricket, a chain-smoker, an expert on Napoleon and somebody who enjoyed working sixteen hours a day without a break.[15]

Barton, too, is a great holder of the belief that you must examine the text with a new eye, without any preconceived conditions. In a rare interview he said, 'I was and am interested in textual and bibliographical scholarship – how Shakespeare's texts came to be what they are – and what went on, on the Elizabethan stage; but that's more like being an archaeologist or a detective – it's not literary at all.' He has a ruthless concentration centred entirely on the play and the actors with which he is working. As a director he has the reputation of being firm, but will listen to what an actor says and if the actor feels very strongly about something, Barton will give way because he believes he can't make an actor do something he doesn't feel.[16] John Andrew says that Tom Henn also had a great influence on McKellen. Whereas Leavis stressed the intellectual basis of the text, Henn stressed the central emotional meaning. He also communicated the idea that literature was a fitting life study. He inspired his pupils.[17]

Although ADC was the busiest drama group – 'more like a rep company than anything,' says Swift – the Marlowe Society was the most prestigious drama group whose productions were shown in the Arts Theatre, Cambridge, went on tour and, sometimes had a London transfer (as did some of the ADC productions). The Marlowe Society's present Secretary Dr Bainbridge, a senior member of the University, says that it is run by 'a largely self-perpetuating committee'[18] of both senior and junior members of the University. Its plays are directed by a professional director. A number of directors are approached each year, and one is selected by the undergraduate president and members of the committee. Rehearsals and performances take place in the Lent term.

When McKellen went up, the previous year's play had been *Edward II*, with Derek Jacobi, the first performance, as far as is known, since Marlowe's day. But for McKellen's first year, the chosen play was to be the two parts of *Henry IV*. Ian, along with about a hundred other Cambridge actors from all the societies went for an audition. He was chosen to be Mr Justice Shallow!

The dichotomy in McKellen's character shows very clearly in his reminiscences about Cambridge. On the one hand he is very confident and speaks about knowing a great deal about acting when he went up. 'I knew more about upstaging and the techniques of acting at fourteen than many of the people I now work with do,' and again, 'I had more experience of acting than even Corin Redgrave,'[19] Then again the diffidence takes over, 'I was rather proud and pleased with myself that I knew how to do it; what I was hopeless at was stepping on to the stage without any aids and just behaving in the style of the play as myself.'[20] Again he stresses his dependence on playing a character when he wrote, 'In character roles, made-up in crêpe hair and padding as Toby Belch, all was promising. But as an unadorned juvenile, as Posthumus Leonatus or as Turgenev's Beliayev, my youth was self-conscious, embarrassed and embarrassing [although Richard Cotterell says the performance was very good].[21] Imitation, mimicry and caricature were insufficient. Prepared to labour as hard as any pro, I did not know how to release and reveal my inner life. My acting was all gestures and no heart.'[22]

Clive Swift implies that Ian was hard to get to know, very quiet about himself. 'He seemed to have no girlfriends, and if he talked about his family, I seemed to remember that it was in a jokey way.' Then he added, 'You know, none of us would have thought that, of all of us, Ian would be the one to have become the great actor he has. A star. Not then – he was the reticent one.'[23]

But even if his contemporaries did not make the right prognosis, other people were more discerning. Writing in the *News Chronicle*, Alan Dent said:

Infinitely the best performance though, is that of Justice Shallow who is genuinely ancient, wheezy, full of sudden changes and chortles and sadnesses ... This Shallow's sighs are half-chuckles and his giggles are melancholy ... The young actor not only plays the mad old gentleman quite brilliantly – he also shows himself a master of make-up, which is the rarest thing in amateurs ... The Marlowe Society persists in its policy of not naming its actors. But one would like to know the name of this Shallow because it might obviously become a name to remember.

The sub-editor picked up this remark and headlined the piece HERE'S A BRILLIANT JUSTICE – BUT WHO IS HE?[24]

W. A. Darlington in the *Telegraph* also noted McKellen's performance but more critically:[25]

'Justice Shallow is another excellent easy performance, and though I thought the Gloucestershire scenes were played too slowly he never allowed them to drag or to lose point.'

It was these notices that made Richard Cottrell stop McKellen outside the stage door of the Arts Theatre in 1959 and congratulate him on the notice. 'Richard said that would be very very useful in getting my first job. Until then I hadn't thought I was good enough to be an actor. But at that exact moment I suddenly realized it was where I was heading.'[26]

'I remember the first time I saw Ian very vividly,' Richard Cottrell said animatedly. 'It was in an excerpt from *The Apple Cart*. He played King Magnus and was all wrong – gangly, awkward, his voice whistly. But I thought, "He's special."'[27]

When Trevor Nunn arrived in the autumn, people were still talking about McKellen's genius in the Justice Shallow part. The next year, McKellen was also chosen to be in the Marlowe Society production of *Dr Faustus* – again a character part, as a very, very old Pope, which was directed by Michael Bakewell, but although the production got excellent notices in the national press McKellen's part was really too insignificant for it to be noticed. But it is noteworthy for two things - Trevor Nunn played the Pope's Acolyte and the play toured, appearing at the Lyric, Hammersmith, and also in the open air at Stratford (McKellen's first performance in that town).[28]

In 1960 McKellen also appeared in *Cymbeline*, the play which he had seen in Stratford when Peggy Ashcroft's performance had so overwhelmed him. He was Posthumus, a part which, as we have seen, he was not too happy about. But he was, perhaps, being a little too self-critical, for *The Times* wrote:

'Posthumus, though less accomplished than Iachimo, more successfully overcame the limitations of the production. Since he seemed to care only for speaking Shakespeare's words, we listened with more relaxation to the words spoken by him.'[29]

The following year – the 1960–61 season – McKellen was elected President of the Marlowe Society and the Society gave the first two parts of *Henry VI*.[30] But the repertoire was not all Shakespeare and Marlowe. 'He got wonderful notices from Harold Hobson playing a lead in a play of mine *Deutches Haus* opposite Margaret Drabble,' says Richard Cottrell,[31] and Clive Swift enthused, 'I remember him with Maggie in a

play of Richard's, she played a German girl and he was the boy in lov
with her, he was marvellous.' He appeared with Margaret again in *The*
Three Sisters when she was Masha and he Tuzenbach and as Warwick
in Anouilh's *The Lark*. Swift continues, ' . . . but the thing I think we all
got the most fun out of was a musical version of *Love's Labour's Lost*
which was such a success that it came to the Lyric, Hammersmith in
1959. I was Musical Director and Richard Cottrell, Corin Redgrave,
and John Fortune (then John Wood, he changed his name because of
the other one) were in it and Ian played Holofernes, in a mortar board.
It was set in 1901 and really only based on the Shakespeare play –
Richard and I wrote the lyrics and I did the music with Corin's assistance.
It was so successful.'[32]

The Times thought so too. Under the headline DISTANT LINK WITH
SHAKESPEARE: UNIVERSITY DRAMA AT ITS BEST, the critic wrote:

Love's Labours [sic] which is to be seen this week at the Lyric, Hammersmith,
is based (very distantly) on Shakespeare, but any fragments of the original plot
and characters which remain are pretty thoroughly disguised in a story (period
1901) of four dramatic dilettantes trying to maintain their rather precarious
misogyny with precepts derived from Ibsen, Chekhov, Zola, and Wilde.

The idea of this fantasy, it will be seen, is full of pitfalls to trap the unwary.
That it will be performed with verve and enthusiasm we might take on trust,
but this sort of airy nonsense needs a really light touch as well – a quality not
always so evident in undergraduate productions. On this occasion, however,
the cast play perfectly in style, with hardly a weak link – though a special word
should be spared for Richard Cottrell's ageing thespian, Mr Ian McKellen's
crusty pedant, Miss Elizabeth Proud's hoydenish schoolgirl, Mr Derek Jacobi's
elegant epigrammatist and Colin [sic] Redgrave's stylish hero . . .

In short, the production represents university drama at its best – fresh,
unpretentious, but enterprising in its subject matter (requiring some knowledge
of Eng. Lit. and such-like arcana for full enjoyment) and with quite a professional attack on performance.

'All the men became actors except Philip Strick who's a film critic,
and Simon Relph who's a film producer,' says Swift, 'but only one girl,
Elizabeth Proud turned "pro".'[33]

'He gave a very mature performance as Halma in *The Wild Duck*,'
says Andrew, 'both under- and overplaying in the way Ibsen has to be.
It was extraordinarily mature for a young man.'[34] He also appeared
with Nunn again in *Twelfth Night* as Sir Toby Belch, and worried about
his beard.[35] Among the ever-changing scenes at any university it is now
impossible to trace all the twenty-one parts that McKellen played in the
nine terms he was there. But it is evident that Cambridge greatly

influenced him in the way that he works on and develops a part, for it gave him a scholarly attitude to the works he has appeared in, and an appreciation of literature for he rarely appears in anything shoddy. He is interested in the best, always: the best writing, directing and acting. Cambridge also gave him a chance to expand his already formidable technique, for he was acting with people who were working to a professional standard, and, indeed, they were to be offered contracts – Swift, as we have seen, by the RSC, Jacobi by the Birmingham Rep, Nunn by the Belgrade Theatre, via a TV sponsorship. McKellen was to go into rep, and there found that university actors were not all that well-regarded: 'Ex-varsity chappies, well, you know, love, they always seem to have rehearsed in front of the mirror,' as he writes in People 'which I stopped doing immediately.'[36]

Academically, he did less well than he, as an exhibitioner, might have expected for he only gained a 2:2 degree in English, but he had made his choices. 'I think we expect too much,' says Andrew, McKellen's tutor in his third year. 'We expect young men to court their girls, act, write poetry, and work. Ian was always courteous, and intelligent. And he was never late with his essays. He is a very organized person – organized in his head – a reasonable man with a radical, searching mind.'[37]

With the learning of all those parts it is little wonder that work suffered. But he had laid the foundations of a career 'which has grown enormously, both in confidence and ability. I so admire what he's achieved,' says Swift, 'He is so articulate, so courageous. We all learnt to act by doing it, and Ian has certainly showed his talent, and though he was quieter than the rest of us then, he has certainly become the best of us.'[38]

So Cambridge then can be counted a success. Or can it? In 1970 he returned to Cambridge as a member of the cast of The Recruiting Officer to be presented both at Cambridge and on tour. In the cast was Trevor Peacock, actor and writer, and Ian took Peacock round the colleges. 'It must have been wonderful to have been up here,' Peacock said with delight. 'And I was amazed: Ian changed in a moment and said "No, it wasn't! It was awful." I don't know why he said it, we never mentioned it again. But it was an extraordinary thing for him to say.'[39]

3
Coventry and Ipswich

COVENTRY

By now, having made up his mind that he was to be an actor, McKellen had been writing to rep companies throughout the country for work. He had three offers but chose the Belgrade Theatre in Coventry, one of the post-war provincial theatres which had built up a reputation for good work. He was to be paid £8.10 shillings a week (the average wage for a male manual worker was £15) which was the highest of three offers.[1] 'I think I had about a month off, then I plunged straight in. I don't think I realized at the time how lucky I was. And I don't think you could do it so easily these days.'[2] His first part was as Son Roper in Robert Bolt's *A Man for All Seasons*.

McKellen recalls, 'The style for much of this [the season of plays] was set by the director of my professional debut, who addressed the first rehearsal: "OK, the play's *A Man for All Seasons*. In your scripts, you'll find the moves they did in the West End production – what was good enough for Paul Scofield for over a year will do us very nicely for a couple of weeks." '[3] And he says of himself at this period, 'Oh, how eager to learn; how happy to be rewarded with some rattling good parts.'[4]

The local paper commented that the Belgrade Company had been augmented by Ian McKellen from the Marlowe Society of Cambridge, but critics and journalists didn't immediately rush to comment on his performances or seek to write profiles about him, and certainly there was no suggestion that a great actor was being hatched. He was an 'also taking part'[5] and *The Guardian*, the most prestigious paper reviewing at Coventry, praised Bernard Kilby (the leading man) and Sheila Keith as More and Lady Alice, and Robert Gillespie as The Common Man but neglected to mention McKellen at all.

Belgrade was pursuing the path that most repertories did in those days, West End hits, the well-made plays from the thirties and the occasional classic. The next play chosen was typical, J. B. Priestley's

northern comedy *When We Are Married,* and again McKellen, as Fred
Dyson, was an 'also taking part' in all three local papers. It wasn't until
his third play with the Belgrade, G. B. Shaw's *You Never Can Tell* in
which he appeared as the ebullient twin Philip, that the *Coventry
Evening Telegraph* commented, '... and there were good performances
from Ian McKellen as Philip, Sheila Keith as Mrs Clandon, Georgina
Anderson as Gloria and Ronald Magill as Fergus'. Neither the *Warwick
Advertiser* nor the *Nuneaton Evening Tribune* commented on his performance, but the *Birmingham Post* gave McKellen his first really good
notice as a professional: 'Bridget Turner and Ian McKellen are outstanding as her irrepressible younger children.'

Philip is a showy part, quick, swift and stylized – a part which could
have been designed to bring out stylish comedy in anyone who has a
glimmer of comic ability. And he was lucky in his 'twin', Bridget Turner,
then a young, struggling actress who has developed into a fine comedy
actress with an impeccable sense of timing that owes something both to
instinct and hard work.

While performing the Shaw play, the actors were rehearsing a real
pot-boiler, one of Agatha Christie's popular crime plays, *Black Coffee*
in which McKellen added to his gallery of old men, playing Tredwell
the Butler in a fine make-up of wrinkles, white wig and an appropriate
bearing. It was an insignificant part which didn't even get an 'also
played' comment from the press.

This again was his lot in the next production which was a double
bill – *Celebration,* the comedy by Keith Waterhouse and Willis Hall,
preceded by *The Man in the Cage* which was written by a Coventry-
bred girl, Susan Hill, soon to become a novelist and writer of some
fame. She was then nineteen, and the papers were far more interested
in proclaiming her prowess and castigating *Celebration* than they were
in McKellen, who, anyway, only had a small part, that of Stan Dyson,
whom the *Stratford Herald* described as 'a moron, with aspirations to
be a Teddy Boy', not exactly, one feels, type-casting. The same can be
said for his next part, that of Mason, a young officer in Barry England's
play *End of Conflict* which was having its premier. The *Coventry
Evening Telegraph* said that McKellen played with 'zeal and dogged-
ness', and it was in this play that he was first seen by Elspeth Cochrane,
who was to become his first agent. 'I thought there was something about
him, even then,' she said, 'I don't remember anything about the play
now, except they all sat round with bare knees.'[6] The play seems to
have been set in the Desert Army and was to lead Barry England to
write another play in which McKellen was to appear later on.

At Christmas the Belgrade put on some lighter entertainment, and with English invariability decided on Dickens's *Pickwick Papers* as being somehow the embodiment of Christmas and put on an adaptation called *Mr Pickwick*. Patrick Newell was brought in to play the eponymous hero, while McKellen was cast as Mr Snodgrass. McKellen got a 'well played' from the *Evening Telegraph* and the *Nuneaton Observer* called him 'poetic' while the *Coventry Standard* wrote: 'Mr Pickwick himself, genial, enormous victim of circumstance, affably bumbled his way through the production in the expert and immense figure of Patrick Newell. Tupman, Snodgrass and Winkle, Messrs Haywood, McKellen and French, partners in the adventure, cavorted, disported and gesticulated.'

All in all, the critics praised *Mr Pickwick* and it was a play which both actors and audiences enjoyed hugely, as they did the next play *Toad of Toad Hall*, with Bernard Kilby playing Toad, George Pensotti as the Water Rat, John Scarborough as the Mole and Patrick Newell staying on to play Badger. McKellen had to be content with the small, but showy part of First Weasel. He was, according to the *Evening Telegraph*, 'a perfectly hateful Weasel,' while the *Coventry Standard* said, 'Highlights of the evening were Ian McKellen's weaselly weasel, Bridget Turner's charming Marigold, and the thistledown dancing of Jennie Lynne.'

McKellen was making his mark but it is interesting to note that it was in the more showy parts, parts that had some bite and which could be characterized. He was though still playing young men in more 'natural' parts, and the test came when he was cast as Konstantin in Chekhov's *The Seagull*. Bridget Turner recalls, 'It seemed to me that the season was being shaped round him. He had certainly done good work. The first time I really remember him was as Tredwell, the Butler in the Christie play. He put on a marvellous make-up, grey hair the lot. And then suddenly he was being given the juve leads. I think I was rather jealous about this, I felt plays were being chosen to show off *his* talent, when I had been slogging away for two years without the same thing happening to me. Though I must admit, when I went out front to see *End of Conflict* – it was an all-male cast – I couldn't take my eyes off Ian. Even when other people were speaking or doing something, you still watched him. Fascination, charisma, call it what you like, he had it even then.'[7]

But if Turner was feeling jealous, McKellen certainly wasn't having an easy time. The life of a repertory actor is remorseless, one play following the other in relentless succession. McKellen was lucky never to have had to work in weekly rep, which is even worse, but the pressure of rehearsing during the day, performing in the afternoon and evening, as well as preparing for the next play, is immense. Just learning the words in whatever spare time you can find is a formidable task, but still the plays roll on one after another. There is no escape, it just has to be done. The first nights come at regular intervals, the press is there judging you and you just have to do it.

Whether McKellen was tired, or whether Konstantin was too great a step forward for him, is now something that cannot be decided, but the event was catastrophic for him. It was, for a repertory company, a good cast: Sheila Keith was to play Irina Arkadina, that self-absorbed actress, and Nina, the girl who deserts Konstantin and causes his death was played by Bridget Turner. The *Evening Telegraph* wrote:

Anyone who has despaired over the Coventry theatre-going public's apparent preference for simple comedies and thrillers would have rejoiced at the Belgrade Theatre last night to see a large audience giving an unusually enthusiastic reception to the opening performance of Chekhov's *The Seagull*.

Such enthusiasm must have given heart to the theatre's director, Anthony Richardson, not so much because he has produced the play but because, if the week continues as it has begun, he must be encouraged in planning his future programme.

One may say, perhaps, that the Belgrade Company have in the past climbed a lesser peak with more to spare, but Mr Richardson may rightly claim that success should be judged as much as on what is attempted as on what is achieved.

Certainly *The Seagull* which brought its author success only after an earlier failure, demands a very high standard from its actors and great insight from its directors. Certainly the Belgrade cannot meet these demands as one would wish. But certainly, it has been worth doing.

This was perhaps a just criticism; to try to do a Chekhov play in itself is daunting, but to try to do it with two or three weeks' rehearsal, and while playing *Toad of Toad Hall* at night might be considered foolhardy. It was slightly unfair to expect an inexperienced actor to pull the part off under such conditions. The paper went on to say, 'Ian McKellen's Konstantin tends to overplay the first two acts, and does not quite convince one of his final anguish.'

It was a perspicacious comment for McKellen can still overplay a part, particularly when the preparation has not been as long as he might have liked. He always 'grows' in a part, even now.

The *Birmingham Mail* was scathing. Under the headline THIS 'SEA-GULL' WON'T FLY VERY HIGH, the critic writes: 'It is doubtful if Chekhov's *The Seagull* at the Belgrade Theatre, Coventry, will be listed high among the season's achievements ...' and he just mentions McKellen playing Konstantin, while the *Birmingham Post* thought that 'no real poignancy came over'.

Gareth Lloyd Evans in *The Guardian* gave a very thoughtful and considered notice to the piece: '...the company almost completely failed to respond [to the play's rhythms and moods]. They have, with two exceptions, committed the fault of either excessive reticence or over-boldness. Bernard Kilby as Trigorin and Bridget Turner as Nina alone seemed to know that to act Chekhov requires a constant compromise between darting naturalism and its patent opposite.

'Sheila Keith as Irina in her regal progress through a banquet of histrionics again unnecessarily reminds us that she has the loudest voice at the Belgrade. But the biggest disappointment is Ian McKellen's Konstantin. This young actor of much promise in voice and intelligent interpretation seems determined to invite disaster with his arms and legs. So often they seemed to be playing one part and the rest of him another.'

The *Stratford Herald* was more encouraging: 'The real pivot of Konstantin is driven, by Ian McKellen, with a fair sense of urgency – not an exalting performance, but at least never overplaying the distraught restlessness.'

Although the critics were severe, at least they were seriously considering McKellen as a young actor who had more than promise, and of whom they were expecting much. They were harsh, but at least they were paying him the compliment of treating him seriously as an actor that would have a future, and an actor that would have to be reckoned with. And it is interesting to note that McKellen is still being criticized for certain faults, for instance overplaying, while he has worked hard to overcome others, such as his gawkiness. He now moves well on a stage, but then awkward movement is a technical problem that hard work can overcome, while correction of overplaying can only come from instinct and judgement.

Elspeth Cochrane remembers Konstantin: 'It was in this part that he *really* struck me – I simply couldn't see anyone else. It was a charismatic performance.'[8] She definitely became interested in representing Ian and got to know him. 'But I didn't ask him right away. Young actors, at the stage he was then, don't need agents, which was exactly what Ian said to me when I *did* approach him. But I knew other people were, or soon would be after him, so I made my bid!'[9]

The next play was an oddball comedy about which there was much confusion in the press and, one imagines, among the actors. Ronald

Millar's *The Bride Comes Back* concerns a magic bowl of faith, a runaway bride, a psychiatrist and a spirit from somewhere or other. 'Bridget Turner and Ian McKellen as her husband [Joe Tilney] add their quota to the general upheaval,' noted the *Warwick Advertiser*. But McKellen and the rest of the company were putting a lot of energy into rehearsals for *Much Ado About Nothing*.

Although the Belgrade Theatre is within half-an-hour of Stratford-upon-Avon and the Royal Shakespeare Company, in those days it used to put on one Shakespeare play a year. McKellen was cast as Claudio and it was his first professional appearance in a Shakespearian role. It was not exactly type-casting, and it is not an easy part for even an experienced actor; it can be insipid or played too romantically. But the press paid the company the compliment of treating the production very seriously. A staff reporter on the *Birmingham Post* wrote:

In the course of a somewhat fidgety season, the Belgrade is giving *Much Ado About Nothing* as one of its most important productions. Last night's opening proved that it is certainly an interesting and enjoyable one, and will be all the more so as it settles down.

But the paper in a long, considered notice did not mention McKellen. That was left to the *Stratford Herald* of 9 March 1962. After giving his opinion on what the play was all about and praising Graham Crowden's direction the critic went on to talk about the actors:

As well as Mr Crowden's production the night is blessed by leading performances of detail and character. Bernard Kilby gives Benedick, harried by the fringes of hysteria, a portrayal which makes an awful lot of sense when he finally gains control of the church scene.

Gillian Raine's Beatrice emerges as a Girton red-stocking fighting for recognition by the Union; a performance of bustling vivacity ... Ian McKellen's Claudio is, rightly, blatantly romantic ...

The *Coventry Standard* paired Bridget Turner and McKellen together saying that they played 'with the assurance we have come to expect'. A small compliment when you first read it, but when you consider that McKellen had been a professional for barely six months, it is a satisfying one. The *Coventry Evening Telegraph* was even more complimentary and said: 'Ian McKellen ... seems to progress in giant strides with every major role,' showing how McKellen was working and taking advantage of the eclectic parts he was being given. Gareth Lloyd Evans in *The Guardian,* however, thought he underplayed, not a criticism which McKellen often hears!

The Belgrade celebrated its fourth birthday with a revue, *Happy*

Returns, with Richard Murdoch imported to take the lead. McKellen was singled out for his 'American Tourist snapping us with his Rollieflex before the "big bang" annihilates "little Britain",' and he also took the part of Romeo in an Alan Melville sketch where he and Sheila Keith showed what happened when Romeo and Lady Macbeth mixed up the dates of their performances. In one sketch according to the *Coventry Standard*, McKellen, Denzil Ellis and Bernard Kilby had 'the audience almost curled up in their seats'.

Next came another Agatha Christie, *Ten Little Niggers*, followed by *Irregular Verb To Love* in both of which he had small parts. That was the end of the regular season: the Company then decided to put on a repertoire season for the rest of the summer. Originally planned to be four plays, one of them, David Turner's *Semi-Detached*, was such a great success that the fourth play was never produced. In *Semi-Detached* McKellen played the young son Tom, and the *Coventry Evening Telegraph* praised him for having 'magnified a small role'. In André Obey's *Noah* McKellen appeared as Shem, a role described as 'lively' by the *Coventry Standard*.

But he was, as indeed was all the Company, playing under great difficulties. Bernard Kilby, the beloved leading man had died following a fall. Philip Grout, now a director, then an actor, told me, 'I was sent up quickly to play Noah and the Company were stunned by Bernard Kilby's death. They had all, including McKellen, admired him enormously. It was a most unhappy time for us all. But I remember, even then, thinking about McKellen, "Lord, what talent!". I had no idea that it was his first job. He was so good.'[10]

Elspeth Cochrane was still keeping her eye on McKellen. And she told another client of hers, Bob Chetwyn, Director of the Ipswich Repertory, about him. Chetwyn recalls, 'Elspeth told me that there was a good boy at the Belgrade. It is, you know, a nightmare trying to get good people for reps at the price you can afford. I was offering about twelve pounds then, sometimes twenty, but that was top salary. Anyway, I went up to Coventry and saw Ian in *Semi-Detached* and thought that he was indeed interesting, so I asked him to come to Ipswich.'[11]

IPSWICH

The Ipswich Repertory Company, in those days, operated in a small hall which is now the Elim Pentecostal Church. As its Director, the charming and direct Robert Chetwyn pursued an adventurous programme which still included the popular successes and thrillers which were then the backbone of repertory companies, along with more serious work. He and McKellen established a firm bond, and Chetwyn was to direct McKellen's *Hamlet* at his request and, later on, *Bent* in which McKellen scored a great success in 1979. Speaking about McKellen at the time, Chetwyn said, 'Ian was always very enthusiastic and hard-working. If you gave him a note (that is a criticism) he would always accept it. But I learnt that I had to have a good reason for it. I might just have been able to con him then, though I don't think I ever did! He was very anxious to learn, and, in fact, had a lot to learn.'[12]

Ipswich produced plays every two weeks and the first play in which McKellen got a notice was *The Gazebo* by Alec Coppel, a comedy play which is hardly subtle, and combining as it does murder and laughter can leave the impression of bad taste. But the company played it deftly and lightly and the *East Anglian Times* wrote: 'Ian McKellen, as Elliott Nash, the writer of thriller plays, has the requisite light touch for the part of the devoted husband driven to murder to save his wife's name. His facial expressions are amusing and he makes the most of planning the murder with frequent reference to his list of things necessary to make a success of it, although, at times, he has a tendency to overplay the part.'

Chetwyn reckons that it was this play that taught McKellen how to play comedy really well. 'He often mentions *The Gazebo* for he did a remarkable job on it. He was totally unsuited to the part: that of a middle-aged man in a very light play, almost a farce, and he was not, then, a natural comedy actor, but he really worked at the part and, somehow, though it was not a particularly good performance in one way, in another way it was very impressive.'[13]

The next piece was headlined BRILLIANT IPSWICH PRODUCTION in the local paper and it was that hoary old play by T. W. Robertson *Caste*. Saying that the play 'has all the traditional ingredients of Victorian Melodrama with plenty of laughs and tear-jerking,' the critic goes on to congratulate Robert Chetwyn on his, 'remarkably fine production,' which,

imbues the dialogue and action with a quality that sparkles with life and vitality ...

The cast was splendid. Notably so Josie Kidd; vivacious, pert and scatter-brained, with an excellent foil in Ian McKellen, her down-to-earth intended who somehow puts across the Victorian atmosphere in the modern idiom with remarkably good effect.

This is the first time that a critic has remarked on another of McKellen's central tenets about acting: that it should be relevant to today, a theory which, as we shall see, he developed and about which he has expressed clear views. Plays should have a point of reference to modern life to be effectively realized to an audience. 'In *Caste*,' Chetwyn reminisces, 'he was superb, and he appreciated the worth of the play, which, though old-fashioned, is a very good piece.'[14]

Next came Philip Mackie's explosive play *The Big Killing* in which McKellen played 'the inevitable young lover hovering dutifully in the background' which the local press found he portrayed convincingly. Then came another comedy, into which McKellen was able to put all he had learnt in *The Gazebo*. He gave a good performance in *The Amorous Prawn* but in *The Keep* he and Gawn Grainger, the other young man in the company, were only adequate.

Then came Christmas and the Company put on an adaptation of *David Copperfield* by Joan MacAlpine. The curtain rose on David Copperfield in early manhood talking to the audience about his life, which was then shown in a series of flash-backs. The *East Anglian Times* wrote: 'Played against a very fine set, an all-purpose affair, with sepia undertones against which subtly-coloured costumes provided all the authentic atmosphere of a Victorian print, this quiet and thoughtful production is a trio of feathers in the caps of adaptor Joan MacAlpine, producer Robert Chetwyn and scenic artist Juanita Waterson.

'Individual performances are in good hands and David Copperfield in particular, is played with convincing sincerity by Ian McKellen. The play takes us no further than his marriage to Dora, but, in one scene, a word and a gesture from him makes brilliantly clear the trouble that lay ahead.' McKellen was to play Copperfield again on television, which he lists among his favourite parts.

Pantomime came next and the choice that year was *Aladdin* in which McKellen played a Chinese policeman and in the ensuing revue, called *How Dare We!* he played in sketches, one of which he had done in the Belgrade and was commended for his comic talent in the press. While all this seasonal frivolity was going on, McKellen and Chetwyn were preparing for a momentous step in McKellen's career – his first major leading part, as a professional, in a Shakespeare play.

This was *Henry V*, a part that he had played at Bolton School. 'I chose this play,' says Chetwyn, 'because I wanted to do it and I thought Ian could do it – and, no, I didn't know he had played it at school. He really worked hard at it. It was a very ambitious production, I suppose, for a rep. As the theatre was so small I decided to use the whole auditorium and have soldiers coming through it from the lighting box at the back. It was quite unusual in those days to do that, and Ian was downstage speaking to them, right out into the auditorium before the Agincourt scene and then the soldiers came forward on to the stage. It was very exciting to do, but caused lots of technical complications. We used to open at Ipswich on a Tuesday matinee, it was early closing day, or market day or something. The dress rehearsals used to take place on Monday afternoon. This one started at 2 o'clock, as usual and it went on *until 5 a.m. the next morning*! Ian never complained once!'[15] And in it McKellen gave a rivetting performance. A.G.G. was very warm about it:

Robert Chetwyn's *Henry V* is surely one of the finest Shakespearian productions yet seen at Ipswich. Produced with a depth of understanding, there is colour, warmth, wit and a wealth of masterly touches. The intimacy of the medieval apron stage is achieved by the characters occasionally spilling into the audience (there is a stirring military invasion from the front row of the stalls) and by this device the audience is drawn into the very heart of the play.

The set (by Juanita Waterson) is simple, impressive and colourful, blending into every mood of the action. Light when the occasion demands, it is darkly sombre as the hour of battle approaches and there is tremendous atmosphere in the brooding tension of the English camp before dawn at Agincourt. The moment of final victory is splendidly achieved.

Ian McKellen's King Henry disturbed one at first by an apparent over-emphasis of youthful exuberance, but, as the action develops, so also does his potential of chivalrous authority and the sum total is a good study of character development. His final scene, the wooing of Katherine, may not in a few of its flippancies please some Shakespearian purists, but it is a gay, happy moment with the touch of a very human producer.

Talking to John Barton, years later[16] McKellen said:

When I played Henry V I worked in a very small theatre and we had no army. So I imagined that the army was in the audience and I knelt down at the front of the stage and whispered, 'Once more unto the breach, dear friends, once more/Or close the wall up with our English dead.' I was able to get just as much passion into that and bravado and patriotism by whispering as I could by shouting. In fact I think I got more because it was more real.

Chetwyn's comment on McKellen's performance is: 'He never stopped working on the part, I mean it was only a fortnightly rep and he had given a very good performance, got good notices. One scene never worked particularly well and he knew it, and ten days into the run, he came running up the stairs, very tiny stairs, to my office. And he said, "Did you see that scene that I hadn't got right? Was it better?" He never lets good notices affect him if he doesn't think a thing is right, most actors would have accepted the glory, but not Ian.' But the good burghers

of Ipswich, in spite of his dazzling performances, had not yet taken
McKellen to their hearts, for as A.G.G. noted the cast at the theatre
had been augmented to twenty-three and almost outnumbered the first
night audience![17]

But they probably felt more comfortable with the next play *Arsenic
and Old Lace*, that dotty tale about two old ladies who murder their
old gentlemen lodgers from the very best of motives. 'Ian McKellen and
Roberta Maxwell put in a nice touch of romance' in this play which
was produced, not by Chetwyn but by Alan Gray. Chetwyn was preparing for John Osborne's tremendous play *Luther* in which McKellen
was to play the lead again. It was again a lavish production for so small
a theatre with members of the St Mary-le-Tower choir providing some
fine singing, and A.G.G. pronounced the production as 'Superb'. And
of McKellen he writes:

> Central figure, is, of course, the great reformer Martin Luther, who wracked
> with ill-health and inner torments is played magnificently by Ian McKellen. In
> his quieter moments he is moving and sincere, although occasional over-
> dramatisation created some effect of superficial suffering rather than a deeper
> spiritual anguish.[18]

Chetwyn recalls, 'The *Luther* I did was the first outside London, Ian
was astounding in it. I remember, though, at one performance I had
two girls in front of me, eating crisps, crunching them loudly, scrunching
up the bags and throwing them about. I was really irritated and I hit
one of them and she screamed. Ian was doing a very quiet scene with
the Pope and he hardly paused, though he must have been wondering
what was going on, what with the scrunching noise and the scream!'[19]

As it was Easter time, the play was performed on Good Friday – a
break from tradition.

McKellen left Ipswich after this production to go back to the Belgrade
theatre again for a production of *The Big Contract* by Barry England
which opened on 13 May 1963.

W. A. Darlington wrote in the *Daily Telegraph*:

> It takes courage these days for a dramatist to tell an ordinary straightforward
> story about ordinary situations, but what a relief when somebody takes heart
> to do it and does it well.
> I left the Belgrade Theatre here tonight full of gratitude to Barry England
> for doing just this. His play *The Big Contract* had just been given its first
> performance.
> The title is as straightforward as the play, for Mr England shows us the
> effect upon an unspecified business organisation in an unspecified part of this
> country of the landing of a contract worth £50 million.

It is a pretty comprehensive study and is full of action. The boardroom's jubilation over their success soon turns to anxiety, for speed is of the essence and the shop-stewards object to being rushed ...

Gareth Lloyd Evans in *The Guardian* was less enthusiastic about the play which he thought needed drastic cutting but acknowledged that the cast, which included David Waller and Julian Curry as well as McKellen, 'drive on with relentless efficiency and pick out unerringly the best of England's writing – his comedy ...'. McKellen's part was the juve lead and the local papers commented on his sensitivity and sincere approach.

It was around this time that Elspeth Cochrane received a telephone call from McKellen asking her to represent him as his agent. 'He rang me from some call-box, on his way back to Ipswich. I was very pleased as I thought he was brilliant, *so* talented – and I knew other agents were after him, more than ever!'[20]

McKellen was back at Ipswich in June to rehearse and then play in another ambitious production of Chetwyn's, *Long Day's Journey into Night* by Eugene O'Neill, the great autobiographical drama of his tormented family, which is filled with bitterness and hopelessness. The family conflicts between the two brothers, and between them and their father, a famous actor, who is both cripplingly mean and wildly generous, and the mother, clinging on to her gentility, in spite of her addiction to drugs, makes a powerful and immense play. In the small Ipswich theatre it must have been overwhelming. The local paper said in its notice:

In the opening scenes the Ipswich Company do not seem too sure of themselves; they fail to sketch in adequately the seemingly ideal family background before the cracks in the surface begin to show. But as the play progresses and the family begins to move obsessively in ever narrowing circles round their pet hells – dope, drink and tuberculosis – the atmosphere builds up well. ...

Ian McKellen and Stephen MacDonald at times fail to convey the strange relationship which exists between the two brothers but individually their performances as a rejected son and a betrayed cynic are moving ...

In the next play, McKellen played a neurotic schoolmaster – it was called *I John Brown* and then came something very light and graceful, *Salad Days* in which 'Ian McKellen and Susan Wherret are (as they say) completely with it as two blue-blooded London Socialite youngsters'.[21]

Then came another leading part, this time in Emlyn Williams's fine play *The Corn Is Green*. Peggy Mount played with him as the school-mistress who was ambitious for her outstanding pupil. The notices were excellent, both players being praised.

His time at Ipswich was drawing to a close, he had experienced much and learnt much. His final notice with them was in the first repertory production of Bill Naughton's *All In Good Time* and he was 'excellently cast as the bridegroom' who 'wilts in sensitive embarrassment'.

Bob Chetwyn sums up McKellen at this time: 'Ian never suggested parts he could play to me, he just accepted them. He was very quiet, but of great intelligence. He was, and is, a wonderful person to direct – always takes it terrifically well, but you do have to be convinced yourself. He queries everything, and when he gets something right he is always excited. He was, even at Ipswich, intensely professional, and never accepted praise unless his performance was worth it. There was one thing I really taught him, that there are always laughs to be had, even in tragedy – Shakespeare deliberately puts them in. It relieves the tension for the audience. McKellen always finds the laughs now – he got that from me.'[22]

McKellen himself felt that he had not yet made the great break-through in his playing that he was seeking. His heart and his head, his intellect and his imagination did not always synchronize. He was still hiding behind characters, finding it hard to pull out his emotions before an audience, and reveal himself. That step was still to come.[23] One person who was in the company was Clare Fox, a West End Producer. 'It was my first job, stage managing at Ipswich, and we all learnt a lot there. Ian was clearly very talented, I particularly remember his Henry v and Luther. But he was more than that. He was wonderful to work with. He was always terribly aware of everyone else and he had some sympathy for *your* problems. And he would actively seek out your opinions – even mine! He was just wonderful.'[24]

4

London, Nottingham and Chichester

'One thing I admire Ian for,' says Clive Swift[1] 'is that he didn't immediately come to London when he had the chance.' After Ipswich, McKellen did indeed have the opportunity to appear in London but he felt that he needed more time to develop his already considerable talents.[2] He was now twenty-four years old and his next step was to be one of the most influential in his life. He was asked to join the company opening the new Playhouse Theatre in Nottingham. The leading man was to be John Neville who, after a decade of acclaimed performances, was a great young star building a legend for himself alongside Richard Burton and Peter O'Toole.

Elspeth Cochrane says: 'James Cairncross who was a close friend of John Neville's had worked with Ian at Ipswich, and I knew Tony Guthrie, so we both talked to them about Ian, and though it was slightly less money at Nottingham than he had reached at Ipswich, it was, we thought, too great a chance to miss, and of course, he did exceptionally well there.'[3] McKellen thought that he was being engaged for some minor role in *Coriolanus* and was gratified to learn that the part was Aufidius. The director was that magnificent orchestrator of Shakespeare's plays, Sir Tyrone Guthrie.[4] On the first day Guthrie read the cast an introduction to an American edition of the play – 'with which I agree to every word'. The essay described the relationship between Coriolanus and Aufidius which was conditioned by Coriolanus's mother fixation, and that he regarded Aufidius as a father/friend figure 'whom Coriolanus worshipped in combat and lusted after in his dreams'.[5] Impressed by the reading, McKellen, the next day, picked up the book which was lying on the stage-manager's table and saw that the Introduction had been written by Guthrie himself!

With this idea the play was built up to show that the two men were sexually attracted to each other, and this became the exciting focus of the play. It was acted in strange costumes, some critics designating them Edwardian, others seeing an eighteenth-century aspect. Guthrie wanted to establish the class distinctions in Ancient Rome in a way that was to be very apparent to a modern audience, and to get the effect of the Roman populace he used local amateurs. To swell the cast even further, everyone who was not playing in the scene of Coriolanus's triumphal entry into Rome had to be on stage. Ian had to carry a banner and was instructed to hide his face behind it.[6] In the cast was Leo McKern who also helped to swell the crowd and a very young Michael Crawford who played the Second Servingman.[7] Crawford accidentally tripped one day in rehearsal, and Guthrie, ever eager to keep in a good effect, encouraged him to do it deliberately.[8] He took special care with McKellen, rehearsing him privately until McKellen got what Guthrie wanted to draw out from him. But McKellen was still having difficulties in fusing mind and action with heart-felt speech. It was still apparent at dress rehearsal, for he was seemingly incapable of doing the speech at the end of the play after Aufidius has slain his lover/enemy.

> My rage is gone,
> And I am struck with sorrow ...

Guthrie wanted this to be preceded by a cry of great anguish and McKellen was embarrassed and nervous about this and the speech. He was cold inside. Guthrie called him down-stage and said to him, quietly but distinctly, 'We are at the climax of a masterpiece. If we haven't convinced the audience by this time that they are in the presence of a great play, they might as well have stayed at home with the television. Aufidius is a man but he can grow, as we all can, to behave like a god. His rage *can* turn to sorrow. Fill your mind, your imagination with your feelings and let your heart wail. If you can't do it, it's all a waste. You can.' This, says McKellen, was a turning point in his life, it was then that he really realized what acting was about, 'to reveal yourself to your audience and make them empathize with you'.[9]

The critics were rapturous about the theatre itself, about the production and about McKellen. Emrys Bryson, the drama critic of the then *Guardian-Journal* and *Evening Post* (now only the *Post* remains) wrote, after describing the theatre:

The first play of the new Playhouse is *Coriolanus* a powerful, distinguished and entirely magnificent production by Sir Tyrone Guthrie – who is himself powerful, distinguished and entirely magnificent ...

The rabble look like film extras out of *A Tale of Two Cities*, the politicians wear Dickensian top hats: the Roman military shake their plumes and clank their swords, while the Volscian military could, in their tight hussar uniforms with furry shakos and dolmans have come straight out of *The Chocolate Soldier* ...

After more about the production Bryson says: 'If Mr Neville never acts again, this Coriolanus will have made him for ever ... and Ian McKellen gives a depth to the Volscian commander, Aufidius, that is twitching in intensity.' *The Times* of 13 December 1963 wrote of '... the first duel with Aufidius when the two enemies circle about each other uttering threats like sensual caresses. Equally responsible for this and similar scenes is the Aufidius of Ian McKellen, a new actor with a prodigious range of hysterical passion which here rises to its climax in a long wailing phrenody over the hero's body.'

Bernard Levin, then Drama Critic of the *Daily Mail* said that McKellen made an excellent contribution and Eric Shorter in the *Daily Telegraph* praised him for 'powerful moments'.

The opening was a full civic occasion and the actors were expected to attend a mayoral reception afterwards. When the actors arrived there was no food or drink, it had all gone, only in the Mayor's Parlour was there anything. Guthrie was, rightly, furious that his actors, who had been working so hard and who had achieved a great success for the town, were being so badly treated that he strode into the roped-off enclosure, ignoring royalty, Mayor and all the dignitaries and picked up a tray of gin and tonics and took them out to the company![10]

Unlike Ipswich and the Belgrade Theatre where plays were rehearsed put on and then discarded, Nottingham presented plays in repertoire, several plays being presented at the same time on different nights. McKellen was not cast in the next play, *The Importance of Being Earnest*, though one would think that he would be excellent as either of the two young men, with his gift for comedy. But in early January 1964 he appeared in a new play by Peter Ustinov called *The Life In My Hands*. Directed by Denis Carey it told of 'a young man who has raped a fifteen-year-old mental defective, who has since died ... with courage and skill, the playwright states his case through the intertwining of characters, a newspaperman, a minister with powers of reprieve, a son whose own life could have ended the same way'.[11] The play examined the issue of capital punishment, and Ustinov evidently wrote a play which made the audience think deeply on such issues and whether society is right to revenge itself to protect the rest of us. 'Find us,' he says, 'any judge or jury that has protected a nation against, for example, the ambition of a politician or the genius of a general.'[12] Leo McKern and George Selway played the minister and the newspaperman and 'Ian McKellen's portrait of the son is toweringly splendid in its questing for truth even though it rips family harmony.'[13] *The Telegraph* called it 'a skilful play', while Harold Hobson in the *Sunday Times* of 12 January 1964 said that 'Ian McKellen turns on a spirited flow of fervent declamation' and *The Times* commended McKellen for being 'eloquently distraught'. Bernard Levin disliked the play but praised McKellen in the *Daily Mail*.

Ustinov himself was there to see the play and later on that year he told Ann Leslie that McKellen had 'a raw, rough-edged quality I find impressive and exciting. He speaks with a Northern accent – and the fact that he has not *had* to lose this as an actor is significant ... the young actors, like McKellen ... are *professionals*, they study everything. This, I think, is part of the influence of television. It has taught extraordinary powers of observation – and as an actor it is very difficult to cheat on television.' While watching Ian rehearse, 'I found him putting inflections into speeches which I, as the playwright, had not even thought of. It was an illuminating experience.'[14]

In February McKellen took part in a play about George Bernard Shaw in which he is listed as playing Winifred Hutchins. Yes, *Winifred*. 'Ian appeared in drag,' Elspeth Cochrane remembers. 'I'm surprised, though, that his name is on the programme, as he said that he was going to do it under an assumed name.'[15] Emrys Bryson writes, 'As you will see from the enclosed review, I was not aware of his being in it ... it's so baffling that I don't give it a line.'[16] The disguise must have been skilful and complete.

The next production on 11 March 1964 was 'A Stark Tale of Human Sorrow' as Emrys Bryson called it. This was that harrowing masterpiece by the seventeenth century Spanish dramatist Pedro Calderón de la Barca, *The Mayor of Zalamea*, translated by David Brett. It tells of what happens when soldiers are billeted on a small town, and the troubles they cause, and of how the proud and arrogant officer rapes the shy and diffident daughter of the local Mayor. The Mayor defies military law and brings the officer to justice and has him executed by garrotting.

In a production by John Neville (assisted by Richard Digby Day) that usually catches the black energy and golden grace of the Spanish character, the tragedy is often melodramatic and patchy.

The adaptation has not fully caught the peculiar Spanish idiom of sombre violence below the surface, the dark storm that erupts suddenly in the sunlight.

One should be made more aware of this pregnant quality of Spanish life and times. The outbursts of the rude soldiers (rude enough they are, too) and the ghastly shock of the garrotted body being trundled forward, are not sufficient in themselves.

Ian McKellen gets the quality over, though, as the haughty, sneering, almost hysterical captain quivering for his prey.[17]

The next part for McKellen was that of Arthur Seaton in David Brett's adaptation of Alan Sillitoe's novel *Saturday Night and Sunday Morning* which had already been seen as a film with Albert Finney. This, inevitably led to McKellen being compared to, and bracketted with Finney. Both northern actors, both retaining northern inflections in their voices, both with an undercurrent of danger in their acting. But the comparison is not an apt one, for McKellen's talent is decidedly of a different kind to Finney's, being a more refined and intellectual one. Emrys Bryson gives a summary of the play, which he calls 'Racy and Rough' in the headline and comments that 'Frank Dunlop's production also packs a wallop, blending the tough dialogue with sets by Patrick Robertson that cram the stage with ideas'. Of McKellen he writes:

Twenty-four-year-old Ian McKellen ... literally packs a punch as Arthur.
Cheekily likeable, untamable, he embarks on his rip-roaring role with the zest of a gladiator. He spins a lathe with the best of them (Raleigh have provided a couple of real ones), gleefully plonks a rat in the tea-urn and gets his face bashed in. An actor with a great future ...

Eric Shorter in the *Daily Telegraph* commented: 'Ian McKellen's performance misses none of the comedy but it also shows the most interesting power to change gear and keep the audience with it.'

'When he did *Saturday Night*, a producer wanted to bring it to London. I don't think Ian was too keen on it,' says Elspeth Cochrane. 'He thought it too soon after Finney's performance, and that there would be comparisons made, but the whole thing fell through anyway.'[18]

Before this though, McKellen had taken part in a lunch-time presentation to celebrate the birthday of a favourite poet, Marlowe, whom he had quoted in that schoolboy debate. John Neville, McKellen and four other actors, entranced a crowded audience who had paid two shillings for an hour of verse, comments and scenes by and about Marlowe. This was one of several such entertainments that were devised and presented by the Company (on Shakespeare's birthday they did 'Sweet Mr Shakespeare').

In June came another challenge: there is a sixteenth-century play about Sir Thomas More written by 'divers hands' including Shakespeare, Dekker and Heywood which the Playhouse decided to revive. McKellen was given the title role. Emrys Bryson thought the play only 'had curiosity value despite director Frank Dunlop's adroit and imaginative manipulation of the material ... but in the first place the play was handled by too many writers and it shows'. He goes on to say:

> Only a theatre like the Playhouse could do a literary curiosity like *Sir Thomas More*. And it is right, particularly in the Shakespeare Quartercentenary, that it should be done.
>
> After a season in which he has done anything from Calderón to Sillitoe, twenty-five-year-old Ian McKellen proves that as Sir Thomas More he is indeed a man for all seasons. Gravely spry, courteously dignified, he gives the role and production an authority remarkable for such a young man.

Benedict Nightingale, then Drama Critic of *The Guardian* thought that 'Mr McKellen's cleverly awkward movements suggest a kind of self-mocking saintliness ... This is a performance of dignity without a trace of mawkishness,' while the special correspondent of *The Times* added to the praise by saying: 'McKellen gives a beautifully modulated performance as More and keeps the jocularity within the bounds of character.'

It was now time for London and the play was *A Scent of Flowers*, a strange, mystical play about a young girl, played by Jennifer Hilary, who caught between love and conscience commits suicide. The play, told largely in flashbacks, starts with the girl's funeral. Writing in *The Times* the dramatic critic explained the play:

> Zoe is the child of a broken home who has been brought up by an indecisive father and a cold-blooded stepmother (Phyllis Calvert) who sent her to a convent school; she enjoys a near-incestuous relationship with her half-brother Gogo (one of the near-Beckett echoes; others including philosophic music-hall cross-talk routines and a fixation on bicycles); at college she has an affair with a married man which drives her to religious self-mutilation and suicide ...
>
> In synopsis it sounds a sentimental story, and on stage it appears even more so, for it is presented as a posthumous record with Zoe herself drifting through the action as a pathetic ghost, sometimes acting out scenes in flashback, and sometimes standing invisible among survivors.
>
> The three acts of the play follow the day of Zoe's funeral from the arrival of the coffin: and within this space of time her life is unfolded in terms of the various people who failed her, her stepmother, who has understanding but no love; Gogo, who can only reason as a scientist; a friendly priest whose charity is limited by his belief ...

It is a slow-moving and over-complicated evening in which one is more aware of Mr Saunders's debt to Beckett than of any expressive urgency behind his adopted techniques. Timothy O'Brien's sets – transparent gold-mesh walls, and soaring metal struts – are beautiful; and Richard Pilbrow's lighting, switching groups of characters from positive to negative illumination does much to clarify the sense of the text. Jennifer Hilary, by resolutely excluding pathos from her own performance almost manages to make one accept Zoe as a figure worth attention and Ian McKellen puts on a fine display of controlled hysteria as the brother.

The drama critic might have also said that the play, in its story at least, had affinities with Graham Greene's *The Living Room* in which Dorothy Tutin had had such a great success.

Harold Hobson wrote quite differently about the play in the *Sunday Times* 4 October 1964:

James Saunders's *A Scent of Flowers* (Duke of York's) was earlier played at Golders' Green and Wimbledon; and before the curtain rose on the first night in London word reached me from those who had seen it, or knew those who had seen it, that the play was offensive and necrophilic, all about sex and corpses and coffins; that in fact (they even went as far as this) the play ought to be suppressed. Factually speaking, these descriptions are accurate. The heroine is dead when the play begins, she steps into her grave as the play ends, and a coffin is on the stage throughout the performance. But to draw from this the conclusion apparently prevalent in the suburbs is as unjust and stupid as to assert that Maupassant was indecently interested in indecent exposure.

To the great credit of the London theatre the first night audience at the Duke of York's did not take this view; it listened to the play with attention and when it was over, gave it one of the most tremendous receptions I have ever heard. There were fifteen curtain calls. It is true that a first night audience is not only the richest and best dressed audience a play ever gets, it is also the most intelligent. But even so the auguries are good.

And although Hobson writes nearly another seventy lines on the play, praising Jennifer Hilary, 'This young actress, by far the greatest acquisition of her sex that the English stage has made for many years,' he fails to mention McKellen or to describe him as a great actor in the making. But the experience must have been a thrilling one, and McKellen's family, father, step-mother and sister were there to share in the happiness with him. Tragically, his father was killed in an accident soon after, and Ian had to take two days off to attend the funeral. His grief can only be imagined, but his courage in appearing on stage night after night in a play that was harrowing in the extreme, and dealt with death so graphically is something that can only produce the utmost admiration.[19]

It was during the run of *A Scent of Flowers* that Maggie Smith, then working with Sir Laurence Olivier at the National Theatre, saw McKellen, and, being greatly impressed by his performance asked Sir Laurence to see him ... but that night McKellen was down with 'flu! But this seemed not to matter for he was being talked about as a potential star, and so the National offered him a contract which he accepted. Originally, the National wanted it to be for three years, but McKellen refused because as he said afterwards, 'people's fortunes vary enormously at the National. It is a chancy business in that it might be very quick, but it might also take for ever. It wasn't as though I was dying to be part of a company, since I'd already been in three. I wanted to see what would happen if I went freelance.'[20] In the event he stayed eight months, playing Claudio in the Zeffirelli production of *Much Ado About Nothing*, Captain de Foenix in *Trelawny of the 'Wells'* by A. W. Pinero and the Protestant Evangelist in *Armstrong's Last Goodnight* – the last two being played at Chichester as well as at the Old Vic.

Claudio, of course, he had already played at the Belgrade, but this was very much Zeffirelli's production, for as well as directing it in a zany, controversial manner he was also responsible for the design, and was meticulous, watching every detail. McKellen was making-up for the dress rehearsal when the exuberant Zeffirelli exploded into the dressing-room, looked at McKellen's blond wig and moustache and, sitting on McKellen's lap proceeded to put rouge and lipstick on Ian's white face while he talked rapidly all the time, about Callas, about opera, about everything.[21] 'He hated working with Zeffirelli,' says Elspeth Cochrane, 'so much so, he wanted to leave the Company.'[22]

Harold Hobson seemed to have enjoyed the play, moving fountains, town bands, and comic costumes and all, though probably thinking it had little to do with Shakespeare. He goes on to say in *The Sunday Times* of 21 February 1965:

The second part of the evening is more valuable. In fact from the church scene onwards, this is the best production of *Much Ado About Nothing* that in my memory England has ever had. The rescue of the performance begins with Claudio's accusation of Hero at the altar. In ridicule and stupidity Ian McKellen finds poetry and rhythm and pain. This leads straight into the play's five minutes of glittering gold in which in a stark and empty stage, the chattering silence and the absurdities laid aside Beatrice reveals to Benedick the hugeness of her indignation at the wrong done to her cousin. Maggie Smith and Robert Stephens are here magnificent.

While the drama critic on *The Times* thought that: 'Ian McKellen's Claudio, a flaxen-haired hanger-on, vacillating between arrogance and servility makes better sense' [than Albert Finney's commanding performance as Don Pedro].

Although this period in McKellen's life produced very little in the way of rave notices or even artistic development it did have one lasting effect, which was to influence the way English theatre was to go, Among the company, along with Derek Jacobi, Albert Finney and Michael York was a tall, young man, who was soon to be proclaimed as one of the finest young actors in England for his playing of Guildenstern in Tom Stoppard's witty, incestuous play *Rosencrantz and Guildenstern Are Dead*. It was Edward Petherbridge, who was to become valued colleague and fast friend. This gentle, kind man has, like McKellen an irresistible sense of humour. Petherbridge says, 'Well, we make each other laugh a lot. We are aware of the eccentricities in each other's make-up. I suppose we are a lesson to each other. Ian always looks on the bright side.'[23] That there is affectionate friendship is apparent if you see them together, and they each go to see each other's performances, going round afterwards to discuss it.

McKellen left the company wanting to see what it would be like to be self-reliant. He says that the only regret he had about the time he spent with the National was that he never worked with Sir Laurence Olivier.[24] He was soon to find a part for he was cast as Alvin in *A Lily for Little India* with the Welsh actress Jessie Evans and the enigmatic Jill Bennett. The play was by Donald Howarth, who according to *The Times* had written a gentle play about the hell of northern domesticity.

A Lily for Little India concerns the escape of Alvin Hanker from his terrible mother – a standard theme to which Mr Howarth gives anything but standard treatment. The first stages of the campaign are fought out as comedy, with the shrewish widow conducting a gross courtship with her lodger on the ground floor, while the luckless Alvin, barricaded aloft in his room, broods on schemes to strengthen his position.

Gardening is the solution he finally hits upon, and thereafter he devoted himself to raising a prize Dragon's Fang Lily, a plant he is ready to defend with his life; and when his mother makes her felonious assault on it through the bedroom window he hurls her to the ground and decamps with the cherished object to the home of a sympathetic girl.[25]

The play also had deeper philosophic tones as it dealt with the questions of self-knowledge and self-reliance, and the three protagonists got high praise from the press, so much so, that the play moved from the little Hampstead Theatre Club to the St Martin's Theatre in January 1966. *Plays and Players* described McKellen as 'a joy to behold. His face, whether darkly framed by a Balaclava helmet or active with pride at the sight of the fast-growing lily, becomes a perfect mirror for the torments and the ecstasies within. Mr McKellen gives as clear an account of the adolescent struggle for independent status as I can remember seeing.'[26]

It was around this time that McKellen had been making *David Copperfield* for the BBC following his success in it at Ipswich and he had also done another television play with Jack Hawkins *The Trial and Torture of Sir John Rampayne*.

In May 1966 McKellen went to the Royal Court for the first time to play in Arnold Wesker's play *Their Very Own and Golden City*, a somewhat polemic play in which 'Ian McKellen, an actor with a hint of Albert Finney, bravely takes the architect from the morning of his world when he thinks every man should have a cathedral in his back garden, to the disillusioned night ... when he realizes that there is no democracy, merely a democratic way of manipulating power.'[27]

McKellen loves working at the Royal Court. It is a theatre which is full of theatrical traditions and, as he said, walking down the stairs from his dressing-room to the stage door, slapping the walls as he went, 'George Bernard Shaw worked here: Granville Barker worked here.'[28]

He was, like many other talented young actors, now making the round of London's small theatres, for next he was to be found at the Mermaid in a Shaw double bill – *The Man of Destiny* and *O'Flaherty VC* (which he says is one of his favourite parts).[29] But it was as the young Napoleon that he got most praise from the drama critic of *The Times* on 15 September 1966 who wrote: ' ...Ian McKellen, whose range of traditional Napoleonic gestures seems to spring from his inner driving force. For all his wispy physique, Mr McKellen has all the equipment for massively passionate roles. In repose he can flood the stage with smouldering energy, and his top notes have some of the same thrill as Olivier's.' He did not mention McKellen in *O'Flaherty*, and the play didn't transfer. Next McKellen went to the Oxford Playhouse to appear in *The Promise* by Alexey Arbuzov, with Judi Dench and Ian McShane.

The play is set in Leningrad from 1942 to 1960 and concerns Lika, played by Dench, pursuing a career as a doctor and the two men Leonidik, a very minor poet (McKellen) and Marat, a dreamy but heroic man. Directed by Frank Hauser, this emotional, intense play caught the imagination of everyone who saw it. The two indigenous Oxford critics could not decide which of the two men had the better part; F. W. D. thought it was McKellen, while Don Chapman thought that it was the easier part, McShane's being the more complex.[30] But they both agreed that the two men and Judi Dench gave remarkable performances. The three, according to Judi, evolved 'a deft, tight cohesion'[31] and on the first night they and Frank Hauser went out to dinner. At the next table was a carp of critics having filed their copy. Normally actors and critics do not mix on these occasion, but the critics were so jubilant at having seen a wonderful trio of performances that the two parties joined and a celebration took place.[32] The play was transferred to the Fortune Theatre in January 1967 and the London critics were equally congratulatory. *The Times* under the headline MOVING PLAY ON ETERNAL TRIANGLE, praised Arbuzov's play and the three protagonists ...

Judi Dench manages beautifully the transition from adolescent impulsiveness to serene maturity; Ian McShane brings to the engineer the right sense of creeping disillusionment: and Ian McKellen plays the nervy and volatile poet to perfection.

Harold Hobson in the *Sunday Times* 22 January said that Dench was giving the best performance of any actress together with the best performance of any actor to be found together. He goes on to say:

There are moments in Mr McKellen's performance ... which must rank with as high achievements of acting as I have ever seen ... and throughout his style, his panache, his vulnerable but never broken gentleness and pride are to be savoured with that joyous sadness which is one of the greatest, and in these days rarest, pleasures of the romantic theatre.

The play transferred to the Henry Miller Theatre in Broadway in November 1967, but ran only ten days and the theatre was picketed by American actors as a protest against British actors appearing on Broadway. McKellen returned to London and opened in *The White Liars* as Tom and *Black Comedy* as Harold Gorringe, a double bill which opened at the Lyric in February 1968, both by Peter Shaffer. *Black Comedy* had already been played at the Chichester Festival, but was being revived with a different cast. *The White Liars* was a curtain-raiser which was dubbed by *The Times* 'not much of a play', but which McKellen thought was superb. Again Harold Hobson wrote a paean of praise about McKellan:

Mr Schaffer's double bill provides an entertaining evening and ten minutes worth of superb acting. It is these ten minutes that make the plays worth seeing. They consist of monologue by Ian McKellen as a pop singer in a fortune-teller's seedy booth at the end of a pier in an apparently decaying watering place. They depend in some sense upon a trick, a change of accent, which, when it comes, revolutionizes the situation, and makes the play in which it occurs, *The White Liars*, instantly exciting and moving.

This adds to Mr McKellen's already great stature: the delicacy behind the suggestion of the uncouth, which is a mark of all his performances makes him without any question the most formidable actor to have emerged from any of the universities since Michael Redgrave, who is also a Cambridge man.[34]

Again the play did not run all that long, but McKellen had had a period where he had tried many things ... classic theatre, comedy, modern plays, Shaw, all of which added to his increasing ascendence as an actor. In four years he had played a series of parts in which he had received good to brilliant notices, had been judged and found meritorious by the London critics. He had, yet, to be proclaimed a star and the comparisons with other actors – Finney, Olivier, Redgrave – were, if flattering, not entirely justified. For we were not seeing a second anyone coming from the chrysalis, we were seeing an actor who was to be great in his own right, someone unique. Already the hallmarks were there ... the excitement, the hysteria, the ability to change an audience from one mood to another, the mannerisms, the ability to stand out among his peers. But something was missing ... but it was just a chance that would make it happen. And that chance was there for the taking.

5

Prospect and Cambridge
Theatre Company

'Since his prodigious debut in Guthrie's *Coriolanus* in 1963, Mr McKellen has been widely credited with star quality. Reviewers are inclined to treat that term as indefinable: actors have either got it or not. In Mr McKellen's case one can go a bit further than that as he is a star of a very special kind. Beyond sheer animal magnetism, he also raised acting from a secondary thing, a reflection of life, into a primary position. He seems not to work with the actor's usual tools of memory and observation, but to build a performance directly from the task in hand. It would not surprise me to learn that he has no private life and no need of close friends, as he appears to be drawing vital experience straight from the stage with no need for outside nourishment. Again and again you feel that his struggle with a text has taken him into temperamental areas he has never explored before. ...' Thus wrote Irving Wardle the theatre critic of *The Times*[1]. He was talking, of course, about McKellen's amazing double, that of playing *Richard II* and Marlowe's *Edward II* in 1969. But before that McKellen had, in 1968, toured in just the Shakespeare play. He had joined the Prospect Company directed by Toby Robertson, with his old colleague Richard Cottrell, who was Assistant Director. 'I said to Toby, "It's *my* turn to do a Shakespeare", for he had done all of them up until then, and he said, "What play?" and I said "*Henry V*". Then Toby rang me at about 11 p.m. one evening and suggested *Richard II*. I sat and read the play and at 3 a.m. I rang Toby and said, "I can't do it – all that talking, all that standing about". Toby talked to me and said I could do it and asked who I would like to play Richard and I said that I would do it if Ian would play it. He was free so it was all quickly arranged,' says Richard Cottrell.[2]

Prospect was a worthy company who toured endlessly round the United Kingdom, bringing sound productions to the provinces with

occasional forays into London. McKellen is always attracted by acting
in the provinces. 'I saw marvellous touring companies when I was
young,' he enthuses[3] and he seems impelled to pay back that debt
somehow. 'There are very few established, famous classical actors on
the road. There are so many inconveniences – not so many good
landladies for example – and it takes a lot of effort. But I am free of
financial and other responsibilities and I enjoy it. It's a wonderful way
to see the country. I have seen most of the major towns in England and
the response of the audience is so unfettered of sophistication.'[4]

Of course, the part is a marvellous one and McKellen's way of playing
it was also inspired. As usual he found inspiration from a modern
parallel:

I went over to Ireland with the costume designs [explains Cottrell] and talked
with Ian about the part, and we read the play together. The central belief in
the play is, of course, the Divine Right of Kings, which is something that we
don't believe in nowadays and which means nothing to modern audiences. So
we tried to find someone in modern life who would give us a clear idea of
divinity and the Dalai Lama was the closest thing in modern society.[5]

Another image McKellen had in his mind for *Richard II* was that of
a modern film star. 'Movie stars do actually have courts, who follow them
around attending to each and every whim. They often hate the stars
because they are utterly dependent on them. But they also love and
respect the star, often just because of the fame. The star is bound to get
disenchanted with all this kind of attention because it's so false. Richard
realized that he needs genuine friendship, something he's never had;
that he has to become a man and not a star. At the same time he regrets
that he has to leave behind his stardom.'[6] 'Another source of inspiration
was a polar bear!' laughs Cottrell. 'Ian went to the zoo one day and saw
this bear padding up and down his cage and thought that that was how
Richard ought to move in the prison scene.'[7]

These were the images that McKellen directed towards the audience.
The tour took a normal Prospect course, attracting notices in the local
papers and on 5 November 1968, Michael Billington, then second-string
on *The Times*, caught the play at the Arts Theatre, Cambridge. Saying
that the main virtue of this solid and sturdy revival was 'that it offers a
carefully rethought interpretation of the central role' and that McKellen
offered a much more virile and varied interpretation than the accepted
effete one. He goes on to write:

The flaw in the Richard is temperamental rather than sexual: he is a
capricious, quixotic despot whose reliance on form and ritual constantly blinds

him to his own inadequacies. When we first see him he is like an overwound toy, gliding smoothly and ceremoniously into court as on castors ...

Having chosen this interpretation, director and actor follow it through with admirable consistency: even in the prison scene Richard paces rhythmically about the perimeter of his cell as if unconsciously harking back to his love of external form and ritual.

My only reservation about Mr McKellen's excellent performance is that he is prone to rattle off the more obviously rhetorical speeches in order to heighten the pathos of a particular line. Otherwise he makes the cracking of Richard's protective shell of majesty extremely moving and incidentally confirms his own pre-eminence among our younger actors ...

A month later, Harold Hobson saw the play in the last week of the tour, at Guildford and under the headline A KING BORN TO BE MAN he devoted most of his column to it on Sunday, 8 December. After praising the production he says that Cottrell found in McKellen 'a supremely impressive' interpreter of the main part.

From the moment of his entry we see that this Richard regards himself not, as we have always thought, as divinely God-protected, but as actually divine himself. Mr McKellen moves on to the stage with a more than human smoothness, and his arms are upraised from the elbows, framing the godhead and the crown, and fixed like the many arms of an Eastern Deity. His Richard is a god, but neither Christian nor Hebrew. He knows no compassion for his creatures, nor at first revenge. His serenity is celestial and appalling, and when he speaks it is with an astonishing swiftness, sweeping aside commas and full stops as imperiously – no, as impotently – as he does the injuries of his angry subjects. And yet, this god, this Deity, when he is with his boon companions, his Bushy, Bagot, Green is not a god at all but only an educated potboy ...

Mr McKellen in fact is a tremendous actor. No player of similar age has such lustre, such interior excitement, such spiritual grace. It is not only I who say this: it is a point of almost universal critical agreement – Michael Billington has gone so far as to call him the pre-eminent classical player of his generation, and B. A. Young says he is a great actor ...

It was, of course, too late to arrange a prolongation of the tour, and McKellen was committed elsewhere, but Prospect planned to take *Richard II* to the Edinburgh Festival and for a longer tour, including the Continent as well as, if possible, to bring this startling performance to London. Toby Robertson says, 'I suppose this is a story against myself. But I thought Ian exaggerated the part. The scene where he speaks about the loneliness of kings which ends

> I live with bread like you, feel want, taste grief,
> Need friends

he wailed those last words and I found it embarrassing. I told Cottrell that I thought they should be toned down. But neither he nor Ian agreed and so he went on saying them like that. Of course, that was the one speech that the critics commended!'[8]

Billington, indeed, had done so, 'I have never heard the line where he says he "feels want, tastes grief and needs friends" [sic] come across with such poignant urgency.'[9]

Cottrell sums up: 'We both saw Richard clearly in terms of a spiritual journey, shallow and heartless at the beginning, then the pivot coming at the "needs friends" speech – that suddenly came out as a great cry at a rehearsal, it was thrilling. That was the turning-point. Then in the deposition scene, Ian was vulnerable then in the prison scene, ...!'[10]

What he went on to do was to make three films and to direct his first play *The Prime of Miss Jean Brodie* for the Liverpool Playhouse and also to appear as Pentheus in *The Bacchæ*.

'Stage and cinema can be complementary,' he said at this time, 'and film producers are impressed with artists who have had success in the theatre.

'So far I've had parts in three films. I regard them just as experience or apprenticeship. Now I hope someone will offer me a leading part.'

'He wasn't desperately interested in doing films and television when he was young, though he saw the necessity of them for reaching a wider audience. I think he always preferred the stage, but I did try to persuade him into doing some small parts, because I think young actors must learn the technique in television and films or else they never learn it and it affects them later on. His first television job was in the Rudyard Kipling series, and Ian had about two lines. He had to sit up a tree on Ham Common, and it rained! He didn't enjoy it a bit and said, "If that's your TV you can keep it!" '[11]

The films, though, were not a resounding success: *Alfred the Great*, *The Promise* and *A Touch of Love* were certainly apprentice performances though it is interesting to note that *A Touch of Love* was based on Margaret Drabble's book, *The Millstone*. 'I've always thought,' says Clive Swift, 'that Maggie [to whom he was then married] might have based the character of George [the part McKellen played] a little bit on Ian.'[12]

Films are another subject on which McKellen appears to have a dichotomous attitude. While recognizing that they are necessary to make a name, he told Catherine Stott that, 'I hope films ... will put me more in the public eye and be useful as such, because whenever I've got to play good parts in films they've not known who I was which perhaps in the future will not be the case. Not that I wanted to be a film star, but it should be useful in the theatre.'[13] According to Stott he found that 'a vicious circle exists in the theatre; to get an excellent part in an excellent play he must first be established to a wider medium than the theatre to ensure the necessary box-office draw to satisfy the backers'. McKellen went on to say to her, 'It is a little annoying when people in the theatre and films who should know you, don't.[14] I am always going after films and not getting them, which is upsetting at the time.' Three years later he told Michael Owen, 'Films are absolutely the worst of all. The actor is never told anything. It is so insulting, so rude and so despicable. I would be glad to not only cut them off but cut their heads off.'[15]

Jennifer Tudor, a young actress, did a film test about this time. 'I was to act a scene with three young actors who were being tested for a part in *Ned Kelly* – Mick Jagger eventually played the part. McKellen was one of them and it all took place in Bushey Park, I think. Anyway, I had to do the scene, the same scene with all of them, several times over with each, McKellen was by far the most inventive and was willing to try all sorts of ways of doing the scene. And what is nicer, he remembers me and always speaks if we run into each other.'[16]

But McKellen need not have worried about his lack of fame, for within a few months his name was to resound plangently throughout the country and forever be associated and synonymous with great acting. Prospect was asked to present two plays at the Edinburgh Festival in that gloomy and uncomfortable Assembly Hall, with grim John Knox's statue looking down and appearing to think none too kindly on such unseemly proceedings. It was Sir Tyrone Guthrie who had the brilliant idea that this dismal place, where the elders of the Kirk of Scotland meet, would make a stupendous space in which to present plays on a thrust, Elizabethan stage and Prospect rose to the challenge. It was decided to revise *Richard II* and to couple it with another play. Toby Robertson after considering *Henry V* with Gary Bond decided on *Edward II*. He had already done a production with the Marlowe Society at Cambridge with Derek Jacobi in the leading part. Ian was asked to take the part of Gaveston in *Edward II*, to which he agreed. Jacobi was unable to take the part of Edward again and Gary Bond was approached. After provisionally accepting, Bond then found that other commitments prevented him from joining the company and no other young actor was prepared to play the homosexual king. 'So I took Ian out to lunch,' says Toby Robertson 'and persuaded him to take on the two parts.' It was thought that to play two such long, draining parts would be too much for any actor night after night, both at the Festival and on the tour that was envisaged afterwards. It was a decision that was to prove a turning-point in McKellen's life.[17]

'He was, I remember, very nervous about doing the two parts,' says Robertson, 'but he worked tremendously hard. It was a tremendous effort to have the double yoke of playing two kings, but it was the making of Ian. He was a terrific success.'[18] The critics and the audiences loved it. 'Ian was tremendously nervous before the opening of Edward,' says Robertson. 'He was very afraid that his voice wouldn't hold out, so I had to talk to him quietly in the dressing-room.'[19]

'I can imagine he would have been,' says Sara Kestelman. 'No one can realize what a tremendous strain it is to have two such large, demanding parts like that to play night after night.[20] The *responsibility*, too.'

'He didn't show too many nerves during the day,' says Elspeth Cochrane. 'I remember that he was most concerned about what to give the cast and he thought it should be bottles of champagne. But he didn't know how to organize it ... obviously he couldn't carry thirty or so bottles himself and he was fussing about this, so, in the end, I went to the off-licence and got them to deliver the bottles. We often laugh about it now.'[21]

But it was not all so easily overcome. The Edinburgh City Fathers always, anyway, grudging about the Festival got wind of the play's theme, and were horrified that in one scene Ian McKellen was to kiss another man. Councillor John Kidd said, 'It is shocking and it is filthy,' as he lodged a protest. 'Can you blame me when I see two men kissing one another. I think it is the sort of play that Edinburgh does not want.' Yet another Town Councillor making a fool of himself over one of the great classics of English literature; from time immemorial they have been fulminating over Chaucer, Shakespeare, Marlowe and anyone else that catches their eyes.

Councillor Kidd asked the Chief Constable of Edinburgh to intervene. Toby Robertson, delighted at the publicity, said that it was a staggering play. 'I think the play is so well constructed and put together that these things are not fortuitous and they belong to the whole concept of the play. To play up the fact that two boys kiss on the stage is, in the context of the play, extraordinarily weak.'[22] Nonetheless, Robertson and his public relations officer, Bill Beresford, had to see the City Fathers. 'It was an extraordinary row,' says Beresford. 'I remember the bother Toby and I had.'[23] The critics were bedazzled. Irving Wardle wrote in *The Times*:

Whatever the dramatic shortcomings of this year's Edinburgh Festival it has at least found the right shows to install in the grim eminence of the Assembly Hall where nightly the lamentable reigns of Richard II and Edward II – a pair of royal playboys brought down by surly baronial backwoodsmen – are being enacted in a setting fully consonant with the dungeons of Pomfret and Berkeley Castle ...

Prospect Productions have more to offer than a mere framework for a star, but the main purpose of their programme is summed up in the double performance of the two kings by Ian McKellen ...

His Richard, with the support of a beautifully coherent production by Richard Cottrell, is a study in ceremony which he takes in deadly sacramental earnest, making his first entry in the midst of a priest-like procession, palms upraised and face chastely impassive, consciously holding himself as a sacred vessel. The point is driven home by contrast in the following scene where we see Richard off duty lounging among his parasites and dispensing cold little smiles and arrogant jokes through clenched teeth. ...

His Edward, matching the geometric progression of the action, does not follow a linear development but a series of bold leaps involving startling physical transformations – the infantile lover, with no interest whatsoever in kingship and hardly able to lift a sword, changing into the blood-drunken warlord, and finally the emaciated wreck in the sewers of Berkeley.

Harold Hobson, already an admirer of the Richard, under the heading A KING ACCLAIMED wrote:

The uncontested triumph of the Edinburgh Festival so far has been that of Ian McKellen and the Prospect Theatre Company in their production in the Assembly Hall, directed by Richard Cottrell ... [Edinburgh] has received Mr McKellen and the production itself, which is all glorious with flamboyant colours of gold and red, with a tumult of acclaim ...

The ineffable presence of God himself enters in Mr McKellen's Richard. As the Deity takes possession his eyes glaze, the real world vanishes from before him ...

He went on to praise, as other critics did, Robert Eddison as York and Timothy as Bolingbroke, Hobson refers to Ian's performance as sensational and, 'in fact, the whole production deserves the rapture with which it has been received'.

Turning to *Edward II*, Hobson went on:

Two days after this triumph Mr McKellen, for his performance in Marlowe's *Edward II*, also at the Assembly Hall, was given as great an ovation as I have ever heard in the theatre. The trouble is that it was not really deserved. The audience after *Richard II* justly alerted by the Scottish critics to the fact that there was a great actor in Edinburgh, went prepared for a masterpiece, and they saw what they expected to see, even though it wasn't there, Toby Robertson's bold and unhypocritical production brings Marlowe out into the open, writing him up large as pro-sodomy and anti-snob. This marries itself easily to the vagaries of our time, but it is not enough.

There is more to the passionate enslavement of King Edward to the fascinating Gaveston than can be revealed by the continuous spectacle of a couple of hippies necking in Green Park. In this production the action is suited to the word with monotonously exhibitionist reiteration that only rarely, in an occasional gash of the wanton loveliness of Marlowe's verse, gives any sense of the destructive tide of homosexual infatuation of which it is the quite inadequate expression. Mr McKellen is an actor of great spiritual grace, but he is not graceful to look at, and all these smacking kisses before his angry nobles suggest little more than that Edward was tiresomely addicted to showing off.

This is worse than disappointing: it is positively boring ...[24]

Looking back on the production nearly twenty years afterwards, Robertson says, 'The production I did up at Cambridge with Jacobi was quite different. It was a *political* play, I felt Ian brandished, *flaunted* the homosexuality in the part. I had had a fruitful and happy time with Derek exploring the play, but I thought that Ian was too actorish, too "we're in the theatre" about it. I missed the interaction of power and suffering which Derek brought to the part. Ian was *too* narcissistic and lost people's sympathy for the part. My lasting memory is of his brandishing a sword over his head as the lights went down at the end of the first act. A typical, theatrical, McKellen gesture.'[25]

'I remember,' says Bridget Turner, 'being in Ireland with Ian before he played Richard and he was on the telephone to Richard Cottrell nearly every evening discussing the play. I'm sure most of the ideas for it came from Ian. Anyway he had a lot to do with the interpretation of the part',[26] and it seems that that would also underline the interpretation of Edward, at least it seems to be from what Robertson says.

'Ian needs a strong director,' Bob Chetwyn says, 'for he is such a strong person himself, so full of ideas, that he has to be watched carefully. He always responds well, though, to criticism, provided that criticism is convincing.'[27]

This is, of course, in great contrast to his days in repertory. 'I don't remember him being at all inventive at Coventry,' says Bridget Turner, 'although he always worked hard, he was rather quiet. But we did become firm friends, he is a wonderful friend. Warm and generous.'[28]

Clare Fox who was up in Edinburgh, working, met Ian for lunch one day and they had to wait a long time before anyone came to serve them, waiters studiously ignoring Ian's signals and attempts to order. He turned to Clare, grinned, and said, 'So that's what it means to be the Toast of the Festival.'[29] And he might have added, 'And all for fifty pounds a week, too!'[30]

After Edinburgh the two plays went on into the Mermaid Theatre, in Puddle Dock, London.

'It was a tremendous experience,' says Eddie Kulukundis, who is on the Board of the Mermaid Theatre[31]. 'I thought Ian played both parts magnificently ... I was equally excited by them both. *Edward II* is a less good play but I had never seen it before, so, then I found it the more exciting for it was a new experience. There is a similarity in the characters of the two kings, of course, but the performances were quite different.'

From there the play went to Vienna and Czechoslovakia. In Czechoslovakia the authorities didn't want visiting plays, particularly political plays, though as McKellen says, 'On the whole we concentrated on the humanity of the characters rather than their political nature. We thought of the political factions as a family, Richard II as a man with cousins and uncles and other relatives, and I think that it was in that sense that we looked at the politics in it.'[32] But Czechoslovakia was at a time of crisis: six months before Dubček had been deposed, which made *Richard II* very topical, and, says Robertson, 'Timmy West who was playing Bolingbroke bore a striking resemblance to Husek, the man now in power.'[33] The effect on the audience was very moving for the actors. McKellen says:

When I came to the speech where Richard II returns from Ireland to discover that his nation has been overrun by his cousin Bolingbroke, and he kneels down on the earth and asks the stones and the nettles and the insects to help him in his helpless state against the armies who had invaded his land, I could hear something I had never heard before, nor since, which was a whole audience apparently weeping. It shakes me now to think about it, because in that instant I realized that the audience were crying for themselves. They recognized in Richard II their own predicament of only six months previously when their neighbours, and as it were their cousins, had invaded their land, and all they had were sticks and stones to throw at tanks.

I would never have talked about the play in those terms. We hadn't seen it as directly relevant to any modern political situation. Shakespeare couldn't have known about Communism, about the East or the West. Afterwards I said to one of the new men, the anti-Dubček faction, to one of their leaders who was in the audience, 'Who did you side with in the play, Richard II or Bolingbroke? The man on the ground or the invader?' And he said, 'Both right, both wrong'.[34]

The play then came to the Piccadilly Theatre in London. 'It was a wonderful time,' says Robert Eddison, 'I remember in my youth people used to come up in the morning and put stools down for what was called the Pit and the Gallery, and when we came into the theatre for the performance there were always all these people waiting to go in. It was always exciting. At the Piccadilly there were always queues at the Box Office and the younger members of the cast got very excited and I thought, poor things, they *have* been deprived.' Eddison loved being in the company and had the greatest 'admiration and affection for Ian. The Duke of York was a dull part, really, but I loved playing it – and Richard Cottrell exercised his considerable persuasive powers on me to do this and Lightborn [in *Edward II*]. I was quite happy to do that as I thought it was the only possible part for me – I couldn't *really* see myself as one of those Lancastrian barons. And, in rehearsals, it was marvellous to watch Ian as he realized the character, became Edward in those rehearsals, very thoroughly.'[35]

Michael Billington in *The Times* wrote: 'I first saw his [McKellen's] Richard in Cambridge a year ago when it was already remarkable but marred by certain repetitive vocal mannerisms: now much simplified and strengthened, it ranks high among the finest Shakespearian performances of the past decade.' One now can add, since it has remained in people's minds and is still talked of with awe, for the last *twenty* years. Both performances were televised and shown on BBC TV.

In July 1970, McKellen appeared again at the Royal Court in the Theatre Upstairs, a studio theatre where experimental plays were performed, in Barry Hines's *Billy's Last Stand*. Irving Wardle wrote in *The Times*:

A lot depends on how the two figures are presented. And at the Court they are shown very much in black and white. John Barrett's Billy is a standard image of the honest working-man, solidly pragmatic, firm-minded and not at all the kind of outsider you would expect to find living in a corrugated iron shack. Ian McKellen's Darkly, with his clipped moustache and silk-lined overcoat is almost an old-style spiv; a plainly untrustworthy character on whom it is surprising to find Billy wasting five minutes. Their dialogue goes with a fine idiomatic swing; and the climax, as McKellen drives his partner to fury by pelting the iron walls with Billy's treasured lumps of coal is really exciting.

Another TV success was *Ross*, which was BBC's Play of the Month in October 1970. 'It's a much more interesting play than the film,' [of *Lawrence of Arabia*] McKellen told Rosemarie Wittman in an interview. 'I think of Lawrence as the first victim of the public relations men. He was built up into this public figure and he couldn't reconcile it with what he felt inside him.'

He was, by this time, working with Richard Cottrell again. Cottrell had left Prospect to take charge of the Cambridge Theatre Company and had collected a bright company to go on an eight-week tour including a season at Cambridge in George Farquhar's *The Recruiting Officer* and Arnold Wesker's *Chips With Everything* earning £45 a week.[36] Among the actors were Trevor Peacock, Meg Wynn Owen, Richard Morant and Susan Fleetwood, soon to become a firm friend and 'an adoptive sister'.[37]

'He was a very gentle person,' says Trevor Peacock. 'He struck up a friendship with my daughter Sally, who was then about seven or eight, he really was very sweet to her. She discovered that he liked jelly and once or twice she made him one and took it to his dressing-room. He loved them and ate them up.'[38]

'He was clearly, from the start, a star performer,' Peacock goes on. 'He doesn't like button-hole acting, he loves acting straight out. He didn't go out with the Company a lot – he was always a very dedicated fellow, acting is the most important thing for him.'[39]

McKellen played two leading parts in the productions – Captain Plume in the Farquhar play and Corporal Hill in the Wesker. Cottrell wanted *Chips* to look authentic so the cast were marched off to a local hairdresser for the regulation short back and sides, but McKellen elected to wear a wig instead![39] Most of the notices were good: *The Stage* (9 October 1970) praised it adding that, 'Ian McKellen leads the company as Corporal Hill, an efficient, small-minded little man, accepting his position without question. This is a brilliant performance, Mr McKellen virtually unrecognized, barking out orders with a gruff northern accent.' However, Michael Billington, in *The Times* was less complimentary: 'The casting of Ian McKellen as Corporal Hill does not help matters. Mr McKellen's brilliance is not in question; but he does not have the natural physical and vocal weight for the goading, humourless NCO and never really suggests he could frighten or intimidate a squad of recruits.' As usual McKellen worked hard, he and other members of the cast learnt to drill properly, coached by John Golightly, a fellow cast member who had been a drill sergeant.[40]

The play toured and notices were very good. The *Croydon Advertiser* commenting on the performances in the Ashcroft Theatre, Croydon said, 'McKellen's playing of Plume has the panache the name implies: but he is never obtrusively showy ... He has splendid vitality and great charm, whether wooing a doxy with impudence or his lady with sincerity.' B. A. Young, catching the play in Cambridge, wrote in the *Financial Times*, 'Ian McKellen makes Plume a true romantic,' while Billington in *The Times* was rapturous, '... the depth and subtlety of Ian McKellen's performance as Plume. Pacing the stage like a restless thoroughbred, he seizes on the character's own admission that his air of cavalier freedom is all a pose. He shows that underneath the bull swagger lies a psychologically complicated figure; and with his reflex production of a notebook whenever a potential recruit appears, he reminds us that for Plume the enlistment business is no fun but an urgent professional necessity. In fact, it is chiefly through McKellen's performance that we become aware of Farquhar's criticism of the hypocrises and dishonesties of recruitment.'

Besides Cambridge and Croydon, the company visited Swansea, Brighton, Leeds and Southampton. McKellen said to Betty Hughes of the *South Wales Evening Post*, 'Being recognized as a good actor is lovely but I do not want the trappings of stardom; I just want to go on with what I am doing now – working in the live theatre and going round the country with good productions. One of the compensations of touring ... is that you sense the audience is pleased to see you.'

But already he was preparing for the next step in his career for he was already working on one of the most tremendous parts any actor can play.

HAMLET

McKellen had long wanted to play Hamlet. In February 1969, he told Catherine Stott in *The Guardian*, 'I badly want to play Hamlet soon, and obviously the place to play it is at Stratford and if Trevor Nunn was to direct me then I can't think of anything I would rather do.' But although Stratford had offered him a contract it was for three years and did not include the coveted part.[42] But the chance to play Hamlet was just about to come – with Prospect. Toby Robertson did not want to direct Ian. 'I had always planned to do it with Derek Jacobi, and indeed, I did it much later on with him,' Robertson says.[43] 'Ian didn't want Toby, nor Richard Cottrell, but he asked me to direct it,' says Robert Chetwyn.[44]

'I think he and Bob had talked about the time that they would do *Hamlet* together,' says Elspeth Cochrane, 'even as far back as Ipswich. It was something they both wanted to do.' So the production was planned, for a tour of the UK and Europe, 'and Ian was very ambitious for his Hamlet to be seen in the West End,' says Robertson.[45] The production was very inventive. Chetwyn explains, 'The set was all mirrors, two-way mirrors, for it seemed to me that that was a recurring image in the play. And it made for some good effects. We had three ghosts, all reflected time and time again, the stage was covered with ghosts and Fortinbras's army, which, in reality, was only about five people, looked like thousands.'[46]

The reason for the ghost is interesting. 'I was brooding on the play one evening and I suddenly thought that there wasn't a real ghost but that it was all in Hamlet's mind. I rang Ian up and he was very excited about the idea and he came round and we discussed it. The voice was done electronically, by James Cairncross, and Ian accepted the whole conception enthusiastically.'

McKellen and Chetwyn did an enormous amount of work before rehearsals began: 'Ian used to come round to my flat for about three or four months beforehand and we really went through the text, word by word and talked over the meaning of it thoroughly; we were locked into it. He was completely open, but he needed to be convinced about any idea, really convinced.'[47]

The concept for the part came from Chetwyn,[48] 'but Ian wanted to discuss every aspect of the part. We decided that we wanted to tell the story as clearly as possible. After all, we would be seen by school kids, audiences who had never seen a Shakespeare play before, so we strove for clarity of the text. The critics, after all, have seen *Hamlet* many times, but most of the audience won't have.'[49]

Patrick Wymark in an interview in *The Times* wrote, 'McKellen says they have no fancy interpretation to offer; the play is quite difficult enough without that. But this is broadly how they are seeing it: Hamlet is first shown as an extremely depressed little boy finding everything possible wrong with his world. Then he sees the ghost of his father which, Mr McKellen says, is a "mind-blowing experience": in the main body of the play Hamlet shows himself ready and fitted for the job in hand.

'Mr McKellen says he finds playing Hamlet more exhausting than he thought he would. "There is a passage when you are on stage for an hour. You are the machine for every theme and you have to fuel that machine somehow. Then, right at the end, you have got to do all that bloody fighting. You are certainly ready for death after that".'[50]

He was of the opinion that it was the best thing he had done so far – whatever the critics would say.[51] The critics, anyway, were becoming very jaded with *Hamlet* – one of them calculated that it was the year of ten Hamlets, but that seems an exaggeration! Certainly Alan Bates had played it recently, as Emrys Bryson was to remark in the *Nottingham Post*. Bryson, recalling McKellen's sojourn at the Playhouse where he showed 'a lean and hungry resolve', comments of his Hamlet:

An unkempt prince with more than a hint of the hippie about him, he is at first gauche and gangling. You'd almost take him for a modern youth – shaggy hair, stark jersey, dirty boots, medallion on chain, a fringed jerkin.

A mercurial, exuberant Hamlet this – a seventeenth-century loner on a mental LSD trip which sharpens his brain and his determination. Horsing around during the play-within-a-play, he stands on a stool and twangs an invisible arrow, like Eros ...

It is a vivid, thrusting portrait of an erratic, even unstable, temperament clarified into action until, in that furious orgasm of revenge, he wounds the king with the sword that is killing himself, forces the poison goblet down his throat, and finishes the job with a dagger stab ...

... and (logical touch) Hamlet is put into a straitjacket when sent off to England to cure his madness.[52]

Gareth Lloyd-Evans in *The Guardian* of 25 March 1971 wrote:

People wait nowadays for an Ian McKellen performance with that breathless anticipation usually reserved for moon landings. His latest touchdown is on *Hamlet* at the Nottingham Playhouse. It is time we were clear about this clever young actor. His recent Shakespearian performances, hailed by the London critics as new discoveries in acting, reveal a slightly more sophisticated kind of competence than Mr McKellen was displaying at the Belgrade Theatre, Coventry a few years ago – displays noted by the provincial critics but at that time unaccountably ignored by London.

Mr McKellen's acting takes us back many decades to the extrovert, mannered days of the old touring companies and matinée idols. His acting is less a committal to the part than a demonstration of personal idiosyncracies. There are so many of them – a vocal quaver, a flashing eye, a leaping leg, a facial quiver, a tousled head, a quivering lip, a winsome smile that, by the law of averages whatever part he plays he's bound to please somebody in the audience. It is a clever, not-to-be-underrated talent as feverish as Kean, as old-fashioned as Ainley, and as calculating as Irving. His speaking is constantly listening to itself, his diction has moments of incredible eccentricity, his movements disguise a basic awkwardness by being incessant and exaggerated. Mr McKellen is a nineteenth century star actor – what he lacks is anything that seems natural, truly felt, interpreted. His is the triumph of artifice over everything else. ...[53]

Irving Wardle caught the play in Edinburgh. Saying that it 'would have needed superhuman restraint not to try to go one better' than the triumphant double of Richard and Edward, he goes on to say,

So it is with some diffidence that I record that Robert Chetwyn's production offers both more and less than a star performance.

Its surrounding framework is that of a treacherous maze; Elsinore, this time, being occupied by sycophantic slapping courtiers and a smirking oily monarch and located in an intricate hall of mirrors in which the natural mingles with the supernatural and the action passes freely between dream, reality and fantasy ...

McKellen's Prince is offered as a jewel in this setting which seems to have been designed as much to allow him maximum freedom as for its appropriateness to the action's requirements ... It is the romantic, neurotic approach, bred almost entirely from within (except in the relationship with Gertrude) and often suggesting adolescent emotional compensation.

It is doubtless irrelevant that McKellen still looks rather like a schoolboy actor: but the depressing factor in performance is his uncontrolled development of personal mannerisms – the ostentatious shows of distress, abrupt village-idiot grins, the tousled explosions of passion and the disconcerting Lancashire cadences that appear at key points (even in the very last line).

McKellen is at his best in soliloquies (here relit to become internal monologues) and in the closet scene where for once he does achieve contact with a partner (Faith Brook).[54]

Elspeth Cochrane says 'As the company wanted a transfer to the West End, and I thought that Ian's Hamlet deserved to be seen, I tried to get several managements interested. But as the notices hadn't been all that good, most of them were simply not interested.'[55]

Also in Scotland at this time was Jack Lynn, actor and then director of Knightsbridge Productions. 'Elspeth rang me at Killiecrankie,' says Lynn, 'and said how interesting the performance was so I went over to Aberdeen to see it. It was among the best three I have ever seen.' Jack says that Gielgud was another of the top three but declines to mention the third! 'I went round to see Ian afterwards and introduced myself. He was, I think, startled to see me in a kilt!' Lynn always wears one in Scotland. 'I found out that the company was to be in Glasgow the next week so I rang Eddie, [Kulukundis] the head of the firm, and asked him if he could come up to see this extremely exciting performance.'[56]

Eddie did and was also tremendously excited. 'For some reason Toby Robertson didn't want it to come to London, I don't know why, but I really thought it deserved to be seen. I took Ian and Bob out to dinner – an Indian or Pakistani restaurant I think – and decided, if I could get a theatre, I would bring it in after the continental tour. I thought it one of the best performances I had ever seen in a British theatre.'[57]

The play was scheduled to go to Holland, Belgium, Germany and to festivals in Rome, Vienna and Zurich. 'Eddie flew me over to Amsterdam to see it, and it was incredible seeing it with a foreign audience. They went wild about it,' says Elspeth.[58]

The *Nieuwe Gids* of Holland wrote: '... Ian McKellen offers us a young Hamlet, emotional and touching. Sober and still dramatic.' While the *Nieuwe Gazet* said that McKellen played 'with incredible flexibility, showing that he has penetrated the heart of Shakespeare's metaphors, and reinterpreted them in a complete pattern of movement ...'.

In Antwerp *La Metropole* said that the interpretation of the play was really astonishing and of McKellen's Hamlet wrote:

It can be said straight away that it was an astonishing interpretation ... a Shakespearian one *par excellence*. Here certainly is an artist who knows Shakespeare's work profoundly and has chosen his personal manner of interpreting Shakespeare's thought ... This is not the romantic Hamlet of the last century. He has given his Hamlet a depth of humanity, and the humorous element is not lacking ...

The *Frankfurter Allgemeine Zeitung* wrote on 19 June 1971, 'A very young Hamlet, sensitive, emotionally almost a manic depressive, clings to the dead lost father, to whom he probably was much less attached when alive ...'

John Francis Lane writing in the *Daily American* criticized the production which he saw in the Teatro Elisso in Rome thus:

I have seen many Hamlets in my time, but I think this is the first which has truly convinced me that it was logical for Hamlet to keep putting off the act of revenge when he has cause, and will, and strength, and means to do it.

This emotionally-strung youth is very much a child of our times. He has nothing but contempt for Polonius and Claudius, the Establishment figures. He loves his Mum but has no patience with her problem ...

All in all, a *Hamlet* worth seeing because it has great emotional impact and contemporary feeling.

On the tour, playing four parts – Player King, First Player, Bernardo and a Messenger – 'changing moustaches all the time' was Tim Pigott-Smith, then a young actor in his third job. 'Ian was a marvellous company leader. I remember one evening in the time that Hamlet is off stage he came into my dressing-room where I was getting ready for the next entrance and took a real interest in what I had done, what I wanted to do, and what my hopes were. Not many leading actors would do that. And he was very good about fan mail too. I went in to say "Hello" once when I arrived at the theatre and saw him writing letters and said "What a lot" and he replied, "O, I answer them all". I made up my mind that when I got fan mail I would answer it all, too. And I do.'[59]

In Vienna, the actor playing Claudius fell ill and Pigott-Smith, who was understudying the part had to go on. 'Ian was exceptionally generous to me about it,' he says. 'He never, ever, made you feel he was unapproachable anyway. And without in anyway being disloyal to the other actor he made me feel that my performance was better.'[60]

'I thought Tim was a very good young actor,' says Chetwyn, 'and he played Claudius very well indeed.'[61] 'Ian didn't socialize much,' said Tim, 'but after I played Claudius he took me out to dinner [Chetwyn was also in the party] and when they came to make some cast changes for London I really believe that Ian recommended me for Laertes, not that he took me on one side to tell me so, not like most people would have, but I feel pretty sure about it.'[62]

'The decision would have been mine,' Chetwyn told me, 'though I would have discussed it with Ian, we were very close at that time, very close indeed. And Tim was a fine actor.'

Laertes has, of course, a fight with Hamlet at the end of the play. 'We rehearsed it again and again so that it wouldn't go wrong,' says Pigott-Smith (Jack Shepherd said in 'An Actor's Life' on BBC 2 that McKellen wasn't very good at fighting) 'but accidents do happen. One night he knicked me by the eye, and blood really began to flow ... it looked much worse than it was. People began to gather in the wings, but it actually wasn't hurting at the time, I suppose that I was concentrating too much on what I was doing. Anyway, at the end, when he lowered me on to the floor, Ian murmured, "Are you all right?" He was very concerned.' Tim had to have a stitch in the cut and the scar is still visible.[63]

There was another incident which he remembers, which happened on tour. The 'Rogue and Peasant Slave' soliloquy was transposed. 'After I did the Hecuba speech we all froze and the spotlight went on Ian and he did the soliloquy, then the lights went up, we all unfroze and he came across to me as First Player and we went on with the scene. One night he came across looking very strange indeed and I thought he was ill, had 'flu coming or something. I managed to ask him what was the matter and he said that a man was sitting in the front row actually following the text and had fluttered his pages over during the soliloquy. He really couldn't stand it, and after a while he just, very quietly, lent over and said something to the man. It was very unobtrusively done, you really wouldn't have noticed.'

In London, at the Cambridge Theatre, the London critics were not altogether impressed. 'Eddie had put Harold Hobson at the end of the row, so that he could get in and out easily,' says Chetwyn (Hobson is physically handicapped) 'and his kindness rebounded on us I think!'[64] In any case Hobson's notice was terse:

> To sit for three-and-three-quarter hours with one's head twisted round at an angle of forty-five degrees is hardly the most convenient way of judging a production of *Hamlet*. To put Hamlet into a strait-jacket and make Gertrude tipsy as happens at the Cambridge hardly seems to me to justify a new production of the play, even if it has the exciting Ian McKellen as the principal part. Despite his fire and passion, Mr McKellen appears to lack any compulsive conception in his performance. The whole evening in fact created the impression of a Wolfit production without Wolfit.[65]

Irving Wardle in *The Times* gave it a longer and considered notice: firstly he commented that the play had been 'clobbered' by critics while it had been on the road for four months, and that it was evidently thought time 'to put the boot in' McKellen, thinking that he had been 'over-sold'. He then went on to write:

> Having seen and joined in the general chorus of derision when the production appeared in Edinburgh last April, it is pleasant to succumb to the sporting instinct and declare that his performance has much improved. Many of his vocal oddities have been corrected and there is no trace of his unconscious Lancashire inflections ...
>
> Gone, too, is the slack village idiot's jaw and the gangling stance. Altogether the performance has more authority, more economy, and more detail that really tells ... Some tricks still need to be cleared up, but on the technical side, McKellen has clearly been getting his head down.
>
> What, alas, remains unaltered is his conception of the part. Hamlet, to his loss, has always been a favourite adolescent role ... And it is mainly on this level that McKellen operates. From his first startled response to the gun salute to the royal toast, he presents Hamlet as a febrile juvenile, capable of rousing himself into furies of self-intoxicated rhetoric (which thoroughly sabotages the point of 'O, what a rogue'), but equally prone to burying his face in the Queen's lap ...

Perhaps the cruellest comment about his Hamlet is the one McKellen himself chose. When Diana Rigg was compiling her book *No Turn Unstoned* she wrote to hundreds of actors and actresses asking them to donate their unkindest criticism. McKellen, to his great credit, submitted this one from Harold Hobson's broadcast on *Hamlet*: 'The best thing about Ian McKellen's Hamlet is his curtain call.'[66]

Speaking about Hamlet in March 1980 when he was in Norway, McKellen said: 'When Hamlet meets the ghost it is immaterial whether the audience believes in ghosts or not. The play is not about ghosts, it is about Hamlet's inner life, about his meeting with his own conscience, about his settlement with his friends, with his family and with himself. It is about a young person's search and that is why this play has always fascinated young people. And Hamlet is no dreamer, he is a person who thinks.'[67]

6
The Actors' Company

After playing Hamlet for nine months, McKellen was asked to open the Crucible Theatre, Sheffield. The actual opening ceremony was a Gala Concert, but the first play was to be *Swan-song* by Chekhov, which was really a one-part play with a tiny supporting part. McKellen discussed this with Edward Petherbridge and was delighted when Petherbridge telephoned him at 1 a.m. and asked if he, Petherbridge, could play the part. Petherbridge, besides being a friend, had recently been much acclaimed for his playing of Guildenstern in Tom Stoppard's *Rosencrantz and Guildenstern Are Dead*, with John Stride at the National.[1] The two actors and the director, David William, rehearsed together in William's flat and there was much talk not only about the play, but about the lot and condition of actors. An idea was born.

1972 was not a good year for work for McKellen – one of the few times he had to go to the Labour Exchange. There was some TV, including an episode of *Country Matters* and a chance to direct Joe Orton's *The Erpingham Camp* at Watford Palace with John Savident in the lead, though the notice was not particularly good. He returned to Liverpool Playhouse to direct *Three Months Gone* by David Howarth and then went to Leicester to again direct, this time Tom Stoppard's *The Real Inspector Hound*. But an idea, which in many actors' opinions was to change their status for ever, was being born. McKellen asked himself the question, if Petherbridge was willing to support him, why shouldn't he, one day, support Petherbridge, who was known as one of the leading young actors of the day. So the two actors and William made a list of twelve actors with whom they would like to work in a small, but high-powered company. And during the rehearsal period of *Swan-song* – in October 1971 in fact – a letter was sent to these twelve asking whether they would be interested in joining a company where the actors were in charge, chose the plays, engaged the directors and helped in the administration. In November 1971 a meeting was held in

McKellen's flat – only one of the twelve, Eileen Atkins, declined, being already committed to other work. After much discussion the aims of the company were hammered out: the actors to be in control, and each actor to be equal with the others, one vote for each person; everyone willing to play leading parts, supporting roles or just walk-on. McKellen felt, and other actors will confirm that this is so, that acting is a job which is interdependent; that even stars need small part players that will give generously to them to make them effective.

There was one problem, a perennial one, how was the company to get money? Where was the person who had enough money to underwrite such an adventure? The Arts Council could be approached, but were not likely to be prepared to subsidize such a radical step. Richard Cottrell, old friend from Cambridge days, and the director of *Richard II*, had recently moved to the Cambridge Theatre Company and he saw the value of having two such consummate actors as McKellen and Petherbridge associated with his theatre, so he was more than interested. 'It was a wonderful idea, and it came at a good time for the Cambridge Theatre Company,' says Cottrell. 'It gave me a smashing autumn season, which was shown by the Box Office – but it did take a long time to set up. We met every week for ages on a Sunday, and people we had asked to join didn't stay the course.'[3] McKellen also approached Bill Thomley, the drama director of the Edinburgh Festival and over lunch Thomley was enthused with the idea of having the Company at the Festival in August. The Company, some of the original names had withdrawn, met with Cottrell who explained the facts of theatre finance to them. At least £75,000 would be needed: he was prepared to sink his own grant for the Cambridge Theatre Company into the scheme and to raise the rest from the Cambridge City authorities and from DALTA, the Arts Council Touring section. The Box Office takings should be guaranteed by the theatres engaging the Company. The actors could have £18 a week during the four weeks of rehearsal and £50 a week thereafter (the average male wage was then £35). Cottrell also produced a list of plays that he thought would be interesting and suitable for the Company to do. The idea was a practicality. McKellen later told Michael Billington:

'A feeling that we ought to be doing more as actors than we are, to help change things, particularly the conditions under which we work. The physical conditions are not very good, And the psychological conditions are often worse partly because of the difficulty of knowing what one's position is within the organization that puts on a play. Actors in the big companies like the National and the RSC for instance, are not in touch with the plays that are going to be done and how they are going to be cast. Obviously there are administrative difficulties if one's running a theatre of up to two thousand people. But what managements could do is take into account actors' opinions on matters of overall policy.'[4]

After the meeting with Cottrell the actors set about reading the plays and having further discussions with Cottrell. Like most actors, reading plays means finding out what are the good parts for them, not whether the play is a viable piece of theatre, but a short-list was drawn up of *The Taming of the Shrew; Measure for Measure; 'Tis Pity she's a Whore; Dandy Dick; Live Like Pigs;* and *The Lower Depths* – which was the one that Cottrell, himself wanted to direct.

Unfortunately, the Edinburgh Festival did not want the Gorki play and as the RSC announced that it was going to produce *The Lower Depths* it was discarded, but the Festival was interested in *'Tis Pity*, the John Ford play which is a blood-curdling Jacobean play of incest and murder. Other plays were looked at, including *The Country Wife* and *The Importance of Being Earnest.*

Petherbridge thought he was to do *Hamlet* and left the Company, but returned when that project fell through. Cottrell then suggested that a Feydeau farce would be a wonderful contrast with *'Tis Pity*. He wanted to translate *Le Dindon* and this idea was accepted by the actors. All the time members of the Company were finding other members, although several directors decided that they did not want to be employed by the people they would be directing and declined to work with the Company, but David Giles agreed.

'I was rung up and asked if I would be interested in joining,' Margery Mason says. 'I imagine that I was about the third or fourth person they had approached for my slot – after Dame Peggy and others had declined [her eyes twinkle]. I was interested so I went along to a meeting in Ian's flat. It was all lovely in those days, we used to kiss and put our arms round each other when we met. It was very democratic, everyone spoke at meetings and voted. The majority vote was taken and kept to.'[5] Directors and designers and principal back stage staff were also given a vote. Edward Petherbridge said to Ronald Hayman:

'Major decisions come to us as the fifteen Artistic Directors. Actually more – including the directors of plays, designers and the administrator, who all have one vote – we've literally got workers' control.'

'Democracies are always more exhausting,' says Cottrell, 'it took a very long time to get everything together, and though people were committed, they did leave – it was always, of course, understood that if people were unhappy they could leave, particularly when we had chosen the plays and they didn't like their parts. But there was, inevitably, some feelings of bitterness when this happened, but not much.'[6]

Casting was also done on a committee basis, for instance McKellen was offered Giovanni in 'Tis Pity, the leading part, but only the Pageboy in Ruling the Roost (as the Feydeau was called). The idea was, as far as possible, for each actor to have a lead or big part in one play, minor ones in the others.

'I was very touched when I was asked to join the company,' says Robert Eddison. 'I was so much older than all the others. But it was all the greatest fun, huge fun, though I did find the meetings endless and ghastly. I never knew what to say!'[7]

'Eventually we reached a point where we needed sixteen actors to finalize the plays, so we then contracted people, and most stayed for the second and third seasons,' says Cottrell.[8]

The Founding Members of the Actors' Company were – in the alphabetical order that they agreed to use for posters, and which now has become commonplace in the subsidized companies – Caroline Blakiston, Marian Diamond, Robert Eddison, Robin Ellis, Tenniel Evans, Felicity Kendal, Matthew Long, Margery Mason, Ian McKellen, Frank Middlemass, Juan Moreno, Edward Petherbridge, Moira Redmond, Sheila Reid, Jack Shepherd, Ronnie Stevens and John Tordoff.

Three plays had now been chosen, for besides 'Tis Pity and Ruling the Roost, the company were offered a play by Iris Murdoch, the distinguished novelist, called The Three Arrows, set in medieval Japan. It had a stunning leading part and the other roles were strong as well. Noel Willman agreed to direct it but there were great discussions about who was to play Yoremitsu, the leading part in the play. Willman thought that there were at least three actors capable of playing the part, so it was discussed in committee and put to the vote.

'Though no one was supposed to have more than one leading part,' sayd Margery Mason, 'Ian managed to get the lead in two of them! He has great powers of leadership!'

'The personalities involved,' says William MacDonald, who was Company Manager, 'meant that there were too many egos in the cauldron. Everyone talked about abandoning the star system, but everyone was a star or a potential star. And people came to see the stars – McKellen and Petherbridge – so, in a way we were obliged to pander to the star system. And to get the confidence of the Arts Council we had to have stars as well. But it was a great privilege to work for them, they were exciting. The excitement, the acclaim, the queues – it was marvellous!'[9] The Company printed a Manifesto in the programmes which said:

> The Actors' Company is a group of experienced actors and actresses who have combined to play both leading and supporting roles in their own Company. Through mutual discussion they have made all artistic decisions concerning plays, directors and casts. Their aim has been to produce a company of equals. The members of the Company have chosen as their first host management the Cambridge Theatre Company.

ON THEMSELVES

A practical experiment in an approach to work in the theatre which *should* be the norm.

These are all people who have *chosen* to work together and this fact generates an enormous feeling of confidence – a buoyancy which is so often lacking when *ad hoc* companies assemble to rehearse.

Firstly it is exciting to be in at the beginning of a new idea. Secondly it is a chance to feel a sense of responsibility towards a project. Thirdly a chance to get back to a way of working which I have not been able to realize for some time.

It's because actors who respect each other and each other's work are willing to support each other.

The proof of the pudding is in the eating – but the cooks have created their dream kitchen to make it in.

It's for the joy of working with and for people I respect to achieve the best possible results for the audience.

The hope that by the principle of equality in the size of parts and a uniform salary, many of the frustrations that beset actors in those classical companies run on 'the star system' will be avoided.

An optimism bred of recognition and respect for talent in each other.

The satisfaction of being involved in the *whole* enterprise of putting on a play.

I always feel that in every field of entertainment, the actor knows best – perhaps about everything except his own performance.

To be chosen, presumably for one's talent and ability, by other actors whose talent and ability one admires, is about the greatest compliment one can be paid. It is an inspiration – and a responsibility – which rarely comes the way of an actor in Britain. I feel that out of this something exciting *should* be produced for the audience to enjoy.

The idea of people working together in a non-competitive spirit seems to me to have everything to recommend it.

I would hope we'd get around to finding out what popular theatre is, one of these days.

From now on none of us will be content with the usual attitude and arrangements in British theatre. A quiet revolution has started.

Work. To the 19,500 members of Equity, work is very important.

Rehearsals for *Ruling the Roost* started on 10 July 1972 in an Arts Centre called The Howff in north London and the assistant stage managers, among them Annette Badland, best known for her appearances in TV's *Bergerac*, were all straight from Drama School, but as the company were already friends and colleagues none of the usual tensions of early rehearsals were apparent. *'Tis Pity* and *Ruling the Roost* were to be rehearsed and the latter play was chosen to be the first to open the Company's season at the Forum Theatre, Billingham. Would the experiment succeed? Already the actors felt it had with regard to their working conditions, but would the general public think so too? Would there, in fact, be enough bottoms on seats, in the theatre's slang, to justify the experiment?

'Within a few weeks they had made the Company itself a star,' said MacDonald, answering all these questions. 'They were a great success – a talked-about success.'

From Billington the Company went to the Edinburgh Festival, then to Leeds, Newcastle and Oxford. Then followed a season at the Arts Theatre, Cambridge (where the Murdoch play was added). Although the critics everywhere were complimentary, the Edinburgh Festival was the greatest test of the Company's worth, for they had to face, not only competition from all the other companies, both official and on the fringe, but also the national critics. They were, naturally, apprehensive but they need not have been. They were captivating and captivated, there was a great air of celebration around. They worked hard, not only on stage but off, giving interviews, photographic sessions and being very co-operative with the media. If the Actors' Company was visiting your town, you knew that they were there, local papers carried pictures and profiles, as well as notices and pictures of the performances.

McKellen himself got excellent comments for *Ruling the Roost*. John Barber in the *Daily Telegraph* wrote: 'Ian McKellen, the pimply seventeen-year-old hotel Buttons, with his trousers too short and his pubescence giving him agony, provides a star performance in a minor role.'

B. A. Young in the *Financial Times* described him as 'brilliantly funny' and Charles Lewson in *The Times* said, 'Last night Ian McKellen's luminous gifts were usefully contained, but not confined, within the role of the seventeen-year-old page boy "suffering from puberty"', and Billington, now at *The Guardian* said McKellen's was 'a genuine comic creation'.

'In the script after the page boy hands the coat to the Robert Eddison character Feydeau writes "business". So I said to them that it must be some business to do with the coat, so would Ian and Robert like to go away and work out something. They disappeared and within an hour they came back and showed me. It was marvellous – they worked something out which meant at the end Robert was wearing Ian's short jacket while Ian had on Robert's long coat. It was very, very funny indeed and always gets lots of laughs,' Richard Cottrell told me.[10]

For *'Tis Pity she's a Whore* where he played Giovanni, the incestuous brother to Felicity Kendal's Annabella, he again got star notices. Allen Wright in *The Scotsman* said, 'Ian McKellen plays Giovanni at a high emotional pitch, as befits a man who feels that he has the laws of nature and the moral code ... McKellen acts as though he were in a trance, his voice sobbing and swaggering in turn. His exalted performance is surrounded by less ostentatious but equally skilful feats of acting.'

Harold Hobson again proclaimed McKellen as the 'most exciting as well as the greatest of our young actors' but a sour note was struck by Nicholas de Jongh in *The Guardian*:

'Mr McKellen has been described as the greatest actor of his generation. He is not and has no chance of being so, until he rids himself of a quavering child-like diction to express absolute agony. In this play he moved from frustrated unhappiness to a childish defiance of the Church, moping rather than being carried terribly onwards by passion. He eats cornets (the production was in modern dress), wears lovely clothes, and mopes like a dissatisfied child. It is hardly Giovanni.'

This was a view echoed, on tour, by the *North Berks Herald* which said: 'As the passionate Giovanni, Ian McKellen never quite matched up to the part. There was a too persistent gawkiness of mien and too erratic and idiosyncratic a vocal quality in this performance for it to have the ring of tragic truth.

'Of all the half-dozen productions of this play I have seen in the last thirty years I have found this one to be the least satisfying ...'

Nonetheless, the Company had established itself as an exciting one, though, unfortunately the third play *The Third Arrow* by Iris Murdoch was not much liked. McKellen himself, was admired in the part, B. A. Young saying that 'Prince Yoremitsu, played by Ian McKellen with the strong glamour the part calls for ...' and he reminded Michael Billington in *The Guardian* of 'some jet-black stallion beating against the sides of a corral and his voice rings agony out of the least expected phrases.'

Iris Murdoch, however, was pleased. She writes: 'McKellen was extremely good (I need hardly say) in the part! But I didn't get to know him, or see him at work for any length of time, and know very little about him or his work.' And she adds, somewhat endearingly, 'In general I am not at all learned in theatre matters.'[11]

The Actors' Company then disbanded for the time being so that they could, hopefully, find more lucrative jobs. It was quite difficult, they had found, to live on fifty pounds on tour, keeping up both a home and paying for accommodation and food. McKellen then went on to direct a play in the West End. *A Private Matter* for which he got a notice, '...is directed sensitively by Ian McKellen' from Hobson. McKellen summed up his feelings about the experiment in an interview with Michael Owen in the *Evening Standard*: 'There is an ego-orientated side of you which thinks of the big parts and top billing. But there is also a more communal side of doing good work with good people. That is exhilarating.'

But as the Company had in itself become a star more people wanted to see it, so it was reassembled for a longer season. Some people had decided to leave. 'Although they were all supposed to be so committed,' MacDonald comments, 'the National, the RSC or a big TV company only had to snap its fingers and they'd run.'

However, good replacements were found and it was decided to take *The Wood Demon* to the Edinburgh Festival with *The Way of the World*, and, later *King Lear* and an adaptation of the works of R.D. Laing, by Petherbridge, to be called *Knots*, was added. McKellen was to play a lead – Michael in Chekhov's *The Wood Demon* and a Footman in *The Way of the World*.

'Although we were all supposed to not mind doing small parts, Ian did,' says Margery Mason. 'I remember in *Ruling the Roost* at the curtain call we were all supposed to mill around the stage and then freeze, take the call. It was surprising the number of times that McKellen was dead centre at the freeze. You must admire his timing!'[12]

Robert Eddison says 'I was very touched to be asked to play Lear. I had been to do a play at Colchester and on my return I found this note from the rest of the Company offering me the part. I wept, amazingly, for I had always wanted to do the part.'[13] Ian was to play Edgar. 'At one rehearsal,' Margery Mason tells the story with a glint in her eye, 'Ian suddenly took off all his clothes in the "Poor Tom's a cold" bit. No textual authority for a naked Edgar, of course, but none of us said anything being perfect ladies and gentlemen, but he decided that that was how he was going to play the part.' McKellen defended his decision thinking that it was in keeping with the whole production. In the event, audiences' reaction was pretty passive, but one night, when the Company did its season at Wimbledon a voice from the audience was heard to say, 'Ummmm, nice one, Cyril!' – a popular catch-phrase at the time.[14]

Between Edinburgh and Wimbledon though the Company was to visit New York. Clare Fox, who had been engaged as Company Manager said 'When the RSC goes to America they take two plays, when we went, we *had*, of course, to take four!' Ian had asked her to join especially 'and they were such wonderful people it was, in spite of all the difficulties, a marvellous Company to be with. But it was such hard work, not only were there four plays to look after, but there were all those endless meetings. Everything was discussed and voted on.' Clare had five stage management staff and a carpenter – 'Peter Price, who did miracles, but then everybody worked their socks off. There was no time to eat or sleep, but nobody regretted it ever. Margery Mason was a great stalwart of the Company, so was Robert Eddison. Loyalty to the Company came before anything, and although, of course, there were disagreements we never washed our dirty linen in public.'[15]

The Brooklyn Academy of Music were the hosts for this remarkable Company of Equals, as they were frequently called, and though the enterprise, in Clare's words, was 'foolhardy' it paid off. The Americans were enthusiasts about them from the first. There was lots of publicity. 'Ian was always very fair about that,' says Mason. 'He didn't do it all himself, but let us all have an interview.'[16]

The Americans were intrigued, worshippers of stars, they could hardly believe that such a company could exist. On 2 February 1974 George Gent wrote about the democracy:

The seventeen members vote on the plays to be produced, the directors to whom they will be assigned and, with the directors on the apportionment of roles. Today's Lear will be tomorrow's footman, and *vice versa*.

This last, in a profession not noted for the fostering of hairshirt humility, seems almost too Utopian, and several members who had assembled over lunch were asked if everyone always acceded gracefully to the democratic imperative.

'We sometimes have some sweat,' admitted Marian Diamond, one of the young founders of the Company ... 'But everyone knows that if he has a walk-on today, he will have a much better role in another production. It all equals out.'[17]

Not washing the dirty linen, in fact. 'Although we were supposed to be so democratic,' says Eddison, 'Ian was very ungracious about being a footman in *The Way of the World*.'[18]

'He said to me, when he was playing Edgar,' says Mason, 'that he didn't really like playing supporting roles.'[19]

British Caledonian had provided free seats for the actors, so they all arrived on time, and they separated to small hotels, like the Chelsea, where Dylan Thomas had died, or to stay with hospitable Americans. McKellen's host was an American actor who had trained at RADA. They rehearsed by day and enjoyed the American Theatre at night, everything seemed to be running smoothly. On 29 January 1974 *The Wood Demon* went off well, Clive Barnes, the most influential critic in New York saying that, 'It was all very Chekhov and all beautifully acted. This play is one of those rarities that does not deserve to be so rare, and the Company is a joy to welcome.' Walter Kerr called McKellen's performance 'beautifully intemperate'. Nearly two thousand people had turned up to see this fresh Company. But next day there was a major upset. The sets for *Lear* had not arrived and the Company wondered about cancelling, but after a Company meeting decided that, come what may, they must not let down the considerable audience who already had tickets. So that night, (30 January) they did that amazing entertainment *Knots* which again had the critics praising their skills. *Knots* was part erudite philosophy, part music-hall entertainment. Juan Moreno juggled, Caroline Blakiston played the organ and Paola Dionisotti turned cartwheels! But the critics were dubious as to whether this was suitable for Laing's convoluted thoughts.

Still the *Lear* scenery and costumes had not arrived so the Company acted it in modern clothes – Eddison finding a long, white suede coat, McKellan wearing some of his own clothes, the girls putting on dresses. In spite of this the play was a great success. 'The play became so clear,' says Clare Fox. 'It was sensational because everyone worked as a unit. I was so proud of them, I was in tears.'[20]

Clive Barnes in the *New York Times* wrote, 'The production is stuffed with good, unobtrusive performances. Admittedly Ian McKellen plays Edgar as if it were a star role, but this is the special genius of Mr McKellen's acting. He has a natural blaze to him that no amount of democracy can douse. His Edgar is deeply felt and beautifully presented. He is that rare bird an intellectual actor with incandescence, so not only does he know what to do, he also seems to know why he is doing it.'

The season ended with *The Way of the World* with McKellen playing his four-line part. Then the Company came home to the large, suburban theatre at Wimbledon. The fame of the Company by now was such that the box-office was overwhelmed with calls for seats, and extra telephones had to be installed. Members of the Company, democratic as ever, actually did stints in the Box Office and many a fan was thrown by hearing McKellen's voice telling them that seats one and two in Row M were the best available.[21] As Harold Hobson proclaimed: 'The Actors' Company pursues its triumphant career at Wimbledon', and even Nicholas de Jongh, not usually an admirer, was moved to say in *The Guardian* of McKellen's performance in *The Wood Demon*, 'all the usual McKellen emotionalism is here exploited splendidly rather than indulged'. John Peter said that 'Ian McKellen's doctor is a fine piece of heady lyrical acting punctuated by fits of petulance that never get out of control'.

Of *King Lear*, the critics were equally complimentary of McKellan's Edgar, John Barber writing in the *Daily Telegraph*: 'McKellen's Edgar has a lovely boyish candour' and Wardle in *The Times* called his interpretation 'imaginative'.

'Tis Pity got a less warm reception, the *Sunday Times* finding it 'as hysterical in Wimbledon as it did in Edinburgh' but Billington in *The Guardian* said that it was the best thing that McKellen had done since the duo of *Richard II* and *Edward II* 'his body quivering with a restless nervous energy, he suggests a man whose bottled sexual passion might explode like a mechanical retort'. But *The Observer* thought that 'Ian McKellan's moody schoolboy Giovanni, his voice even more tousled than his hair has grown since I saw it two years ago ... but this Giovanni is such a narcissist that his love for his sister is hard to credit.'

For McKellen that was the end of his acting with the Actors' Company though the Company itself continued to go on for several more years, Petherbridge being faithful to it. Eventually though he left, too, and without its two stars audiences fell away though the work continued to be both interesting and good. However much actors like to think that the general public will turn up to see good work it simply is not true - we all go to see stars. The RSC, it is true, tends to make its own stars, either on its own stage, like Roger Rees, or gives them the necessary technique to become stars, and then it re-employs them, like Donald Sinden and Ben Kingsley. The National imports stars like Anthony Hopkins, Dorothy Tutin, Judi Dench or, even, McKellen himself. It has made no stars of its own.

About this time, the Marlowe Society at Cambridge wrote to McKellen asking him if he would like to produce its next play which would have meant McKellen spending time in Cambridge. He wrote back charmingly to them saying that he had had enough of administrative work for some time and felt that he must get back to acting, and recommending his old colleague from Cambridge days, Clive Swift, for the job. A typical McKellen gesture.

What was McKellen to do next? He had in 1972 refused to go to the National Theatre again to play in *The Bacchae* and *The Misanthrope* as he felt so deeply committed to the Actors' Company, so that way might be closed to him.[22] There was always television, his performance with Janet Suzman in a BBC production of *Hedda Gabler*, also in 1972, showed another possibility. But, perhaps, it was time for him to do something that would satisfy him completely. He had found out that he didn't like playing small, or supporting parts, that his personality burst forth, tearing the part asunder. 'I remember when we, at the RSC, thought that we should make our leading players play walk-ons as well,' Ronald Eyre reminisced. 'We asked Judi Dench to play a maid or something in *Much Ado*. She went to great lengths to disguise herself, found a dark wig, put freckles on. She didn't want people to recognize her and say 'That's Judi Dench' and so upset the balance of the scene. Now you'd never get Ian to do anything like that. He would always want to be recognized. You were only too aware that it was McKellen playing the footman.'[23]

David Giles, the director, who had worked with the Company was to say in *The Times* in June 1975, 'There was a feeling of creative energy about them [McKellen and Petherbridge] which no amount of democracy could change', and Robert Eddison said, 'Ian was always the star, nothing could change that'.[24] Margery Mason relays, 'When we were re-rehearsing *'Tis Pity* with a new member of the cast Ian was being very selfish and taking up far too much of the time, after all poor John Bennett hadn't played the part before and he had, and there was quite a lot of feeling about it in the Company.'[25]

'Margery was absolutely splendid at one meeting,' chuckles Eddison. 'She said, "Ian, you're rehearsing like a star".' 'I didn't get much thanks for it,' says Mason, but Eddison says that, 'Ian was quite humble and after thinking it over was very apologetic. He has humility'.[26]

Eddison thinks that what was wrong was that you just couldn't satisfy everybody and Mason agrees. 'It was all lovely at first, then people began wheeling and dealing to get parts, the atmosphere was spoilt and we all had to spend too much time on administration.'[27]

McKellen obviously thought so too, for he decided to return to playing only leading parts again.

7
The Royal Shakespeare Company

LONDON

What happened was that John Barton, his mentor at Cambridge asked him to play Dr Faustus in a production of Marlowe's play. 'When he said that it wouldn't be at Stratford and Emrys James was going to play Mephistopheles it all just seemed unavoidably right.'[1] He had always, for some reason been rather afraid of being in a large company, his experience with the National had not been all that happy, and as a young actor he could have been quite easily lost in one, but he was now to be eased into the RSC gently. After *Faustus* at Edinburgh and a short tour, McKellen would come to the RSC's London base, the Aldwych, play the lead in *The Marquis of Keith* by Wedekind, an interesting and fascinating play, with the equally fascinating Sara Kestelman; and take over from Richard Pasco as the Bastard in *King John*, again with Emrys James. An interesting package, and an interesting situation. His salary was to be around £250 a week.[2]

He had always envisaged the RSC as a monolith, but he found the reality quite different. 'I found it broke down into various groups of fairly intimately working people. From inside it was much smaller than it appeared from outside ... the RSC is not actually a company in the sense that I think of a theatre company as being. It's a company in the sense that it produces a product, a limited company in which a group of people all work together. It's hierarchical, that's its structure.'[3]

Caryl Brahms, an astute lady of the theatre, summed up McKellen at this stage very shrewdly in *The Guardian* (26 January 1975):

McKellen has sufficient tricks – what Olivier, Guiness or Gielgud has not? – but he is too true an actor to integrate them into the part and they are left twirling in mid-air, like a flight of conjuror's bottles, keeping their spangled master at their mercy ...

It is not that, like a great many actors, he wants to appear at the apex of a constellation; nor that he feels his light would shine the brighter from an otherwise dim cast. He is concerned only to be surrounded by a company playing to the top of its talents, as his work with the Actors' Company has proved, so that the play may glitter along with its star and he bends his intelligence, which is manifest in all he does on the stage, and his skill, which is considerable, to this end ...

That he is an actor of high style and accurate delineation is not in dispute. ...

His face, in no way arrestingly handsome, is indeed his fortune, in that the blob nose and the unarresting features are splendid for disguise and are not forever pulling one back from his characterizations to his own personality. His voice is strange, a little disturbing. It seems to come from a cranny high in the back of his throat.[4]

Another critic Benedict Nightingale also assessed McKellen placing him among his peers thus:

I have my reservations about McKellen. He is an actor very prone to trills and cadenzas, unafraid of the extraordinary gesture or outrageous intonation: and that means he seems sometimes overblown or 'stagey'. The smaller the stage the more apparent this is apt to be. I was thrilled by the Richard II and Edward II he did in that gigantic pulpit, the Assembly Hall in Edinburgh, a little worried when he took both performances to the relatively intimate Piccadilly Theatre and deeply embarrassed when he repeated them on TV. Eyeball to eyeball his elegant movements can seem stilted, that oboe of a voice gratuitously gasping. And yet, discretely directed, carefully controlled he's as subtle, daring and versatile as any actor we have.

Nightingale goes on to say that McKellen, John Wood, Alex McCowen, Ian Richardson and Anthony Hopkins were, at that time, the most exciting actors of their generation.[5]

Faustus was an exhilarating *tour de force* – the dark evil of Emrys James's Mephistopheles, quiet and menacing as only he could be: the use of life-sized puppets for the Deadly Sins Masque, and, above all McKellen's glittering, glamorous *young* Faustus made an exciting evening. Alan Ridell, writing in the *Sunday Telegraph* described the galvanizing death scene thus:

Twitching convulsively, McKellen achieves a spectral insubstantiality as the spirit drains from him. When finally dead, the weight returns to his body, which slips limply off the chair, his scholar's robe a sack-cloth shroud.

Harold Hobson was characteristically enthusiastic in *The Sunday Times*:

Eloquent and soaring performance uncontaminated by any craven fear of tearing a passion to tatters. But for once God is not on the side of the big battalions and the thunder of Mr McKellen's Faustus is less impressive than Emrys James's quiet Mephistopheles.[6]

As usual McKellen had worked very hard on the part, actually taking lessons from a ventriloquist and learnt how to manœuvre puppets so the Masque scene was very real. His voice also improved, mainly due to the intensive work that the RSC's voice coach, Cicely Berry, puts the whole company through. McKellen admits his debt to her, saying that she relaxes mind and body and that she prepares an actor to be tuned, like an instrument. She lengthened the range of his voice and gave him confidence in it.[9] 'We all owe a lot, a *very great deal,* to Cicely Berry,' declares Sara Kestelman. 'Our debt is enormous.'[7] Judi Dench describes what happens:

'At Stratford before a performance, we all lie out on our backs with our eyes closed and do Cicely's breathing techniques, starting by breathing on a vowel and building up. She then comes round and when she lifts up one of your arms, totally limp, suddenly you know all about relaxation. It's all about conserving breath and energy.'[8]

The next production that McKellen took part in was Ronald Eyre's production of Wedekind's *The Marquis of Keith*, a strange play which Eyre now feels was performed too soon. It centred round a self-styled Marquis who wanted to build an arts centre in Munich. The period was roughly art nouveau and the costumes, stunning and stylized, were by Voytek. Sara Kestelman played Countess Anna, a glamorous widow who was also a singer and for whom the arts centre was to be a showcase. As B. A. Young said in the *Financial Times*, 20 November 1974:

'The entertainingly depraved society has been nicely realized by Mr Eyre in his production, and the piece, though a little bewildering, was a very good evening's entertainment.

'We found a modern parallel in the building of the National Theatre,' Kestelman says beguilingly. 'It seemed to us a valid resonance',[10] while Eyre admits that 'it was difficult to discover Wedekind's style'.[11]

'Ian and Ronald were wonderful together,' Kestelman goes on. 'They really bounced things off each other. Both of them and Ian Richardson were absolutely fearless about experiment in rehearsal. Ian seized on things in the play which I simply had not seen. Ronnie worries brilliantly, while Ian worries in a big way, his are not tentative worries, they are *explosive* worries. It was sometimes agonizing, exciting and dangerous. I had the feeling that I was working with dangerous explosive personalities that might explode out of existence! And I was afraid that the underlying seriousness of the play was being eclipsed by the high style of presentation, a very real anxiety. But, underpinning it all was, after all, real observation, it was all well-observed and somehow we all managed to pull the whole thing together. It was so full of inventive business, daring, expressionistic – but it was pulled back.'[12]

But Eyre says that it was a near thing. 'After the first preview I realized that the play wasn't working at all, so I went to see Ian and there and then he just turned on a sixpence and accepted a new way of playing the part. He somehow keeps his work at a distance, he had no ego about it, said that he wouldn't let me down, and, of course, it became one of his best performances. *He was quite ready to shed one vision of the part and do another*. He is very skilled technically, and is dazzlingly assured in that way.'[13]

'He is an outrageous corpser, so am I,' says Sara, (corpsing is theatrical slang for laughing on stage when you are not supposed to) 'and it was always an explosive situation on stage with us. At the second preview, I think it was, it might have been later, in the Ball scene, Ian suddenly walked in front of me and went off-stage. He mumbled something as he passed me and disappeared into the wings. I wondered "what on earth is going on?", struck a pose or two, hummed a tune, looked decorative and vacuous, thinking perhaps he's ill, then he came on again, muttered something and went on with the scene! But he is totally supportive when you work with him – and as a man he is tremendous fun, witty, entertaining.'[14]

Another thing that Kestelman likes about him is his honesty. 'He can say quite tough things about a performance, and he is wonderfully astute about knowing what is wrong with it and he is not afraid of stepping on dangerous ground. I like him coming to see me at a preview for he has a keen eye for what is wrong, but it is all said with love, and taken with love as well.'[15]

The critics were divided, of course:

'It's title role is etched by Ian McKellen in indelible acid. His bogus Marquis is, as his pathetic mistress says: "A sheep in wolf's clothing". But he is the black sheep, one who would sell his own dam if it would raise him above the flock. And McKellen plays it with restless energy and punctuates each sentence with an intake of breath that might well be his last ...' so wrote Jack Tinker in the *Daily Mail*.

B. A. Young described his performance in the *Financial Times*: 'Ian McKellen has put something of Hitler into Keith, which seems to me to be going too far.'

Billington in *The Guardian* said that he was 'bursting with firework energy in his ascent. Shrinking into his ill-fitting Chaplinesque suit into decline and all the time giving the kind of inventive performance that demands the spectator's attention.'

Yet Frank Marcus in the *Sunday Telegraph* felt that McKellen 'does not convince me that his manic energy is fuelled by evil and corruption'. Robert Cushman in the *Observer* said that McKellen was 'as charismatic as they come'.

In *King John*, an odd production by Barton with a text that upset the purists for he had edited it heavily, McKellen took over the part of Philip, the Bastard from Richard Pasco and again divided the critics:

'A strikingly heroic Bastard,' proclaimed Michael Coveney in the *Financial Times* but Wardle in *The Times*, 10 January 1975 was scathing: 'as it is still played as a Pistol-like bumpkin one must ascribe this weird reading to the director'. Shulman in the *Evening Standard* said that it was 'vigorously bold, but too perky by half', though Cushman, ever-loyal, said in the *Observer* that McKellen's was the best acting in the play.

But McKellen soon after the opening was off round England again taking *Faustus* to Manchester, The Forum, Billingham – which first housed the Actors' Company – Cardiff and to the main house at Stratford-upon-Avon, a useful testing for what was to come.

He was then asked to direct again, Alistair Sim in *The Clandestine Marriage* by George Colman and David Garrick at the Savoy. It is interesting to note that this was one of the plays that Margaret Drabble chose for her imaginary company to perform in the novel *The Garrick Year*. Writing at the time in *This Week in London*, I said:

'The eighteenth century, like our own, was much obsessed by money – and in those days one's daughters were pawns to be used to further the aims and aspirations of the family. In this play by George Colman and David Garrick, Mr Sterling, newly rich, desired to ally himself with the minor aristocracy by marrying one of his daughters to a baronet – if the elder daughter Betsy does not suit, well, her sister Fanny will be the bride ...

'In this jolly romp, the cast play for broad comedy, ignoring the social satire that underlines the play. The production ... concentrates very largely on the comedy business and it is a pity that the cast do not let the cutting edge of the lines speak for themselves.'

Martin Connor, a young actor in the cast, says, 'Ian was an exhilarating director. Very inventive, always letting you try things out. But sometimes he would come in and re-do the previous day's work in a totally different manner',[16] which probably explains why the production was ultimately unsatisfying and did not realize the real purpose and satire of the play.

In June McKellen was cast as Colin in *Ashes* by David Rudkin which had earlier been tried out at the Open Space with Peter McEnery and Lynn Farleigh. McKellen was teamed with Gemma Jones in this grim, dour little piece which concerned a couple unable to have children and the humiliating process that has to be gone through if an infertile couple decide to do something about their infertility. Irving Wardle writing in *The Times*, 12 June 1975, thought that the documentary approach and emotional power fully transmitted the experiences of the couple where none of the physical indignities was glossed over. 'It is, at the same time, a nakedly personal piece of writing; and the further it develops the more it changes from a controlled theatrical statement to a wild scream of pain ... But for much of the time it is extremely, and unhelpfully, specific about character; at least the character of the man – a bisexual failed writer with ancestral ties to Protestant Ulster.' He was critical also of McKellen's performance. 'Mr McKellen, alas, has taken the husband's Irish background very much in earnest, and has mashed his delivery into a stew of Belfast, Birmingham and Lancashire; the voice takes precedence over character and the meaning of the lines. It is an energetic and committed performance; but not easy to listen to.'

Harold Hobson in the *Sunday Times* also castigated McKellen on his inability to present an acceptable accent interestingly and commented that, 'while clearly working to prevent his highly mannered style externalising everything [he] imparts a fearful complacency to the sexual discontents of a man determined to be disappointed, even without the help of fate.'

It was a grim evening, not helped either by its grey setting and claustrophobic atmosphere of the Young Vic.

Around this time (the plans were actually finalized in November 1975)[17] McKellen rang Trevor Nunn and said, 'I would like to go to Stratford. It always seemed to say in Michael Redgrave's autobiography, "I rang up Glen Byam Shaw and in the afternoon we decided I should play Henry V, Prospero, Falstaff, Peer Gynt, and an evening of Strauss". Well, I asked Trevor what he was going to do, and fortunately he was just working out a season and was able to take me into account.'[18]

His awe of the company had faded a little as he realized that the company as such did not actually exist, rather it was a group of companies under a nomenclature. He had also discovered that 'if actors like me feel they can offer something, they do generally offer it, and the person to offer it to is Trevor. I don't go to planning meetings. But one has the ear of the general.' But he also noted that none of the actors was in the group running the company nor had they official titles.[19]

The package offered to McKellen was a demanding and dynamic one – Romeo and Leontes in *The Winter's Tale* in the main house, and Trevor Nunn's own production of *Macbeth* in the Other Place, that tin shed where the RSC did experimental work and intense, studio productions to small audiences. But first there was another exciting project, a renewal of his partnership with the incomparable Judi Dench, which had proved so exhilarating in *The Promise*.

The play was to be a little-known one by George Bernard Shaw called *Too True to be Good* and McKellen was to play a burglar, Judi was Nurse Sweetie Simpkins and Anna Calder-Marshal her patient. It was catalystic casting with three strong personalities in the cast. Added to that Joe Melia, John MacEnery (later to be replaced by Michael Williams, Judi's husband), John Phillips and Dorothy Reynolds, the cast was a formidable one. McKellen was again surrounded with the excellence he likes. The director was Clifford Williams, a subtle and accomplished Shaw director.

McKellen isn't altogether happy with Shaw, finding him difficult to learn. 'He writes very rhythmic sentences but they're too long and they're complicated.'[20]

However, the part of Aubrey Bagot, the burglar, was to be one of his great successes. The play was full of Shavian politics and wit, rather confusing at times, but gave all the actors splendid chances, and McKellen took his excellently, and, it must be said, that the partnership between him and Dench was as charged as ever. He played up the elegance of the part superbly curling a pearl necklace sexily through his fingers, wearing an old-fashioned striped bathing-suit in a way to make one wish that all men would wear them again and speaking the lines with the clarity and precision that Shaw demands. His comic timing was as exquisite as his appearance, the melding between man and part, and the fusion between him and Dench made for a fine evening.

Jack Tinker in the *Daily Mail* spoke of his 'spell-binding potency' while Hilary Spurling in *The Observer* wrote that McKellen was 'throughout a treat to watch: his elegantly carved thirties profile and Dornford Yates postures ironically expressive from his quiff to the balls of his feet'. Bagot has a long, impassioned speech at the end of the play and Mrs Spurling said that she felt a palpable sense of fright and despair emanating from the stage.

B. A. Young in the *Financial Times* thought McKellen 'in particularly good form, good alike at grave and gay ... and quite free of the mannerisms that sometimes creep into his performances. The long speech at the end of the play, when all the rest of the company have gone, needs special magnetism to retain full attention and as Mr McKellen gives it, interest seems to increase rather than diminish as the minutes go by.'

The play was a success and the RSC asked if Eddie Kulukundis would be interested in a transfer to the West End. 'They wanted, I think, to keep Judi and Ian together for a bit longer, and, as you know, I love Shaw, thought the production marvellous, and so I found a theatre for it. It did reasonably well,' Eddie told me.[21]

The Dench/McKellen partnership was being prepared for something very special indeed which was to erupt on to the world later in 1976 at Stratford ...

STRATFORD

McKellen was still dubious about playing at Stratford. He seems to have little or no affection for the big theatre there and finds the audience difficult. 'You've got all those foreigners, bless them, who know as little about Shakespeare as I do about Wagner. One senses that the audiences at Stratford don't get involved. They don't know whether they're going to see Mr Shakespeare. Is it his theatre? Did he build it? It's that variety of audience that people who like working there are very enthusiastic about, the challenge of melding those disparate parts into a whole.'[22] That was written in 1977. The previous year he seemed to have thought that the audiences were more homogenous though acutely sensitive to the jokes and laughter of schoolchildren who came to see GCE texts in action.[23] Another actor, Donald Sinden, who has had experience of Stratford audiences for over forty years admits that you do get a lot of tourists there, 'but you must also remember that a lot of the audience is also composed of scholars who know the text very well and take it seriously. It's a marvellous audience.'[24] Before the company went to Stratford, in January 1976, they met in the RSC's rehearsal rooms in what could only be called a decrepit warehouse in Covent Garden, stuffed full of dusty chairs, old sofas and other gradually decaying props. Trevor Nunn gave an introductory talk about the humanity and breadth of Shakespeare's plays that said that the policy of the RSC was not to limit and categorize the work. Also in the company were Donald Sinden and many of the great young actors that the company was then producing like Roger Rees, Bob Peck, Ian McDiarmid and Greg Hicks, all of whom were to make names for themselves in the coming years. It was a strong company, McKellen was surrounded by excellence.

The texts were minutely examined, in the Leavis tradition – precise analysis of the preciseness of the poetry, the way it conveys meaning, the text paramount in importance. As John Barton puts it, actors like to know how the verse *works*. And this is what has become known as the RSC Method and which is explained, worked out and illuminated in Barton's book *Playing Shakespeare* based on a South Bank Series of programmes which were transmitted in 1984 and in which McKellen took part. In the first broadcast Barton said:

There are few absolute rules about playing Shakespeare but many possibilities. We don't offer ourselves as high priests but as explorers or detectives. We want to test and to question. Particularly we want to show how Shakespeare's own text can help to solve the seeming problems in that text. We will try to distinguish between what is clearly and objectively so and what is highly subjective ...

That was the underlining theme of the TV programmes and may be considered the blueprint underlining all the work at Stratford. Barton further defines the problem that the actors have to face, was the text written at a particular time and for particular actors and that they are also actors with modern habits of mind and a different acting tradition. The two have to be brought together. 'Our tradition is based more than we are usually conscious of on various modern influences like Freud and television and the cinema, and, above all, the teachings of the director and actor, Stanislavski. I suspect he works on us all the time, often without us knowing it ... I think the most basic thing ... is the importance of asking the question "What is my intention?". If we had to reduce our modern tradition to one single point I think it would be this. It is practical advice which always works and always helps the actor.'[25]

McKellen's contribution to the discussion was a very typical one. He said the actors must be 'concerned with other people, our audience and other characters on the stage, impersonated by other actors. It's not enough to be aware of our own thoughts, our own feelings, our own words. We must listen to the words and understand the feelings and thoughts of the other characters.'[26]

The first part that he was to tackle was that of Romeo. He had always felt that this was not his part and that by now, at thirty-four he was too old for the part. 'Although I have never seen a young actor bring off the part; in fact I've never seen any actor bring off the part. Although Romeo is young his immaturities are nevertheless expressed in complex verse. Unless you can appreciate that language and have had some experience in dealing with it, you're unlikely to bring out what is fascinating in the play.'[27] He was worried about his age and rang Sara Kestelman. 'I knew that was really what was behind his call asking me if he should play Romeo. So I said to him, "I'm not going to say the obvious to you",' she says. Indeed, Kestelman encouraged him to take the part.[28] There is, of course, the old dictum that an actress cannot play Juliet, understand Juliet, until she is too old to appear physically credible in the part, and the same is true, perhaps even more true, of Romeo, who is the less mature of the 'two-star-cross'd lovers'. But appearance problems were overcome. Visiting him in his dressing-room John Andrew's wife asked him how he managed to look so young. McKellen grinned, 'It's a kind of magic: it's to do with the theatre.'[29]

John Barber described McKellen's Romeo in his notice of 2 April 1976 in the *Daily Telegraph*:

At first, Ian McKellen works far too hard to establish Romeo's extreme youth.

A kerchief round his curls, this scampering, impish, long-necked adolescent deteriorates too soon into the hair-teasing, breast-beating Romeo of convention.

But he is always an immensely likeable personality – clearly Verona's favourite odd-ball. We quite understand why his lady falls for him on sight.[30]

But how did McKellen achieve this mastery over this part, generally considered to be most difficult?

When Maggie Norden of Capital Radio was preparing her programmes on Shakespeare for the 'Set Book Series', *Romeo and Juliet* was one of the plays to be discussed and she asked McKellen to contribute to this and other plays in the series. She writes in the Foreword of *Shakespeare Superscribe*, the book based on the series, 'with Shakespeare's plays, our "cast" often suggested modern parallels, lending relevance and immediacy to daunting texts. I remember giving Ian McKellen a cup of coffee and asking, "How can we wake up some of Shakespeare's sleepier stuff?". He replied by reciting the *Romeo and Juliet* prologue, changing the word "Verona" to "Belfast"':

Two households, both alike in dignity
In fair Belfast, where we lay our scene,
From ancient grudge break to new mutiny,
Where civil blood makes civil hands unclean.
From forth the fatal loins of those two foes
A pair of star cross'd lovers take their life;
Whose misadventures piteous overthrows
Does with their death bury their parents' strife.

In the programme itself he mused on the effect of playing Romeo in modern terms in Belfast at that moment, indicating that he thought it would be a foolhardy thing to do, but letting his imagination work on the effect that it might have. Again, this shows his ability to find modern parallels – one of the hallmarks of a McKellen interpretation.

Another hallmark is that instilled in him by Cambridge – that of examining the text minutely though he says, 'I'm not good at working at home. I do it all in rehearsal – doing my analysis out loud.'[31]

Another principle is to take nothing for granted, always trying to find things out for yourself. 'Rylands instilled in me, and in everyone else, the most scrupulous attention to the classic texts, transforming their understanding.'[32] He pointed out to Maggie Norden that nowhere in the text is a balcony mentioned and that in an Elizabethan theatre Romeo would have to talk to Juliet with his back to the audience and thus could not speak the lines to them. It seems, though, that he has forgotten that the Elizabethan Theatre was similar to that at Chichester in that the audience sits around the stage, and, originally, often on the actual stage! And when he says that the romantic couple should be able to make love, he is perhaps forgetting that boys played female parts in Shakespeare's day, and if you examine the plays in detail you will find that Shakespeare rarely gives his actors any opportunity for physical love (for example, Antony and Cleopatra are parted for most of the play), probably to save any embarrassment to his actors, or from respect for the law. Even recently we have had a case before the courts, when Mary Whitehouse brought an injunction against the National Theatre for presenting The Romans, citing a law which forbids one man to procure another for the purpose of homosexual acts. The theatre has always had to be careful.

McKellen, though, has said that he would like the balcony done away with so that the couple can fling themselves into each others' arms.[33] Of course, McKellen might have had another, more practical reason for disliking the balcony. During the run of the production in September, as he was about to clamber down from the balcony a rung of the ladder

Bolton School: (*above left*) Margaret in *Friar Bacon and Friar Bungay* (1953); (*above right*) Henry in *Henry IV* (1956); (*below*) Alfonso Fernandez in *The Strong are Lonely* (1958).

As Evans with Peggy Mount in *The Corn is Green*, Ipswich (1963).

Richard II, Prospect
Theatre Company
(1968).

As George in the film *A Touch of Love* (1969).

Romeo and Juliet, Stratford (1976).

As the Marquis of Keith with Sara Kestelman as Anna, the Aldwych (1974).

Bernick in Ibsen's *Pillars of the Community*, the Aldwych (1977).

Rehearsing with John Wood for *Every Good Boy Deserves Favour* (1977).

McKellen (Max) with Tom Bell (Horst) in *Bent*, the Royal Court (1979).

Walter, Central Television (1982).

Pierre in *Venice Preserv'd*, the National Theatre (1984).

McKellen with Greg Hicks,
Coriolanus, 1984.

As Schulmeister Platonou in *Wild
Honey*, the National Theatre,
1984.

McKellen as Iago with
Imogen Stubbs (left)
and Willard White in
Othello, Royal
Shakespeare Company,
Stratford, and the
Young Vic, 1989.

broke and he tumbled an estimated fifteen feet to the stage. A member
of the audience, George Bartram said, 'Mr McKellen did not seem badly
hurt. He picked himself up, rubbed himself and went on. Francesca
Annis was concerned but, being aloft, could not help. Later, taking his
call, McKellen brandished the offending rung.'[34] Speaking in Bucharest
years later McKellen described how he actually analysed a particular
speech:

'I think Shakespeare wrote in this wonderful language particularly to
give directions to the actors. For example, there is a line in *Romeo and
Juliet*, a timeless play, full of poetic charm. Juliet and Romeo have
just spent their first night in bed together. Romeo has to leave the city,
but Juliet, of course, does not wish him to leave. So, she says to
him,

> "It was the nightingale, and not the lark,
> That pierced the fearful hollow of thine ear ..."

' "What does this mean?" the director asks the actress playing Juliet.
"In modern English it means the bird you have heard was the nightingale,
the night bird, not the lark, the bird of day; so you must stay here with
me, it is still night." But the director asks a further question, "Why did
Shakespeare have to write 'pierced the fearful hollow of thine ear'?
What does it mean?" "Oh," the actress replies, "this is an example of
Shakespeare's poetic charm." But this is not so. It is a very exact
expression and has to do with reality, it is not poetry. How near the
hollow of an ear do you have to be to see that it is hollow and not that
it is pink, beautiful or ugly? In other words when the two lovers heard
the bird, whether it was a nightingale or a skylark, they were very close
to each other, they were in bed, they were making love. Juliet doesn't
speak it poetically; remember that you're in love with Romeo and that
you're making love with him. In other words this line is not "nice" but
sensual, real, passionate and youthful – and only then does it become
beautiful. Of course, this is Stanislavski's concept. It is the return to
reality.'[35]

His Romeo was very hot-blooded, very sexy. At the end it was very
moving when he gathered the supposedly dead Juliet in his arms and
did a stately dance round the stage with her corpse until he sunk slowly
down on to the stage.

'At the end, when he was holding her in his arms and he took the
poison, do you remember, her hand just moved, though it was behind
his head and he couldn't see it, I wanted to call out, "She's alive, she's
alive" – I was so caught up in it,' remembers Sara Kestelman. 'He was

wonderful, so was she. I have never seen such a clear, beautiful reading of the part.'

The critics were often harsh. Robert Cushman in the *Observer* 4 April 1975 commented:

An actor who in his mid-thirties essays Romeo must expect double-edged compliments: having acknowledged him the best adolescent of his generation, I must express familiar misgivings. He is given to sulks, which suit some of Romeo but not all; he defies the stars with a violent twist of his mouth, sounding like tragedy and looking like toothache. Like Miss Annis, he is good at dread, hurrying a line to its end with a kind of vocal shiver.

Michael Billington in *The Guardian*, 2 April 1976, wrote a perceptive notice:

... I found for the first half the play obstinately failed to take wing.

Ian McKellen as Romeo seemed to be compensating for his own maturity by overstressing the lad's moonstruck teenage rapture and, with his feverish running exits, put one more in mind of Pirie than Petrach ...

But after the interval, a minor miracle occurred; this defective tragedy, which owes more to bad luck than fate, actually started to grip. Instead of implanted hysteria one got the feeling that these characters were, in Keats' phrase half in love with easeful death ...

And McKellen's Romeo, too feverishly tousled initially, made 'I am fortune's fool' the desperate cry from the heart and acquired in death an ironically belated maturity.

Felix Barker described McKellen's Romeo in the *Evening News*:

Ian McKellen treats us to a Romeo of such moody and mannered eccentricity that he is impossible to accept as one of history's great lovers.

In crumpled shirt, ill-fitting velvet jerkin, a black band round his head, the actor takes off in psychotic hysterics. In the transport of frustrated love he is reduced at one point to a rustic dolt with a nodding head.

But it is characteristic of McKellen that he works steadily on a part, and in this case, he refined his original interpretation. In the *Sunday Times Magazine* which did a feature on what happened in Stratford on Shakespeare's birthday it was noted:

At 6 p.m. Ian McKellen and Francesca Annis, the stars of Nunn's production of *Romeo and Juliet*, returned (they had been to Nunn's earlier to rehearse for a recital), this time to discuss their play. Mr Nunn had seen it the night before after an absence of a week and had made copious notes as is his habit during the run of any play: 'There are some things I want to change. A play can jump the rails in just a week. Some cues are being taken too slowly. Some of the text has been mislearnt. On the whole, it's in very good shape.

John Barber, who had rather dismissed McKellen's performance at Stratford, calling him 'Verona's favourite odd-ball' though liking the performance, was very enthusiastic when the play reached the Aldwych the following year:

Romeo is not a good part until he thinks Juliet is dead. Till then, most actors rely on youth and good looks. Ian McKellen a puny and cadaverous figure among strapping friends, aims instead to create a charming adolescent, a little like Stan Laurel in his comical calamities.

Believing Juliet dead, he shows his quality as a classical actor and achieves both manliness and pathos.

The comic element was one of which McKellen was quite proud. Remembering Bob Chetwyn's dictum that even in a tragedy you can get laughs he claimed that he and Francesca Annis got twenty-seven laughs in the balcony scene, all of them planned.[36] One laugh certainly was not planned. Realizing that there was a pun in the last line 'Thus, with a kiss, I die!' (*die* being an Elizabethan euphemism for an orgasm), he made a very explicit gesture which led to embarrassed laughter. He quickly cut it out.[37]

He admits that, 'It is a very, very difficult part to bring off. It sets so many problems. But as Nureyev said in an interview the other day, "The critics have one view. I have my own". So whatever happens with Romeo critically I have to put that against what I have learnt ...' Francesca Annis, whose Juliet won almost universal praise says, 'The marvellous thing about Ian is his enormous confidence. On stage you feel you are not alone. He would be in control if anything went wrong.'[38]

His next play was to be *The Winter's Tale* in which he was to play opposite Marilyn Taylerson as Hermione and Cherie Lunghi as Perdita. He gave, according to Harold Hobson, a 'masterly performance' while Michael Billington said that he had never seen the Sicilian scenes so convincingly played:

'Shaw said of Leontes that, compared to Othello, this is an unmistakable study of a jealous man from life. And Ian McKellen remarkably suggests a man seething with "diseased opinion". Into an idyllic image of family life, he suddenly injects a racked sexual anguish, spitting out words like "sluiced" and "bedswerver". And when his newborn daughter is deposited in his lap, he lifts his curled, white, knuckled hands above his head as if fearing physical contamination.

'Yet the key to his interpretation is, "I am a feather for each wind that blows"; and he suddenly switches from demonic tyranny ... to the pathos of a man destroyed by his own sexual fantasies. And it is this feeling of a good man afflicted by sudden sickness that makes the final reconciliation scene deeply moving.'

John Barber in the *Daily Telegraph* admits to tears in the last scene. Benedict Nightingale in the *New Statesman* felt that there was a strange gap in the middle of McKellen's reading of the part. 'He proved with his Romeo earlier in the season that he could project sexual longing, but sexual envy, sexual violence and sexual disgust leave him at a loss. He throbs and broods and occasionally rages, but he doesn't give the impression of a man whose stomach is being eaten away by an acid that reason, sense and all the usual alkalines cannot check ... Mr McKellen gives ... an exterior grief and not an internal laceration: a man wounded in the head and heart, not one mutilated in the abdomen, bowels and groin.' Richard David in his book *Shakespeare in the Theatre* says: 'The extraordinary utterances of Leontes' jealousy, colloquial phrases and speech-rhythms spun into the most elaborate rhetorical patterns of marched parentheses and repeated aposiopesis, were given an exquisitely sensitive reading with every twist and turn of the meaning made clear, appearing deeply felt, but deeply felt as if in a dream, the logical connection between cause and feeling somehow dislocated. Even when Leontes emerged from his solipsistic self-communings and engaged with other characters the remoteness of the dream-world was hardly lessened, sometimes on account of the directors' (Barton and Nunn) deliberate manipulation, sometimes on account of a curious quality in the writing that is Shakespeare's own.'

David Nathan writing in the *Jewish Chronicle* 11 June 1976 summed up what people were feeling about McKellen at that time:

The theatre world seems to be divided between those who like McKellen and those who cannot stand him. Certainly, he can, at times, display a whole rhetoric of gesture and grimace. But the best actors take risks. Not that he does here [in *The Winter's Tale*]. The rage is controlled and comes from within as does the anguish at being thought a tyrant.

It may be too early to say for certain that he is a great actor, but he is capable of great performances, and this is one of them.

But the season was not yet over. Besides playing his parts, McKellen was also giving recitals and workshops and all the time taking in the RSC method, with which he concurred, of studying and finding out all possible meaning in the text. His last part of the season, when he was again to be cast with Judi Dench was to be the most explosive of the lot, in a production which Robert Cushman proclaimed the best Shakespeare production he had ever seen and of which Sir Peter Hall was to write that it was refreshing, invigorating, utterly clear and original, and to record that his admiration for the subtlety of the acting was unbounded.[39]

MACBETH

The play was *Macbeth*, that play which is considered so unlucky in the theatre that the superstitious refer to it as 'The Scottish Play'. It was to be Trevor Nunn's third attempt at it and it was to be played, not in the main theatre, but in The Other Place, that tiny shed along the road from The Dirty Duck, the actors' pub in Stratford. Its budget was around £250,[40] the props were minimal and costumes contrived from already existing ones. It seemed an interesting studio production, no more. But the melding of McKellen, Dench and Nunn was to prove electric, and the effect on the whole company which included Bob Peck, Roger Rees, Ian McDiarmid and Greg Hicks was to prove a very fruitful one. 'From that company,' said Peck, 'came the touring company, and then that led to the nucleus of the company that devised and performed *Nicholas Nickleby*.' This production, which became a legend, played not only in TOP but transferred to the main theatre and then went to the Warehouse, the RSC's London equivalent of TOP. Finally it went to the Young Vic – 'where I think we gave our best performances,' judged Peck.[41] It was then televised by Thames TV and is now on video.

Nunn had a very clear idea of what he wanted. It was a great play about faith. Lady Macbeth is motivated entirely by her faith in her husband and his ability to be great, while he is equally convinced and sustained by his faith in his own invincibility promised him, as he thinks, by the witches.[42] 'Trevor was very much in control, as far as I remember,' says Peck. 'For instance, I had conceived of MacDuff as a family man, a farmer perhaps, but Trevor asked me to play it almost as a pastor. And it worked. Of course, there were arguments between him and Ian, but that's not unusual in rehearsal, you know. There are always animated and heated discussions then, but Trevor persuaded him to simple ideas, anchored him down. He had his own style, which isn't always admired, but it is undeniably powerful. He tends to thresh around in rehearsals but Trevor anchored him down. Trevor's very clever!'[43]

The bad luck that traditionally surrounds this play – there is a story that someone was killed in a duel after the first ever performance –

continued in this production. After an early rehearsal Ian, Judi and Trevor walked wearily from the theatre and Judi slipped and fell in the street *twice*. It seemed ominous. 'We won't be able to do this play, will we?' she sighed to Trevor, who characteristically rallied his players and steadily built up a rapport whose closeness was essential for his conception of the tragedy.[44] And during the run, John Woodvine's seat stuck to him; someone made a false entrance; Bob Peck got injured in the fight too. 'One night a sword which was thrown into the ground leapt up again and my ear got sliced,' Peck remembers. 'I don't think it was anybody's fault, we were very tired at that point, the work was so concentrated and we were working at speed. But I enjoyed doing the fights.'[45] That the play was about faith, the disturbance of the existing moral and physical order, and the erosion of that faith is an idea that F. R. Leavis taught. Writing in *The Common Pursuit* he says:

Macbeth is possessed by the devil: the tragic dignity and moral finality of Shakespeare's world are focussed in Macbeth's cry of 'animal despair' only in so far as this refers us, inevitably (one would have thought), to the quite other effect of the total action – the total action in relation to which the speech has its significance. By his plunge into crime, taken in fatal ignorance of his nature

> If it were done, when 'tis done, then 'twere well
> It were done quickly

he has confounded 'this little state of man' and the impersonal order from which it is inseparable. It is not on his extinction after a tale of sound and fury, signifying nothing, that the play ends, and his valedictory nihilism is the vindication of the moral and spiritual order he has outraged, and which is re-established in the close.

Nunn, as is his wont, worked with his leading players separately as well as with the whole cast.[46] An example of the way that the text was examined occurs in *The South Bank Show*'s programme *Word of Mouth*. Again, taking one of Leavis's precepts from *The Common Pursuit*:

The control over Shakespeare's words in *Macbeth* ... is a complex dramatic theme vividly and profoundly realized – not thought of, but possessed imaginatively in its concreteness, so that, as it grows in specificity, it in turn possesses the poet's mind and commands expression.

McKellen said in *Word of Mouth*:

You have to think and have analysed in rehearsal totally so that your imagination is being fed by concrete metaphors, concrete images, pictures can then feed through into the body, into gesture, into timbre of voice, into eyelids, into every part of the actor's make-up, so that it does seem ... that he is making it up as he goes along ... But to start at the top with the first line ... Seyton says to Macbeth: 'The Queen, my lord, is dead', and Macbeth replies, 'She should have died hereafter', which is a short line. 'She should have died hereafter.' Indicating that there should be a pause, I think, and during that pause in performance with the audience gathered round me as you are now, I used to take advantage of that pause to catch the audience's eye and begin this soliloquy which is Macbeth, me, talking directly, sharing my thoughts with the audience ...

Then he goes on to analyse the beginning of the speech line by line:

'Hereafter' introduces one element of time, the future. Then we get a regular blank verse line, 'There would have been a time for such a word.' There would have been a *time* – stressed – *time*. This speech is about time. 'For such a *word*.' Word is the last line. What word? Is it about 'she', the Queen? Is it hereafter? Is it time? There's something about the line which trips, in Hamlet's words, tick-tocks like a clock. There would have been a time for such a word. It's leading to the next line. And here comes the word which is important – 'Tomorrow and tomorrow and tomorrow'.

There are only two words in that line, an irregular line, given weight by its repetition three times and the tripping of – 'There would have been a time for such a word' – slows down on 'Tomorrow and tomorrow and tomorrow'. The rhythm is important. It's also a nonsense word if you say it three times or if you say it twenty times like a kid skipping. 'Tomorrow and tomorrow and tomorrow ...'.

What does that word mean – 'tomorrow'? It's beginning to have the lack of meaning, I think, that Macbeth detects in his own life at this point: 'Creeps in this petty pace from day to day'. And here comes the first metaphor, the first image, and the rhythm is beginning to creep, is beginning to plod along a country lane. It's footsteps now. Not the tick-tock of a clock. 'Creeps in this petty pace from day to day'. Well, we've had tomorrow, we've now got today – at the end of the line 'from day to day', but it leads on to the next line, to not day but 'the last syllable of recorded time'. And it slows up even more, ending up with a very important word 'time' at the end of the sentence. Sylla -*bell*. I wonder if bell isn't the bell of a clock which records time.

Then we get a regular line. 'And all our yesterdays have lighted fools'. yesterday. We've had tomorrow. We've had today. We've now got yesterday. We've got the whole complex of time. Macbeth is not just talking about himself, he's talking about eternity and going to say something about it. . . .

This continues for another three pages of the transcript – all for one short soliloquy!

Besides this intensive work on the text, McKellen as always had to find a modern man to whom he could relate, to get the key for the character. Macbeth is a general, an extremely able, even gifted fighter, so two people came into his mind – Moshe Dayan and Mohammed Ali. And even John F. Kennedy was used as a source of inspiration.[47] Talking to John Barton, a conversation recorded in *Playing Shakespeare* McKellen explained his feelings about doing Macbeth:

... I must believe in what I'm doing. So I had a problem when I was playing Macbeth. I don't believe in witches and I don't believe in God, and Macbeth clearly believed in both these concepts. I've never killed a man, and he is a professional soldier. I've never murdered a man and he does. I've never been married, and so I have to imagine my way into all those aspects of his life by thinking of people I know, or it may be by thinking of a modern man, a contemporary whom I don't know personally but who's vaguely in Macbeth's position.

When I was rehearsing I tried to think of generals who had gone into politics in the way that Macbeth seems to be wanting to go into politics. Then I thought, wait a minute, it's something more than that because Macbeth is the glory of the world, he's the golden boy. So who would be a modern parallel? At the time, in the late seventies, Mohammed Ali was the greatest athlete in the world, so I asked myself what it would be like if he were to decide that he wanted to be President of the USA. I thought about it and then forgot about it ... it's useful to think like that and to base things on modern life.

And as Judi Dench says: 'At the beginning it's not a King and Queen of Scotland or even great people, it's people who you can recognize. Anyone who is driven to the extremes of greed and passion or lust or ambition can go this way. There but for the grace of God can go anybody. We don't tell a great epic, tragic story; we try and tell a psychological story about people.'[48]

Richard David describes the setting in *Shakespeare in the Theatre*:

The playing space was defined by a dark circle marked on the boards: outside this circle was a ring of fourteen beer-crates on which the actors, entering at a signal that the performance was about to begin, took their places, rising and moving inside the circle, sometimes taking their stools with them, as the moment came for each to act his part. The wall at the back of the stage was clad with two large upright rectangles of natural wood, which formed between them a narrow dark slit. Through this slit Macbeth passed to murder Duncan, and pursued a Macduff apparently worsted and disabled in the final fight. From it Macduff eventually returned with his own and Macbeth's bloody dagger in either hand (no 'usurper's cursed head' was exhibited). A large coppery thunder-sheet hung stage-right and almost under the spectators' balcony, was a table from which actors drew such few props as were necessary.

The whole aspect was sombre. Lady Macbeth wore a long black dress, her hair bound in a black scarf: Macbeth a black tunic, trousers tucked into boots, also black. The other actors were in an assortment of black clothes, the only exceptions being Lady Macduff who was in a twin dress to Lady Macbeth, but in white, Duncan who was in a white robe, the hem of which was kissed by the court, and Malcolm who wore a white Arran sweater. The Royal Robe of Scotland, worn by Macbeth at his coronation, was a priest's cope, resplendent in white and gold. The witches' two middle-aged bodies and an epileptic girl were in a rag-bag of garments, including moth-eaten fur. The play was acted without a pause or interval, the audience sitting around or aloft in the small gallery. The effect was almost claustrophobic, the effect of evil apparent from the first moment, when against the muttered prayers of the saintly Duncan (Griffiths Jones) the witches keened in an unearthly way before starting their spells. After Judi Dench had made her incantation – 'She actually asks to be made cruel,' says Judi in *Shakespeare Superscribe*[49] – the evil became palpable. 'A priest used to turn up regularly,' McKellen told me,' and hold up a crucifix. Not to protect the audience or himself, but to protect the cast. He really thought we were liable to be assailed, evil was really present.'[50]

He and Dench wove a magic. He says, 'When I work with Judi I really have to pull myself up to her level', and she says, 'I'm so lucky to have such a smashing actor as McKellen to act with'. Although she is sensitive about her height, she is five foot one-and-a-half, nearly a foot shorter than he, this never seems to matter. Like most actors they can manipulate their heights successfully. In fact, one of the great surprises in meeting Judi is her smallness, she towers on the stage. Here the disparate heights worked for them, the image of Judi kissing her stage husband is a memorable one. 'I have to go right up on tip-toes to reach him,' she said 'right up on to the toes of my boots.'[51] The erotic charge of their performance was immense and, for once, McKellen seemed to act with regard towards his leading lady. 'This was, I'm sure, due entirely to Judi,' says Ronald Eyre. 'She is a very special person, and a very great actress. She brings the best out of anyone. She and Ian have magic together which, I believe, is largely due to her.'[52]

Both the airborne dagger and Banquo's ghost were internal images in Macbeth's mind, and he played the scene when he drank the potion the witches had brewed as if hallucinating. The ghosts were puppets held by the witches which he took with him, discarding them as the prophesies proved false.

Another effective piece of production was, what Richard David calls, 'the twirl'. 'When Macbeth and Banquo entered, from the back, the circle on which the witches were already huddled down-stage, they at first looked back leisurely along the way they had come and then, suddenly aware of the witches' presence, twirled rapidly round, with daggers drawn to face them down-stage.' It was used when Lady Macbeth finished reading the letter and turned to face the Messenger heralding Duncan's approach, and again before her incantation. And during the battle scenes it occurred.

The whole production was pared down and made extremely simple, but this made the text more intense, an intensity that was also apparent in the acting. It was unsparing both of actors and audience. Unremitting in its agony. Great attention was paid to detail. 'Ian was meticulous in the way he put the blood on to his hands. He trickled it on so that it ran in rivulets down his hands,' Peck said. 'He sleeked back his hair at the beginning, and then half-way through wetted it so that it would look more tousled at the end.'[53] In the pictures, taken at rehearsal his hair is wavy, so this must have been a later detail which McKellen added. Certainly, he was at first unrecognizable as he sat on his stool. Even the Porter's scene, though obviously a space to laugh, seemed less of an intrusion than usual, and the 'English' scenes, played with great poignancy by Peck and Roger Rees also had an almost unbearable intensity. 'It was, of course, a very strong cast, full of strong person-alities. And although Ian is, himself, a strong person, he had equally strong people with him. Judi generates her own charge. But then, Ian needs someone as strong as he is or else he takes over,' Peck continued.[54]

The critics were practically unanimous: Michael Billington in *The Guardian*, 11 September 1976, wrote:

The simpler the better; that is my feeling about Trevor Nunn's ceaseless quest for the ideal *Macbeth* ... Now at Stratford's The Other Place in a production played without an interval, he has hit the right balance between verbal clarity and depraved religiosity. I have never seen the play come across with such throat-grabbing power.

Partly this is the result of the auditorium's intimacy. ... But the effect is also due to Ian McKellen's overwhelming Macbeth which charts, stage by stage, the character's self-willed disintegration. If I had to pick the key to his performance I would say it lay in the line about making 'our faces vizards to our hearts', for what we see is the gradual tearing away of Macbeth's public mask until we reach the driven psychopath beneath.

With hair swept back like Toshiro Mifune in a Samurai epic and poker-back stance, McKellen is at first your perfect soldier. But when he talks of his 'single state of man' being shaken his body gives an involuntary shudder ...

He is at his best, however, when after his coronation he assumes the mask of tight-lipped courtesy ...

If this is not great acting, I don't know what is ...

Robert Cushman in the *Observer* remarked upon his expressive use of his hands and said also in a very long notice:

Mr McKellen, with the reputation of a self-conscious Sensitive Plant, is actually surprisingly burly: a believable fighter and a bulwark worth undermining. This time he never slackens or wallows, freshens the most jaded lines; 'tomorrow and tomorrow' are separated by a silent chasm, beyond which wake sickening vistas of despair. If not absolutely my ideal Macbeth (too much the toy of fate, not assertive enough in his last battle), he is the best I have seen.

And later, when the production reached London he called it, 'The best Shakespeare production I have ever seen' and remarked upon the way McKellen 'flooded the stage with energy'.

J. W. Lambert writing in the *Sunday Times* 12 September 1976:

... seldom felt the woe of a man facing disaster more poignantly transmitted than in Mr McKellen's chill, staring end; but even at his first entrance one felt that his triumphs on the battlefield were the gestures of a hollow man, his mounting ambition a substitute for life rather than a mark of vitality.

Gone are the physical vocal flourishes which for me have too often spoiled enjoyment of Mr McKellen's powers. Reflective, natural (in, needless to say, a way possible only to a highly-skilled actor) he marvellously achieves that blend of the practical ... and the introspective; and establishes with his wife a rich relationship, full of affection, desire, awe, inspiration and protectiveness.

There were some dissenting voices. A year later when the production reached London, Bernard Levin was to write:

Faced with the RSC's *Macbeth* (The Warehouse) I can only echo Hermia's 'I am amazed and know not what to say'. Trevor Nunn's production was seen last year in Stratford, and there acclaimed a work of genius: its reception in London has been no less hosannic. Yet it struck me as hideous and empty ...

... I can see nothing in Ian McKellen's Macbeth other than a ranting and twitching, and he speaks the verse with inexcusable coarseness ...

B. A. Young also commented on this in the *Financial Times*: 'His speaking of verse ... is eccentric beyond the bounds of acceptance.'

For his performance McKellen received the *Plays and Players* Award for Best Actor of the Year. Trevor Nunn summed up what Judi and Ian had done. 'This was,' he believes, 'to make the play genuinely tragic, not just melodramatic, about brutality and blood. There were times of quite amazing exhilaration in their work together. Shakespeare's words were the articulate, visible tip of the iceberg.'

LONDON AGAIN

While playing at Stratford McKellen also took part in a Festival Hall (London) recital with the Russian poet Yevtushenko – he reading in his native speech, McKellen reading translations. As Ned Chaillet said in *The Times*, 23 September 1976: 'They bounced the reading back and forth with all the confidence of an experienced vaudeville team in the ribald poems ... and moved with dignity into the sombre works.' The recital was repeated at the Round House.

The season at Stratford ending, the Company went to Newcastle to give the plays together with recitals, workshops and educational talks and demonstrations, in which McKellen took part. Then *Macbeth* did a short season in the main theatre in Stratford. Next McKellen moved to London where he played Romeo again in the Aldwych and Macbeth in The Warehouse. It is also customary for the RSC to add other productions, not by the house dramatist, to the London Season and the plays in which McKellen played were *Pillars of the Community* by Ibsen, *The Days of the Commune* by Brecht and Ben Jonson's farce *The Alchemist*.

Pillars of the Community was that rarity, a play that had been neglected for years which was really good. It was a John Barton production and McKellen was again appearing with Judi Dench, who glittered in the glamorous role of Lona, and again their compatibility, their ability to produce an extra dimension to anything they do together was apparent. Karsten Bernick, the character McKellen played, was a prosperous ship-owner and consul in a small Norwegian sea-port. Seemingly a good man, his past conceals much that is to his discredit. The man has been, and still is, cheating and conniving, and although he sees the shameful side of capitalism he is not above manœuvring it to his own benefit and gain. McKellen seized on this part avidly.

Michael Billington in *The Guardian* described his appearance as Bernick as being:

Ramrod-backed, wavy-haired, perpetually busy, he is at first the model *entrepreneur*. Gradually he gives way to fluster and hysteria (notice the way the hands depend heavily from his wrist) as his life-lies are exposed. But his final speech, in which he atones by creating a public company, hits just the right note of arrogant modesty, exemplified by the conspiritorial look he gives the free-thinking Lona Hassel when he dares to say 'Let him that is without sin cast the first stone.'

Irving Wardle in *The Times* called the performance superb and went on: 'We first see him as a briskly affable public man, changing his face in private into long-practised off-hand cruelty with his wife, and simulations of his younger spoilt self with the old friends he has betrayed.'

John Peter in the *Sunday Times*, calling it a 'Great Bomb of a Play' in his headline said: 'This is the finest performance I've seen Ian McKellen give: a sleek self-made buccaneer defensively encased in a smooth frock-coat, his fixed, steely gaze hooded with insecurity. His bearing and his gestures reveal the nervy tidiness of a secretive nature, and like most secretive people he is most convincing in moments of evasion.' It was a brilliant success for McKellen and won him the SWET (Society of West End Theatres) award for 1977.

Unfortunately the next play *The Days of the Commune* did not find favour with the critics – it is not one of Brecht's better plays, being naive and dour. But McKellen, and indeed all the company, received good notices, Billington saying, 'Ian McKellen, as the older, more liberal Langevin meanwhile suggests age without adding one streak of grey to his hair but simply through the compulsion with which he clutches his battered, document-filled suitcase.'

The Alchemist was to provide McKellen with one of his finest roles, that of Face. This rumbustious farce tells the story of three people, Face, Subtle and Dol Common who take advantage of their master's absence to dupe Sir Epicure Mammon and get a large sum of money from him. John Woodvine was playing Subtle and Susan Drury was Dol. Together they made a wonderful comic team, acting with amazing speed and dexterity. McKellen with smooth face and sleek hair took on disguise after disguise and his witty playing contrasted well with Woodvine's drier wit, and they all gave delightful details to their parts, such as McKellen's gesture when he caught Abel Drugger's foul breath. Bernard Levin pinpoints McKellen's characterization, saying:

'Ian McKellen's Face, changing in an instant from swaggering Captain to shambling menial (Jonson hardly called him "Face" by accident) is so charged with energy that you would get an electric shock if you touched him.' While J. C. Trewin, writing in *The Lady* summed up his feelings so:

> [McKellen] has never been more expertly amusing. Mr McKellen is always a surprising actor. He is a man of peak-and-valley. You never know how you may find him. Now he is a foaming delight as the fellow who is, successively a swaggering military man, a shambling alchemist's assistant (with Lancashire accent) and, finally, the suave servant on his master's return.

There was some controversy over the play as Bernard Levin in *The Sunday Times* 18 December 1977 took exception to the way Trevor Nunn and Peter Barnes, whom he called jointly Bun, had edited and modernized the text. 'When they are faced with a word or phrase they do not understand ... [they] replace the offending expression by one which they have heard of, on the assumption that their audiences need as much help as they do themselves. How kind! How thoughtful! How civil of them thus to piece out our imperfections with their thoughts!'

Castigating them with a lack of integrity for diminishing Jonson's play Levin pleaded 'intolerable provocation on the part of Barnes the Booby and Nunn the Noodle' for butchering the play. He went on to say that it would serve them right if he refused to review the play 'in which Jonson's work is butchered on the altar of Mr Barnes's vanity with the blunt knife of Mr Nunn's misunderstanding'. But he did return to the play, as we have seen, giving it an ecstatic review. This previous notice, of course, brought forth a spirited reply from Mr Nunn defending his and Barnes's action in the name of clarity in production.

The end of the play was truly memorable. Face, all his peccadilloes and rogueries found out, is left on stage and the lights dim slowly, leaving just a spotlight on him. McKellen sat there quite still, his face an awful, terrifying blank. He was a hollow man without anything behind the eyes.

It was for Face that he received his second consecutive SWET award; 'he is always very good at award-giving ceremonies,' says Tim Pigott-Smith. 'His acceptance speeches are always just right – but after all, he has had more practice than the rest of us!'[55] Sara Kestelman remembered, 'He asked me to accompany him to a SWET Award Dinner, I think it was 1978. Anyway, he had to present one of the awards to an actress and he came back and sat down beside me again and they announced the Best Actor Award. He knew he had been nominated, of course, and he was up against some pretty strong competition. But he was genuinely amazed when his name was called – his jaw literally dropped. He really was very, very surprised!'[56]

Around this time McKellen took part in a performance of *A Miserable and Lonely Death*, a play about the South African political prisoner Steve Biko which was given in aid of the South African Defence and Aid Fund in which he was 'excellent'[57] and he also took a one-man show to the Edinburgh Festival.

Another interesting and socially-conscious entertainment in which McKellen appeared was *Every Good Boy Deserves Favour*, a Tom Stoppard and André Previn piece for orchestra and actors. It concerns brain manipulation in a Soviet mental home. It was a single performance, though afterwards televised. McKellen was then living in Camberwell, a house which he had bought some time ago, and some preliminary work was done in his unpretentious sitting-room. 'We had a rehearsal here one night and sitting in this room were Stoppard, André Previn, Trevor Nunn and John Wood. It constantly surprised me that people like these are prepared to listen to me. It must mean something,' he said to Michael Owen.[58] Bernard Levin was excited by the piece, which entailed a whole symphony orchestra, besides several actors and wrote in the *Sunday Times*:

> In it, Stoppard used all his glittering verbal felicity and warmly mordant wit to mount a savage indictment, filled with icily-controlled hate, of the Soviet Union's incarceration of sane dissidents in torture-hospitals; I have never before seen a play with so directly salutary a purpose that was at the same time a work of such true theatrical genius ...

They had been good years for McKellen and he summed them up by saying:

> 'The RSC is a friendly company. I feel I can go and try to interfere and then be told to mind my own business. That's fair enough. It is possible they might listen to me more as I'm playing Macbeth rather than Second Messenger.[59] It is the studio work that I have enjoyed so much and which has been such a corrective to my work. I know, you know, I used to do all these things.' He swings an expansive arm towards the ceiling in a gesture towards the so-called mannered acting he has been accused of by some. 'There is a new fashion now for intensity at close quarters. I say fashion and I mean fashion. Instead of pushing the play towards people now we just lay it open and let them take what they want. But when I started playing big parts I was acting in big theatres. If you are in a large theatre trying to reach the people in the back circle it is possible the people in the front stalls will think you are overdoing it.'[60]

As he was so enamoured of the studio work he told Nunn that he did not want to return to the main theatre at Stratford for another season, so he and Nunn devised something that would continue the studio work and combine it with Ian's missionary feeling that he must take good drama to the provinces and to people who would be otherwise starved of it. It was new, daring, and was to prove a great success both for McKellen and the RSC ...

8
Travelling with the RSC

After playing with the RSC for three years McKellen's next move was to return to something he was always happy to do – tour. 'I told Trevor Nunn I didn't want to do a season at Stratford this year,' writes Michael Owen.[1] He thought that both the RSC and the National Theatre had an obligation to tour but, of course, the costs of big scale touring and the requirements of repertoire work made this extremely difficult. So a neat formula was worked out. McKellen was enthused by *Macbeth* realizing that the discipline of small-scale work was what was needed. As he said, it was a 'corrective to my work'[2] and he wanted to continue to grow as an actor. So what was devised was two small-scale productions of classic plays that could be given in halls, gyms or any space that could seat no more than a few hundred people. The plays chosen were ones that were familiar to McKellen. The first was *Twelfth Night* in which he had played as a boy in Bolton and again at Cambridge. The other play was to be *The Three Sisters* in a translation by Richard Cottrell. 'When I did the play at Cambridge I couldn't find a translation which I thought spoke well, so I did one myself,' Cottrell told me. 'I wasn't involved with the production – though I would have loved to have been – because I was busy doing something else. But I did spend a day with the cast asking all sorts of acute questions about the text. The same kind of examination of text had been going on as with a Shakespeare play. It was a stimulating day, being quizzed by these highly intelligent actors.'[3]

Instead of Tuzenbach, which he played at Cambridge, McKellen was to play Andrei, the brother who through his misalliance did not fulfil his sisters' dreams for him. There was also to be an anthology entertainment, *Is there Honey Still for Tea?* which would be done as an extra or in places where the space was too small for the other productions. The company was to play in over twenty places including the Edinburgh Festival on a tour lasting fifteen weeks. McKellen was to be Artistic

Director, though this was not stated on the programme. The sixteen actors were composed of a nucleus from the Stratford Company: McKellen himself, Roger Rees, Bob Peck, Clyde Pollitt, Griffiths Jones, Patrick Godfrey. They were to be joined by Suzanne Bertish, who had been with Prospect, Jeremy Blake, Christopher Hancock, Rose Hill, Susan Tracy, Bridget Turner – who had worked with McKellan at the Belgrade – Alec Wallis who looked after the music, Emily Richard (now Mrs Petherbridge) and McKellen's old friend and associate, Edward Petherbridge. It was a mixture of old mates and new friends. Caroline Mackay was Stage Manager, the Tour Administrator was Jean Moore; Brian Harris, known as 'Basher' was in charge of lighting, the Wardrobe Mistress was Carol Deary, the driver was called Ted, and the carpenter ("simply marvellous" according to Peck) was John Bluck. The unit was to be self-sufficient, taking minimal scenery, their own lights, and the Wardrobe Mistress took her own washing-machine and wig-cleaning apparatus. Everything went into Ted's truck. Stray journalists who came to report on the venture found themselves roped in to make tea or coffee, help put out seats or black out windows. 'We all mucked in,' says Bob Peck, 'we all helped, for instance, with the get-out' (i.e. dismantling the scenery, putting the costumes into skips, and loading the truck).[4] 'Ian was marvellous,' Bridget Turner remembers, 'he would often go ahead of us and we would arrive finding him putting out the chairs.'

The chairs were a permanent problem. The company arrived at the Edinburgh Festival to find several hundred more tickets had been sold for each performance in the Daniel Stewart and Melville College gym hall than they wanted for the production to have great effect. And they were arranged in a way that did not suit the production, so the company got to and moved them.

The company journeyed to places that had no drama, let alone anything as magnificent as this troupe. In small places like Paisley, Dunfermline, Horsham, Poole, Blandford, Exmouth, Glastonbury they went, bringing pleasure to people who had not been to the theatre for years, if at all. And everywhere they went they would attend civic receptions, put on a workshop for children, if asked for, and shake hands with the audience as they went out. And McKellen was everywhere, using his charm and energy to make people feel that this was a special occasion, that their expectations were not let down, that they had had a good time. It was a remarkable performance.

Then there was the publicity. As always, McKellen was unsparing of his time with journalists, telling of the venture, himself, the company. As one journalist remarked in the West Country, 'With amazing humility

Ian McKellen, one of Britain's top actors, stood at the back of the former church after the performance and actually *thanked* people for coming ... he is totally committed to getting out to places where they do not normally have actors of this calibre. He also likes performing in small intimate surroundings – hence his warm and welcome enthusiasm for St George's.'[5]

They were courteous, also, to the people who prepared the halls for them. In Edinburgh the head porter at Stewart Melville was presented with a signed programme, an RSC T-shirt and a bottle from the company[6] – all organized by McKellen. The dressing-rooms were *alfresco*, often just a space with a curtain down the middle, and a shower if they were lucky. There were no proper dressing-tables, no proper lights for making up. So they improvised, using what they had and this led to closeness. 'With all the actors in one room, we can comment on one another's performances and resentments don't build up,' McKellen explained to Victoria Radin.[7] He went on to give his reasons for undertaking this tour:

'There is a sense in which acting is more than just earning one's living. We're not claiming to bring the best of British theatre to the culturally stunted, but we are giving people who might not normally go to the theatre an enthusiasm for the great plays. For us, it's good, because they're not an audience who've put on their best clothes and are sitting there grimly telling themselves they'd better enjoy it. They generally take it in quietly and at the end they often behave in quite an abandoned way – they cheer, stamp and shout, "Come back soon".'[8]

To Heather Neill of *The Times Educational Supplement* he said, 'I'm very much against buildings. Theatre exists for the night you see the play, and that can happen anywhere', and he was proud that audiences were getting the best 'which isn't always true of touring productions'.[9] Ipswich was another place where tickets had been oversold and McKellen, in a sky-blue vest, rearranged the seats. The arriving actors were dismayed both by the acoustics and the fact that the audience was widely spread. Heather Neill was roped in to make tea, the company having lost its all-important tea urn. In Bury St Edmunds he and 'Basher' had a real theatre to work in and they quickly went through the lighting plot together during the afternoon. And it was here that the company dogs, belonging to John Bluck and Griffiths Jones had a fight over a dinner. The company lost its flag, and had a competition to design another one, and there were constantly letters to answer. 'The company has had *such* letters, sometimes from quite old people who had never seen Shakespeare before,' McKellen told Heather Neill. In Canterbury, where the performance coincided with the Lambeth Conference, the company had the pleasure of seeing a group of bishops queuing for return tickets.[10]

The tour was sponsored, of course, partly by the Arts Council, mainly by Hallmark Cards and, in Edinburgh, by British Petroleum. Although in one or two places some publicity was needed to get people to come to *The Three Sisters*, the Box Office was doing good business and the performances were generally sold out. In some places, special offers were made for the matinée performances in collaboration with local newspapers[11] and McKellen and other members of the company were always ready to give interviews and generally help to make citizens aware of the presence of the RSC. In Peterborough, where the company appeared in the Key Theatre, one of the few actual theatres it played, McKellen talked to Harold Hodgson of the *Peterborough Evening Times* emphasizing the modernity of Shakespeare. 'Shakespeare,' he declared, 'is as modern as punk rock. There is nothing in modern life that Shakespeare did not know about. Punk rockers fall in love don't they?' He might also have added that 'punk' is a word used by Shakespeare (in *Measure For Measure*). 'Shakespeare knew more about people,' Ian went on, 'than any other man who lived. All the human passions: jealousy, hate, love, youngsters' relationships with their parents.' He again stressed the motives behind the tour, 'Our show is designed so that we can put it on anywhere – in theatres, village halls, schools – and our message is that Shakespeare lives.'[12]

The third entertainment offered was *Is There Honey Still for Tea?*, an anthology of words and music about England. He said, again to Hodgson who ran a series of features on the company's visit, 'I suspect the word anthology frightens people. It reminds them of their schooldays and examinations and learning huge chunks of long boring verse.' The programme in fact seeks to find out whether there is such a thing as Englishness and if so whether it is still alive. 'It makes people think, "Does my country mean anything to me?" in a slightly old-fashioned atmosphere of the garden party and the picnic on the lawn. We leave people to make up their own minds. We don't supply the answers or come to any conclusions.' The entertainment, in which McKellen sported a striped blazer and boater, did not only use classic texts, but drew from the works of Noel Coward and used excerpts from Captain Scott's Diary.[13] It proved to be an amusing, if somewhat light-weight, evening.

In *Twelfth Night*, McKellen again played Sir Toby Belch but this time without the addition of an uncertain beard and he gave an insight to Hodgson on his ideas on the part. 'Who says Sir Toby Belch should be fat? Shakespeare doesn't. And, furthermore, who says he should be an old man? Again Shakespeare doesn't.' More textual study had been done.[14] His Sir Toby was a somewhat wistful country gentleman who drank too much to soothe the sorrow in his heart. It was nicely paired with Roger Rees's delicate pale loon of a Sir Andrew. They were both, regretfully, wasting their lives. But Sir Toby was trying, according to McKellen, to pull himself up by his bootstraps. He was not yet a hopeless case, not yet too far along the path of dissipation. He wore country tweeds, a knowing look, and one of the great joys of the production was the expressions on his and Rees's faces watching Malvolio (Bob Peck) read the letter. Alan Wright in *The Scotsman* thought that:

'Ian McKellen's performance as Sir Toby Belch sets the exuberant tone of the production. This swaggering squire refuses to be his age and seems to be desperately defying Feste's warning that "Youth's a stuff will not endure". He may be an amiable buffoon but McKellen reminds us that he can also be a boorish bully.' B. A. Young of the *Financial Times* said that McKellen brought his 'matchless comic talent to as funny a Toby Belch as I can remember, the lines adorned with well-placed frowns, giggles, yawns and side-long winks that polish them to a new brightness. This Toby, a sportsman in tweed plus-fours, is a man of high intelligence; whatever he does, he does with complete foresight of the consequence. Mr McKellen *has cast all the accepted qualities of the part overboard and erected a fascinatingly different character from the same material.*' (Author's italics.)

The provincial press was just as complimentary. Charles Spencer writing in *The Surrey Advertiser* of the performance in Christ's Hospital Arts Centre in Horsham noted that: 'Ian McKellen is in classic form as Sir Toby Belch. He presents the figure as a dissipated clubman, the kind of bloke who is forever pouring whisky into his tea and pinching serving-girls' bums. What makes the performance special is the way he manages to make his character both sympathetic, contemptible and enormously funny at the same time.' And he commented further that the scene between McKellen and Rees 'in which they get a drunken attack of the giggles in the middle of the night is marvellous stuff because it has the ring and tone of absolute authenticity'. Cushman described them simply as 'the best'.

It was perhaps daring to bring so Russian a play as *The Three Sisters* to the Edinburgh Festival for a company from Russia, The Moscow

Drama Theatre of Malaya Bronnaya Street was also there with Gogol's *The Marriage* and Turgenev's *A Month in the Country*. In Russia they are considered a very daring company giving, as they do, modern interpretations of the texts. Their style is much more akin to what we are used to in the West than the State company which visited London in the sixties. Although the direction of their production was not received particularly well, the acting, which was splendid, was. And it was all, naturally, very, very Russian.

But no one who saw Trevor Nunn's searing production is ever likely to forget it, its poignancy, and the way it drew the audience into its atmosphere made it remarkable. One simply sat there with tears pouring down one's face, and went out silently, moved to one's core. At least, if one had any sensitivity, that is. Nothing would have stopped the brash Americans on my bus discussing whether Andrei should have pushed the pram or not – they were certain it wasn't in the text! It was a simple production in one way. A backcloth with icons painted on it, a few pieces of furniture and a lot of mime. A brilliant scene was acted for the meal; the stage was not big enough to show both the seating and eating parts of the living-room, so the company performed a wheel-like turning movement in which they left the sitting area and evolved themselves round an invisible dining-table. Yet it was all so subtly done although there was a feeling of claustrophobia, of fustiness. It is, of course, very much a play needing a team of actors who are more than good, and there are no star parts, just parts that are longer than others. But it must be said that the three girls were played beautifully. Bridget Turner, care-worn but with an edge to her, unlike most Olgas you could really imagine her a head-teacher; Emily Richardson, delicate like steel, was Irina; and, above all, the brilliant Suzanne Bertish as Masha. Her scene of farewell with Vershinin (Petherbridge) was 'almost unbearable as Suzanne Bertish expresses her agony with a rending animal cry'.[15] McKellen played Andrei, the shiftless brother looking 'podgy and piggy-eyed'[16] and very shabby at the end. B. A. Young wrote: 'Andrei, the unworthy head of that family, is played by Ian McKellen with his usual resourceful invention and a crumbling into tearful self-pity that is a masterpiece.'

It had been an exhausting tour. Heather Neill recorded that the get-out would last until 2 a.m. when Ted would drive off, and then start getting-in at the next place at 9 a.m. the next morning, McKellen often in attendance. He is a wonderful leader, time and time again other actors say that of McKellen. And certainly in this tour he had been an inspiration and bulwark dealing with multitudinous details as well as giving splendid performances. But what went wrong? Why didn't he stay with the RSC? In June 1978 he said to Sheridan Morley in *The Times*: 'I sometimes wonder what would happen to me if the RSC didn't exist or if, naming no names, it got taken over by somebody who didn't care for my work. Plenty of RSC stars have left the company and had a rough time in the outside world. But where else would I want to work? It seems perverse to give up something you enjoy just to prove your independence, and this small stage work really is very important to me. I know now that the RSC can be divided into those who actually revel in the big Stratford and Aldwych stages and those who don't, and I'm with the latter half. I know too that my Romeo and Leontes would have been vastly better on smaller stages ... If I have one overriding fantasy it is to be charging round the country in a circus tent doing plays in a way the audience will never forget.'[18]

The tour had certainly been a success: the RSC Touring Group is now part of the company's usual operations, and the work at TOP went on until late 1989, when it was closed to be re-built. Why did McKellen leave? In saying to Morley that 'This type of company needs a certain kind of actor: often without family ties, willing to rehearse long after the play has opened, and to take part in every aspect of the production from the shape of the acting area to the kind of publicity',[19] he was giving a blue-print of himself. So why *did* he leave? To do a murder thriller for television! It doesn't make sense. McKellen has only admitted publicly that he left because he wanted a change of direction,[20] but it seems strange that an actor who said that, 'I will only work with committed people, people who are positive and who I respect',[21] having found such people, and an organization of equal enthusiasm and integrity should not want to go on working with them. But he did leave and it wasn't until May 1979 that the theatre was to be rapt by a McKellen performance again.

9
The Commercial Theatre

'He doesn't like the bricks and mortar much,' Clive Swift said.[1] 'Bricks and mortar' is the term the theatre gives to the owners of theatres and the producers who operate in the West End, risking their own, and other people's money to put on plays. The bricks and mortar tend to play safe – that is what most actors think. Lately though, some of the producers have been collaborating with the subsidized companies and transferring successes from them to the West End, as indeed happened to McKellen with *Too True to be Good*. 'It's good for us and the actors,' Bill Wilkerson of the RSC told me. 'Both they and we get some money that way, and it's good for our work to be seen by people who might not come to the RSC'.[2] The play which was to be such a success for McKellen very nearly didn't get staged at all.

It was called *Bent* and the author, Martin Sherman, had written the part of Max with McKellen in mind.[3] He sent it to various managements who turned it down. Its theme was a grim one – the treatment of homosexuals in Nazi Germany – the cast large and the whole of the second part took place in a concentration camp. Not a family play, definitely not. Sherman then sent the play to Bob Chetwyn, McKellen's director for *Hamlet* who says: 'I read it one summer afternoon in the garden and was gripped by it. It is a wonderfully dramatic, interesting play and I knew Ian would be perfect casting. I sent it to him immediately. He was on that RSC tour – in some drill hall somewhere. But I didn't get any response, then I had to go to Brussels. It was ten weeks before McKellen telephoned me and said he loved the play and could we talk about it. Then Sherman rang me and said that he had sold the rights to a New York Management, so it would now be difficult to put it on in England.'[4]

However, Eddie Kulukundis did one of his Father Christmas acts. Eddie, for those who do not know him, is the most genial of people and when he is enthused by anything moves quickly and decisively. As he combines being an impresario with being a ship-owner he has financial backing and the contacts. 'When Ian and Bob brought the play to me themselves I twisted the Royal Court's arm to do it there [Eddie is on the committee] and did a deal with the Americans who had bought the rights. It was Sherman's first play and I thought it stunning. It did well too.'[5]

'I read the play and was very excited about it,' said Clare Fox now working for Eddie. 'It was a very strong play, you either loved it or hated it. But whatever you thought of the play, Ian was just marvellous in the part.'[6]

There were two other main parts besides Max: Rudy, Max's young lover whom he kills at the behest of the SS, who was played by Jeff Rawle; and Horst, the man Max meets and falls in love with in the concentration camp. Horst was played by Tom Bell. As usual, Ian as leading man was an inspiration to the company. 'He was very good with Tom Bell,' says Eddie, 'they had a rapport which was, I think, very much due to Ian. They both gave magnificent performances.'[7] 'Having Ian in a company,' says Jack Lynn who was then Eddie's partner, 'is marvellous for everyone around. The way he behaves is a wonderful lesson to any young actor. Watching him rehearse is so interesting, he is very generous in giving scenes that ought to be given to other people, to them – he's like Gielgud in that respect. They both think of the play before themselves.'[8]

There was one scene in the play about which everyone was apprehensive, Max and Horst, discovering their mutual love, actually stood on stage, looking out to the audience, and made verbal love to each other to the point of orgasm. It could have been acutely embarrassing, causing the kind of high-pitched squealing laughter that an English audience uses to cover its puritan but prurient unease. McKellen and Bell did it superbly. When I congratulated him on it he looked relieved. 'Did it really come off?' he asked eagerly. 'We were so worried about it. We thought people might laugh.'[9] But they didn't – it was played with such tenderness, one of the few times that McKellen has shown that quality on stage. 'I thought they did that scene beautifully – I don't know how anyone could have been offended by it, how could anyone be offended by love?' asks Jack Lynn.

The play opened at the Royal Court in May 1979 and transferred to the Criterion Theatre in July. The critics, though divided by the play, were enthusiastic about McKellen's performance. As usual he worked hard on the part. His physical appearance changed startlingly. His wavy, luxuriant hair was almost shaven, he lost weight, letting his cheek-bones

sink in and he had a stubble. And this was not just effect on the stage,
seeing him in his dressing-room he was almost unrecognizable. Not all
critics liked the play, and one, John Barber actively disliked it. His
notice read:

I am usually suspicious when a pamphlet is thrust into my hands at a theatre
to explain or fortify what is happening on stage. A play should speak for itself.

'This happens at the Royal Court where Ian McKellen leads the cast in *Bent*
by an American writer new to me, Martin Sherman.

'Here, however, the pamphlet seems justified. It supplies facts about the Nazi
persecution of homosexuals and suggests half-a-million died in concentration
camps.

'The piece begins as a rather jejune thriller, with the brutal Gestapo hounding
down suspects and persecuting those they catch. In the better second half it
settles down into a grim study of a friendship in Dachau between two inmates
condemned to carry stones back and forth.

'For a naive account of the gay life, lissom young men start things jealously
bickering or performing in a transvestite club . . .

'After arrest Max, determined to survive at all costs, accepts orders which
result in his friend's death in an outburst of blood and off-stage screams. Max
is now clever enough to get himself branded a Jew and wears a yellow star
instead of the dreaded pink triangle worn by the despised homosexuals.

'The Dachau sequence is remarkable for McKellen's performance – his hair
cropped, eyes at once furtive and wolfish, the whole body locked in a hideous
tension as if to keep a nervous panic under control . . .

Barber then described the love scene and commended Bell for his part
and noted that the reception was particularly warm. He returned again
to the subject in a feature written in July under the headline WHAT
MAKES A PLAY? Asking what attracts people to the theatre Barber said:
'The presence of Ian McKellen in the cast at the Criterion might get me
there. Unless, that is, I was put off when told more about the play.' He
then outlined the plot, the torture, the necrophilia, the murder of the
lover and the suicide at the end of the play when, on the death of Horst,
Max decides he can no longer live and so, pinning on the pink star at
last, he hurls himself on to the electric fence and dies agonizingly. Barber
went on to say that he resisted such material but, in spite of McKellen's
'mesmerizing performance' . . . 'he did not alter my belief that a degrad-
ing spectacle cannot be made to serve a serious cause. The peddlers of
titillation have removed torture from the tool-kit of the serious artist.

'*Bent* seeks to glamorize homosexual love by presenting it as coming
to valiant birth amid the most succulent horrors in recent history. I
admit the play packs a thrilling punch but it seems to argue that

being a homo is all right because it blossomed even in Hitler's torture chambers. The torture chambers are too hideously alive in the century's experience to be used to promote any sort of thrill. They must not be *used* at all.'

This feature provoked a reply from McKellen saying that Barber was making the kind of protest that people had always made. He pointed out that younger theatre-goers welcomed the semi-documentary revelations in *Bent* and that the play used horror in the way that Shakespeare did. He also commented that the audience's reaction to the love scene, which was applauded every night, showed their response to the tenderness and joy underlying the scene.

What, of course, McKellen ignored in his well-argued letter was that the play *was* titillating, as Barber had pointed out, and that Mr Sherman, though a competent writer who told his story quite well, lacked the power and beauty that are found in Shakespeare's writing. It is unfortunate that excepting that one scene, the whole atmosphere of the play was shoddy and vulgar, for it is a theme to which a Shakespeare could and would have done justice. But, as McKellen said to Paul Donovan in the *Daily Mail*, 'It is an achievement to get a play like this on in the tourist season in the West End.' The play lasted until November when Ian Albery, the bricks and mortar, took the play off feeling it was not right for the Christmas season. 'When we transferred to the Criterion,' Clare Fox explained, 'business dropped off a bit, but then word went round and it grew and grew.'[10] Certainly audiences were enraptured by the love scene and the performances by Bell and McKellen. Nightly flowers were thrown on the stage, something that generally only happens at the ballet and opera. It was a great triumph for McKellen both as an actor and because he created such rapport with Bell that the whole love scene became believable and transcended indifferent writing. For his part in *Bent* McKellen received a SWET award – and one it should be noted, that he had now won for three successive years, something no one else has yet achieved.

He also received the CBE in the Queen's Birthday Honours, June 1979, as a recognition for his work. As he said, 'I received a letter from 10 Downing Street ten days after the Tories won the election. The first two things that Mrs Thatcher did were to give me a CBE and to knock £1.5 million off the Arts Council Grant. There is, I suppose, a side to myself which the Establishment wishes to recognize.' John Andrew said, 'When we gave Ian an Honorary Fellowship of St Catharine's [which happened a year or two later] there was an anarchic look in his eye. I think he was pleased to get the Fellowship but there was a side to him which was decidedly anarchic about it. But he has good manners and didn't make it obvious.'[11]

It was the following year, in January 1980, at the *Evening Standard*'s 25th Drama Awards that McKellen showed his rebellious streak again. There had been further cuts in the Arts Council Grants. 'We were all very angry,' says Tim Pigott-Smith, 'and Ian made an excellent speech about it, short and to the point. Much better than Peter Hall's which got all the attention, but Ian is an excellent speaker – a good leader.'[12]

After *Bent* McKellen had three months out of work, something very unusual for him, then he went on tour with his one-man show and signed a contract to make a film, *A Priest of Love*. For this he again lost a stone in weight and grew a beard, which he dyed red as he did his hair, for he was to portray a controversial figure from another time, D. H. Lawrence. The film co-starred Janet Suzman as Frieda Lawrence and Penelope Keith as Dorothy Brett. As Charles Spencer of the *Evening Standard* said, 'It is the uncomfortable hunching of the shoulders, the hollowing of the chest and edgy energetic movements of the actor which best suggest the turbulent tubercular writer.'[13] McKellen commented humorously, 'Have you noticed how Freud, Shaw, van Gogh and Lawrence are the same person? When I put my beard on, I could be any of them.'[14] He played Lawrence very noisily, unable to assume success. 'North country people often cannot handle it. They brag.'[15]

'When we were up at Cambridge,' Richard Cottrell remembered, 'F. R. Leavis was in his D. H. Lawrence phase. I don't know whether Ian heard any of his lectures on Lawrence – I was a year ahead – but Leavis did seem to turn the subject, whatever it was, to Lawrence's works, so I presume Ian did hear something.'[16] Some of the film was made in Mexico and Margaret Drabble went out to see the filming, as did Gerald Pollinger the trustee of the Lawrence Estate, who is a literary agent. He was introduced to McKellen who said 'I hate agents', and walked away.[17] McKellen had some years before left Elspeth Cochrane for James Sharkey, at that time with Fraser and Dunlop, but who subsequently set up on his own and is still, at the time of writing, representing McKellen.

McKellen had got the part because Christopher Miles, Sarah Miles's film-making brother, went to the last night of *Bent*. He rang Ian and asked him if he were interested in playing Lawrence. After some discussion Ian read the script, was delighted with it and agreed to make his first film for thirteen years.[18] He was also thrilled to be co-starring with Ava Gardner with whom he established quickly what he called 'a mutual admiration society'.[19] What attracted him to the part? 'He was a radical in every sense, he fought his background, he fought the Establishment, he fought his disease, a man constantly battling, supported by his amazing wife who was his friend, companion, mistress and mother.'[20]

Christopher Miles was so sure that McKellen was right for the part that he didn't even test him for it 'even though everybody in America said "Ian Who?",' said Miles.[21] Another visitor to the set in Italy was Frieda's daughter who gave Janet Suzman, who was playing Frieda, a bracelet that Frieda used to wear. But the film, unfortunately, did not take off. The *New York Times* called it a 'foolish film' (11 October 1981) but praised McKellen saying, 'he uses most of his vocal tricks to make Lawrence seem more interesting than he is actually written'. The film did not get a wide distribution and McKellen has yet to play a major part in a really successful film, though recently he has taken to doing cameo roles, notably in *Plenty*, starring Meryl Streep where he plays a scene with Sir John Gielgud and, of course, John Profumo in *Scandal*.

Then came the excitement of being asked to play Salieri in Peter Shaffer's *Amadeus* on Broadway. The play, a piece of great theatricality with a long, highly dramatic central part, had been an acclaimed success at the National Theatre, where Peter Hall had staged it with superb panache. Then the leading part had been played by Paul Scofield. When the play starts Salieri is an old man, rambling on about the past and his feelings of guilt because he knows that he has ruined Mozart and claims actually to have killed him. Salieri is on stage most of the time and changes from age to youth and then back again.

It is one of the most succulent parts written in modern times for a star actor, and Shaffer had considerably rewritten the play for Broadway making Salieri's part even more important. It was something that McKellen relished. 'I have no intention of giving a carbon copy of Paul Scofield's performance. The difference in our ages is crucial. I went and saw it at the National Theatre and shut my eyes whenever I thought a piece of great acting was coming up.'[22] At the National Theatre the play had been acted in the Olivier Theatre, with its amphitheatre shape and open stage with no proscenium arch. This made the New York production in the The Broadhurst, according to people who saw both, a different experience. The space, of course, was a different size and there was more of a barrier to cross to reach out to the audience. In the Olivier, Scofield seemed in our midst and actors had made entrances through the audience. One felt very much drawn into and part of the play. But Peter Hall enthused the cast to play with high energy and

brilliance. Pictorially the play looked wonderful and the ambience of
the theatre, though very traditional, suited the play. Some critics thought
that McKellen's performance was just a box of tricks, technically pyro-
technic, but one that was utterly heartless. Walter Kerr in the *New York
Times* on Sunday 4 January 1981 gave a long and considered description
of McKellan's Salieri:

We have already met actor Ian McKellen, met him as the dying eighteenth-
century Viennese court composer Salieri, a crumpled ghost in a wheel-chair
looking as though his shawling and tight grey nightcap had already provided
him with a shroud.

We had watched him lurch to his knees in memory of his youth and retrace
an agreement he thought he'd then reached with the God of Bargains. If he
could be given the gift of music – of writing it and *knowing* it – and if fame
and fortune were to come of the gift, then he would live honourably, chastely,
productively, an almost ostentatious advertisement for virtue. When, the very
next morning, he'd been whisked off to Vienna and blessed with a scholarship,
he was certain the compact had been sealed. And so it seemed to be.

Stripping away his old man's rags to adopt a proud but genial stance
alongside the Emperor's harpsichord, dressed in silks and munching Viennese
macaroons, Mr McKellen cheerfully – and with only a faint trace of irony as
yet – takes us back to the hours of glory as his country's most popular and most
honoured musician. Being a man of his word, he is also its most trustworthy and
most faithful.

Until the moment he hears the music of a drooling, lustful, slovenly young
jackanapes named Mozart. Mr McKellen is seated in a high straight-backed
chair as he begins to recall the incident, flippantly dismissing Mozart's pipe
organ as a 'rusty squeeze-box' while he attends, mesmerized, to the sounds that
come out of it. We hear the sounds, too: tape recordings billow at us from
beyond chandeliered palace walls, just sufficiently muted to keep the spoken
word dominant. The spoken word must be dominant here because it is *telling*
us what the musical sound seems to mean to the stunned man grasping its
intentions, its achievements.

As one piercing sustained note from an oboe penetrates the sighing fullness
of the organ chord, Mr McKellen can contain himself no longer. He is on his
feet, lifted there by the juxtaposition of tone no one has conceived before, and
he is caught – bound and freed at once – by uninvited ecstacy. He has always
held that music is God's art. Here, unbidden and irresistible is the voice of God
and it has come, not from Salieri himself but from 'a man whose voice is that
of an obscene child'. For the moment, though, rapture is enough . . .

Further on in the notice, Kerr mixes and mingles the names of Salieri
and McKellen as though he were not sure whether there was one or two
people, so much does he identify the actor with the part. He comments

on McKellen's 'extraordinarily interesting small gesture – a mere tic of the head, out of nerves and near despair'. And, discussing Mozart's music saying that it cannot be removed asks, 'Would *Mr McKellen* erase it if he could?' where one would expect him to write, 'Would *Salieri* erase it if he could?'. In such a precise and brilliant writer as Mr Kerr this is an interesting mistake – he has undoubtedly been mesmerized by McKellen and has forgotten that he, McKellen, is an actor playing a part, is not the real Salieri. He says that the end of the play did not live up to the beginning which robs McKellen of 'the opportunity to enlarge upon his first striking ecstasy. Mr McKellen remains accomplished throughout' and he goes on to praise Tim Curry, the Mozart.

New York, though, loved McKellen's performance and the play was a big, big Box Office hit. He was to receive numerous awards for the part, including the coveted 'Tony' award for Best Actor, The Drama League's Delia Austrian Medal for the Most Distinguished performance by an actor or actress on the Broadway Stage, the Drama Desk award and the Critics Circle award. In all *Amadeus* won five 'Tony' awards, made half-a-million pounds for the National Theatre, three-quarters of a million pounds for Sir Peter Hall and gave McKellen a taste for stardom and an opportunity to make a million dollars. This was the sum he was offered to tour in the part – and which he turned down saying that his roots were in England.[23]

Richard Cottrell, who saw the performance, thinks that it was 'thrilling. Ian was in total control of his audience, really had them eating out of his hand'.[24] Jack Lynn thought that, 'Ian was more realistic than Paul Scofield and that the partnership between him and Curry was more even than between Scofield and Callow [Mozart in the London production]. He was rather toned down and subdued for Ian, but it was very understandable why he won the Tony. Brilliant actors and a brilliant director make for brilliant theatre, after all!'[25]

At the beginning of the play (the curtain is up when the audience enters) Salieri is sitting in a chair with his back to the audience. 'It was amazing,' Bridget Turner said, 'one moment the chair was empty, the next Ian was there. I don't know how he managed it!'[26] The wait was some fifteen minutes before the play actually began. It could have been boring, or he could have nodded off. How did McKellen fill the time? He used to read, slipping the book in a secret pocket which he had made into the costume, before he turned to the audience.[27]

'They know how to treat a star in New York,' enthuses Richard Cottrell[28] and McKellen was given the full star treatment: a limousine to take him to and from the theatre; acclaim and recognition from everyone, including the ominiscient New York taxi drivers; the best table in restaurants; the whole panorama of social recognition that that city which worships success gives to those that have the talent to achieve it. But underneath the North Country boy was still there, startling reporters by arriving on a bicycle for interviews, though he did live in a splendid downtown apartment with views of the East River. Friends went over to see him and nearby was Jane Laportaire a friend from Ipswich days, who was in *Piaf*, also on Broadway. For McKellen it was a realization of a dream for writing in the *New York Times* he said, 'this month (September 1981) marks my twentieth anniversary as a professional actor. Looking back, I realize that I always wanted to be on Broadway, right from the beginning.'[29]

Talking about the glamour to John Heilpern he said, 'Much of what's delightful about New York seems to me to be what was delightful about childhood. There's always something to look forward to. A parade. A birthday. And they give you such wonderful presents. Gift-wrapped. None of this is very important, but it's so *nice*.' He was, though obviously pleased, quite cool about getting his Tony, saying that they were really more important to American actors, though he had found it very convenient for getting things done: 'I went to the laundry and the man said he couldn't get my suit back till Monday. I said, "But you've got to! I'm on the Tonys on Sunday." "You're on the *Tonys*! Great! Sure!".'[30]

But *Amadeus* wasn't enough to occupy McKellen, he learnt to tap-dance, in case he did a musical. 'There's a man in the company,' he said, 'who's a first-rate hoofer and he's going to teach me. When I come back I would like to do something unusual rather than going straight back into Shakespeare and I may as well take advantage of being in the City of Musicals and find out whether I can sing or not.'[31]

He also gave a performance of his one man show on Shakespeare, for the Globe Theater Center (*sic*), the theatre that is the dream of Sam Wanamaker, who wants to reproduce Shakespeare's Globe Theatre where it originally stood. He altered it slightly to suit the American audience, but basically it was the same as he had done for the last five years and was to do again.[32] Tickets ranged from $35 right up to $250 and besides McKellen, the audience also saw Princess Grace who came with Sam Wanamaker. It was, as always, a great success.[33]

Yet in spite of the fun and the acclaim, McKellan refused the tour offered him, saying that he had no wish to appear in great barn-like theatres holdings thousands.[34] He was also very tired, 'I can't convey what a hit on Broadway's like. It's overwhelming . . .'[35] He also found that he had lost all interest in work, 'I lost all interest in the theatre. I couldn't even think about work. If I'd been cleverer and interested in investment I think I could have retired.'[36] He was less than kind, though, about the Americans, saying 'Americans are still forty-niners at heart. They like to dig for gold. They're always *mining*. They are not good gardeners. To create fine theatre you plant little seeds. You should nurture and cross fertilize your plants, and try to produce a black tulip.'[37]

Of New York he said, 'New York is just like a village. It's not the capital city, it's small and it's an island. It has a local newspaper the *New York Times*. Its TV and radio stations are local and Broadway and the Mayor's office and the Tony awards are all there to sell New York. People who see you in private are genuinely thrilled by the sight of you. It confirms they're in the right place.'[38]

So he came back still feeling committed to England and to the feeling that the theatre must mean something to everybody, not just the few who visit the West End, or the Broadway theatres. And he came back to take stock, to a new house, and a hiatus in his career.

10
One Man Show 1980–1983

Ian McKellen has always seemed to enjoy doing recitals either by himself or with other actors. He has two One-Man Shows, *Words, Words, Words* and *Acting Shakespeare*. He also took part in the RSC's *Is there Honey Still for Tea?*, and with Sheila Allen did a recital about D. H. Lawrence at the Edinburgh Festival in 1980.[1] The recital that he has performed the most is *Acting Shakespeare* which, in this country, appeared at the Edinburgh Festival and in Belfast, Oxford and Newcastle. He also performed it in New York as we have seen and on the university circuit on the West Coast of America for which he won the 1983 Drama Desk award. He recorded it for American TV and in 1985 took it to Canada. He has also taken it on several British Council sponsored tours. In 1980, in February and March, he visited: Israel (Haifa, Tel Aviv, Jerusalem); Denmark (Copenhagen); Norway (Oslo, Bergen); Sweden (Karlstad, Gothenburg, Uppsala, Stockholm). In September 1982 he visited Rumania (Bucharest), while in January and February 1983 he went to Portugal (Lisbon), Spain (Madrid) and finished up in Cyprus, where he appeared in both the Chanticleer and the Municipal Theatres. In May he was at the Atheneum Theatre in Poland, while in November he gave ten performances in Le Petit Odeon in Paris, and such was the demand for seats that a final performance was given in the Main House where people were fighting to get in. He often did special performances for actors who enthusiastically watched a master of their craft, and, as always, he gave long and thoughtful interviews to the press both in the actual countries and before he went.

He told a reporter in Norway, 'Shakespeare is not primarily a poet or a philosopher but a professional theatre man. I try to present him from an actor's point of view. He is universal, very modern and extremely relevant today. To me his plays are far more topical than much written today.' And in Romania he explained that 'an actor on stage, in front of an audience, can show that theatre is the most direct form of art'. And that is exactly what audiences get, McKellen in his own clothes, tweed jacket, open-necked shirt, maybe jeans and T-shirt, with a chair, in front of the curtains. No more, but he conjures up a parade of characters, and an 'exhilarating mixture of solo turn, textual explication, potted Shakespeare biography and acting-display'.[2] He tells anecdotes from his own career, like the story of *Richard II* in Czechoslovakia.

He is, of course, well-known abroad for his televised performance of *Macbeth* for it has been shown in many countries so the analysis of Macbeth's speech, also given here, makes one of the climaxes of the recital. He plays his famous parts, of course, as well as *Richard II*, Hamlet, Romeo, *and* Juliet, too. But he gives a foretaste perhaps of things to come: Coriolanus was included, now, of course, it is a part McKellen has played; Richard of Gloucester from *Richard III* also a part he is playing in 1990 at the National Theatre; Mistress Quickly, indeed Michael Billington thought he was the best Mistress Quickly ever seen; and he did the Eastcheap scenes from *Henry IV*, playing both Prince Hal and Falstaff – a McKellen Falstaff is something else we have to look forward to. He also interspersed these scenes with pieces about the plays from many sources; Ellen Terry playing Puck with a broken toe; passages from Samuel Pepys's diary (where he seemed like Pepys himself to a critic in Norway). He played Jacques, Polonius, Hamlet's advice to the players, of course, doing the Player King as well, a Protean performance which drew forth not only admiration but intelligent understanding from the critics. Tito Livio writing in the Portuguese newspaper *A Capital* said: 'And above all this, a healthy irony; intelligence in the service of Art.' While Fernando Mideos wrote: 'Ian McKellen was at one and the same time an extraordinary comedian and virtuoso who put before us many of the male characters in the Shakespearian Universe; and a connoisseur and critic, who, naturally and fluently spoke to us, unfolded ideas, revealed personal views on his country's most famous writer.'[3]

In Israel McKellen said, 'I am well aware that an audience enjoys seeing an actor moving from one role to another, even if it is only myself all the time without costume or make-up. I also mean to speak a bit here and there about my own relationship to Shakespeare, about my experience as a Shakespearian actor. I prefer not to assume that my audience knows very little about Shakespeare even though the reverse is no doubt true ... There is a side of Shakespeare in which I claim to to be an expert, an aspect about which most people have probably never thought much: Shakespeare the professional man of the theatre. I have no intention of speaking of Shakespeare as a philosopher or a humanist, or of Shakespeare the Renaissance poet or the English National Hero. My intention is to speak of that fellow who lived in central England four hundred years ago and fell in love with the theatre to such a degree that he decided to devote his life to it. In the second half of the performance I intend to offer a brief perspective on the manner in which Shakespeare has been presented in Britain during the last four hundred years.'[4]

Eliakim Yaron, writing about a performance in Israel wrote:

'Ian McKellen is a marvellous actor full of feeling for the material he deals with ... and a complete mastery of the two chief means of expression at the disposal of an actor: his body and his voice.

'His body never imitates: his changing positions suggest the dying Romeo, the crippled Richard Gloucester, portly John Falstaff. But above all, he excels in his wondrously musical voice. The vocal variety with which he characterizes the poet king *Richard* II, or Macbeth's confusion, or the courageous Henry (v), testifies to a remarkable voice full of rich and limitless possibilities.

'The evening as a whole is not an ordinary anthology of Shakespeare. It is a distinctly personal evening stressing the man behind the various roles ...'

One of the pieces of virtuoso acting that McKellen brought off was the acting of both Romeo and Juliet – though when he was growing his D. H. Lawrence beard, one journalist wrote that though Shakespeare's women had been played by men he doubted whether he had a red-bearded man in mind! He did both beautifully ... Hava Novack saying that 'every word, every gesture proof of what a first-class actor is capable of doing ...' and he went on to write:

'I was most enchanted by his extraordinary ability to play with the spoken word. Each syllable is enunciated with exactly the right emphasis. He rolls the words around his tongue, tastes them and produces them each with exactly the right interpretation. This isn't simply a matter of perfect diction or of playing with the various possible vocal registers, *but a thoughtful and emotional comprehension of each word, an internalization of each phrase, profound analysis of each sentence.* In this way it is possible to play Shakespeare without exaggerated gesticulations, without unnecessary pathos, and still communicate the least shadow of meaning ...' (Author's italics)[6]

In Sweden they thought he lacked Alan Howard's authority but that, 'McKellen gets there through consistent analysis; the methods he uses are refined pauses when one leasts expects them, a sudden explosive gesture, an unexpected faintness and new vibrations in the voice or a strange heat in a pause. All this enables us to see life in new dimensions, without difficulty.' And the same anonymous writer gives a sketch of the last moments of the recital:

Appropriately Ian McKellen ended with a piece from Shakespeare's last play *The Tempest* ... Finally Ian McKellen places a red rose, from the huge bouquet he received, on that place which he has enabled us to imagine to be Shakespeare's grave on the empty stage which in two hours has been an arena for the whole world.

Thank you, Shakespeare. Thank you, Ian McKellen.

Another critic in Sweden described McKellen thus: 'He had a well-worn jersey with RSC on the front; Royal Shakespeare Company ...' and remarked on the untidy beard![8]

In Paris they were just as enthusiastic about him. Anne Laurent in *Liberation* called it 'two, almost miraculous hours with the best Shakespearian actor of his generation, king of stage, another Olivier ...'[9]

Le Figaro wrote:

Groans, laughter, fury: the art of Shakespeare is recreated within three blue curtains and thirty square metres by the skill of an actor at the service of the theatre: Ian McKellen.

... [he] has no equal for leading us into his Shakespearian voyage ... An actor occupying the scene by sheer force of voice, look, body. A fine show. The performance, without flaw, cleverly balanced between laughter and emotion, is extended into a pedagogical initiation ...'[10]

Michael Billington writing in *Drama* summed it up like this:

Afterwards a man from *Time* magazine asked me what kind of actor I thought McKellen was. 'Rare', was all I could say. He has a touch of the pub-comic (like Olivier), a love of language and emotion, an ability to shift physically between male and female, youth and age, gawky and heroic and a well-trained analytical mind. McKellen, a great Protean stage presence, had the Paris audience eating out of his hand....[11]

The performance was a virtuoso one – it encompassed a wide range of emotions for both actor and audience. It was hard-edged in its analytical approach but was not afraid of the romantic. When he conjured up Shakespeare's spirit from his tomb, it was something that could have been pathetic but was so beautifully controlled that the tears pricked the back of your eyes; it was so skilful a manipulation of an audience, a whole galaxy of audiences, many of them with little knowledge of English, it was exploitation in the best meaning of the word ... it was Ian McKellen.

The tiredness was working itself out for in Romania he told a reporter, 'I haven't worked in any theatre for a year – and this is because I want to find a play about nuclear disarmament, [his family supported CND] because I'm obsessed by this problem. You see, there is a risk that nuclear arms will destroy the future. There is also a risk that nuclear arms will destroy the past – because when life is destroyed, books are destroyed too.'[12]

But the nuclear disarmament play is still to appear and what McKellen did when he returned to this country was a play for Channel 4 which was chosen to open that channel. It was based on a novel by David Cook and was filmed mainly in a derelict hospital in Islington, by Central TV.[13] It was a story about a mentally handicapped man, called *Walter*, which had some very realistic and distressing scenes in it showing the disturbed man in some harrowing situations: sleeping with the corpse of his mother and being dragged screaming to a mental hospital where he is attacked by a homosexual dwarf. The Spastics Society help by introducing the producer Nigel Evans to intelligent people who understood what they had to do and although they were themselves handicapped, they appeared in the play.

As usual McKellen's research was impeccable – he went to psychiatric hospitals and day-centres for the mentally and physically handicapped, talking to patients, observing their behaviour and trying to find out what it was like to have a mind that was impaired. The physical movements were there to see and could be imitated, but the mental characteristics were harder to delve into. Then, one day, just before filming was to start he decided to play Walter in Marks and Spencer. He pushed by a queue of angry people, and was so convincing that after an initial angry reaction the queuers took pity on him. This was the release he needed to become Walter.[14] The performance was painful, in that the viewer actually felt that he was seeing into a disturbed mind using its strange logic. Of the character McKellen said, 'Ideas go round in his mind like goldfish, as David Cook puts it. It's difficult for us not to think, and we do so with a full vocabulary of words, symbols and images. A quality of his sort of mind is that for much of the time it's blank. All the same, when he does something that looks insane he doesn't seem lunatic to any onlooker who's felt what he has gone through.' And he stressed the comic elements in the part, too.[15] He was, according to Nigel Evans, the only actor who could have played the part and McKellen describes it as, 'The most amazing job I've ever had.'[16] About working with handicapped people he admits that he was very apprehensive at first but it was very, very moving. 'You very quickly forget what the outside is because the inside is so radiant and welcoming. In one room, on the days we were filming ... there were actors, nurses, ex-nurses, mentally handicapped people, physically handicapped people, a blind man, a legless man. And then there were the technicians with their paraphernalia.' And he commented how wonderful it was for these people to be earning money, thirty pounds a day of their own, which enabled them to buy things which they could never have afforded before. 'They'd found out about the right to work.'[17]

The television programme *Link* made a detailed documentary of its filming, and the play was presented in two parts over two consecutive evenings at the beginning of November 1982. For his part as Walter, McKellen won the Royal Television Society's Award for Best Performance.

Then followed, as we have seen, another tour of his One-Man Show and in March 1983 he appeared at Hampstead Theatre in a play by the director, Michael Rudman, called *Short List*. It concerned a group of actors, directors and administrators meeting in a Hampstead flat to discuss the awarding of a prize for the best new writing of the year. It was considered amusing, but trivial and never made the West End. Francis King in the *Sunday Telegraph* described McKellen's performance as a 'prancing, preening, smirking juror, who, in the end, always gets his own way' while the *Sunday Times* commended him for his 'magnificent portrayal of fifties' theatrical camp'.

The next play was even more disastrous. It was called *Cowardice* and was written by a friend, Sean Mathias. 'The play was sent to me,' says Duncan Weldon of Triumph Apollo who presented it, 'with Ian's name on it and also Janet Suzman's. We had worked with Janet before, and we, obviously, would like to be associated with Ian. So I decided to do it.'[18]

The play concerned a brother and sister who used to dress up as Noel Coward and Gertrude Lawrence. McKellen had decided to do the play because 'I didn't want to be trapped in the classics – that rigorous exercise, the poetry and the rhythm – or to be in their two huge, uncongenial houses. I thought about the commercial theatre and how few new original plays go on there, the sort of play that really is original.' So he did *Cowardice* and for 'only two hundred pounds a week'[19] Several managements turned him down before Weldon decided to do the play. However, the play was not liked and closed very quickly, though Sean

Mathias has gone on writing and won a prize for the Best Play in the Edinburgh Fringe for 1985.

That then was a disappointment for McKellen – 'He is not yet an actor whose name can appear on a marquee and sell tickets,' said Weldon that same year. 'He cannot yet overcome indifferent material. But I still place him among the three best actors of his generation.'[20]

11
The National Theatre and ...
to 1989

In the past, McKellen has had hard things to say about the National Theatre. In 1976 in *The Observer* he said. 'I'm against the notion of building theatres that will stand for eternity, like the new National Theatre or the monstrous building at Stratford. When that went up in the 1930s it was thought to be the end, what a theatre should be. Five years later it was out of date, just as the National soon will be.

'I think it'll be a pity if people get the notion, which is slightly being sold at the moment, that anything that happens in the National is, because of that, bound to be better than what is going on elsewhere. But that is the sort of assumption behind building a cathedral to drama on the South Bank.'

And in the same year in *Plays and Players* he pointed out that a lot of good work originated in huts, and pubs and church halls and that buildings were not necessary to produce good theatre, and though 'London may still make an actor's name, it won't necessarily, any longer, make him happy or make him a living ... The national theatre of Great Britain is spread throughout the country; it belongs everywhere; a spirit dispersed throughout the body of work going on all the time, all over the place. Don't the new buildings in London contradict, in their location, this continuing process of decentralization?

'If we are too impressed by the new National (its cost, its size, its site, its expansiveness, its potential) we are in danger of assuming that it is the be-all and end-all ... the more successfully the National exploits its new resources, the more it will pre-dominate and the more expendable other companies will seem to be to the money-savers and the philistines ...

'We now have a symbol amongst theatres: a cathedral, not a chapel; a head office, not a corner shop. How will the workers within this symbol be able to reconcile themselves to their official position? Probably by ignoring it and continuing much as before. Outside the building will frustrate them. Inside, let's hope it will be different.'

And he later told Anthony Holden, 'I was very wary of coming to the National.[1] From the outside, I *hated* the place, and all it stood for.' It was then surprising that he decided to join the company, especially as the company was led by a strong director, Sir Peter Hall who has, rightly or wrongly, the reputation of not paying much attention to what his staff says. It is only right though to point out that, in his *Diaries*, Sir Peter denies this charge. But actors, anywhere, do not generally have much right to say anything about their conditions, the work they do or the policy of the management for whom they are working. McKellen described Hall in a Radio Forth broadcast as ' ... the prime example of the "artistic director" – that new breed which runs the British, and indeed the world's, major theatres ... he is a mighty administrator, planning overall policy and employing almost everyone involved – that means meeting after meeting after meeting! All artistic directors of my acquaintance are workaholics, divorced and very charming.'

Describing his first impressions of the National he said 'It's still too early for me to speculate as to how Sir Peter balances his burdensome responsibilities as the leader of such a large army. Sometimes you see him in the staff canteen, concentrating a little too hard on his plate of French fries, as if avoiding a stagehand with a grievance! At the other end of the canteen, there is likely to be a huddle of actors complaining, as actors tend to do, sometimes justifiably – although once a play reaches the stage, we hog the attention of the critics and the audiences; the director slumps neglected and lonely at home or, just as probably, gets down to planning his next show.'[2]

But in spite of calling it a 'robot factory' – other actors refer to it as 'The Lubianka' – McKellen engaged upon an interesting programme of work. The first play was Thomas Otway's little performed work *Venice Preserv'd*, last seen in the legendary season at the Lyric Hammersmith in Peter Brook's production with John Gielgud, Paul Scofield and Pamela Brown. It is a production that still lives in the memory of those who saw it. This time the director was Peter Gill and though it was sumptuous it did not supersede the memory of the previous incarnation. McKellen played Pierre (the part Scofield had played) and Michael Pennington played the other protagonist, Jaffier. It was perverse casting – McKellen seems more natural casting for the tortured Jaffier, torn between love and duty, while Pennington seems to fit Pierre more. But both men, being excellent actors, played their parts with intelligence and vigour and it was as McKellen said 'a gentle way of slipping into the National

Theatre.'[3] Emrys Jones writing in *The Times Educational Supplement* said, 'Pennington's Jaffier is another impressive feat of control – intelligently spoken throughout its great length and never monotonous in delivery. Unlike these two bravura performances [Jones had previously praised Jane Laportaire's Belvidera] Ian McKellen's excellent and unselfish Pierre works through restraint and through tense understatement. His gritty honest, disillusioned solder is at times a valuable counterweight to Jaffier's volatility.'

B. A. Young in the *Financial Times* (13 April 1983), thought it McKellen's best performance he has yet achieved 'and that is about as high praise as I can find ... He can fill a single word with vibrant meaning and he speaks Otway's verse to perfection in a manner that retains all the poetry while allowing for everyday speech.'

Irving Wardle in *The Times* of the same date remarked that, 'Pennington burns and McKellen smoulders'. It was a notable debut, but a quiet one – two excellent actors giving performances that were no way above what one expected of them. Although McKellen obviously likes working with good actors, if there is too much competition it sometimes seems to dampen his ardour and ability to transcend his part and he himself seemed to feel that as he said, 'I wish I had a more spectacular death'.[4]

But in the next play *Wild Honey* adapted from Chekhov by Michael Frayn there was no doubt as to who was the star – McKellen had found a marvellous part for his comic genius. Writing in *Drama* McKellen said, 'We recognize of Chekhov, what we don't yet, in our hearts, accept of Shakespeare, that only when every part – each lazy valet, each stoical nanny, each gypsy violinist – has been perfectly cast, costumed and acted, can the whole play be fully realized. Actors climb up Chekhov like a mountain, roped together sharing the glory if they ever make it to the summit.' Certainly the National found an expert team of actors to support McKellen, including the ever-reliable Basil Henson and Brewster Mason. Nicholas Jones gave one of his best performances and in the female lead a vibrant Charlotte Cornwell played with great style.

Christopher Morahan directed, recently highly acclaimed as a co-director on Granada's *Jewel in the Crown* on television. He and his cast immersed themselves in photographs and paintings of Czarist Russia and Christopher and Ian went to Moscow and attended a rehearsal at the Moscow Arts Theatre of *Uncle Vanya* and noticed that the rehearsal room walls were covered with almost life-sized pictures of Chekhov and his family and friends. Ian missed, though, the research on the social background of Russian life before they started rehearsals, that he and his group had done on *The Three Sisters*, a common RSC practice[5] and he comments:

'*Wild Honey* takes place at the onset of spring in Russia and the two of us were there to witness the seven-month winter ending and the countryside everywhere turning green ... The sweet air was full of birdsong and lilac scent. Wild flowers, wild bees, wild honey. Each time I now come on stage as Platonov, welcoming Anna Petrovna's return with a huge bouquet of wild flowers, (nightly culled from the car-park alongside the National's stage door), I can feel again the mud on my boots, the sun on my face and hope to bring on too, some genuine sense of that re-awakening after the long winter's hibernation.'[6] He also commends Michael Frayn's adaptation of *Wild Honey* saying, 'For *The Three Sisters*, the RSC read five translations before voting Richard Cottrell's the most speakable, and, we hoped, the most accurate. Not a word of Frayn's script was altered during eight weeks of rehearsal. We must have been the first non-Russian actors ever to feel we were doing a Chekhov play in its original language.[7] And yet he was intensely unhappy about the part while rehearsing – even up to the First Night.[8]

The Press was ecstatic – Irving Wardle in *The Times* (20 July 1984) wrote, 'Ian McKellen's Platonov excels, partly through his volatile contrast with the surrounding company. Switching in an instant from moral denunciation to teasing and from high-minded restraint to reckless seduction, his reactions are always two steps ahead', while Milton Shulman wrote in the *Evening Standard* 23 July, 'McKellen is superb, and then superbly funny, as Platonov lancing his self-frustration by taunting the company with eloquent supercilious humour and placating the women who love him with increasingly desperate stratagems until finally vodka and self-pity take control. His Platonov manages to be both Chekhovian and Fraynian and still utterly true to life; it is a brilliant dual creation.' McKellen himself says that 'you can't begin to be funny without being truthful'.[9]

The *Sunday Times*, while giving most of the notice to a critical appreciation of Frayn's work in translating and editing an unwieldy original text, said of McKellen's performance that it 'dominates' and so it did. This heartless creature, Platonov, was given a febrile, energetic performance which was brilliantly conceived and executed. It continued to dominate the play even towards the end of the run when the excellent cast had changed in one or two parts, but was, I thought, stronger than the original. The audiences loved it, the play doing excellent business. For his performance as Platonov, McKellen won his fourth prize presented by the Society of West End Theatres, now called the Laurence

Olivier Award, this time for the Best Actor in a Revival. He found the experience 'bewildering. I don't know how it happened'.[10] Both these plays had been presented in the Lyttleton Theatre, the National Theatre's proscenium arch auditorium. Next McKellen was to tackle the open apron stage of the Olivier Theatre, perhaps the most difficult in which to play of the three theatres which make up the NT complex. The part was a notoriously unsympathetic one too, Caius Martius in *Coriolanus*. It was to be directed by Sir Peter Hall and was to prove one of the most distraught productions in which McKellen was to appear.

There is something about the character which is repellent: a blood-thirsty soldier dominated by his mother who is arrogant, a turn-coat and possibly bi-sexual. However, actors love playing such a faceted character, although the play is not a favourite with audiences. All actors seem to want to establish themselves as a notable Coriolanus rating the part just below the 'must' parts of Hamlet, Macbeth, Othello and Lear.

Before that, though, Sir Peter Hall had announced a radical change in the construction of the National Theatre. Several times in his *Diaries*, he says that he, Trevor Nunn and Peter Brook all consider the ideal acting conditions to be a company of twenty to twenty-five actors of high standing who could work in small places. This they feel would produce excellence in a way that they cannot obtain working in large organizations. There is a feeling that administrative work holds up the real purpose of their companies – the creative work. With this, no doubt, McKellen would agree, with the added comment that the actors should have a large, if not equal share in the decision-making. When Michael Owen asked him in March 1984 to what extent he (McKellen) would want to become part of the decision-making process or whether he would like to join the directors, McKellen answered, 'Peter and the other directors do seem to be talking to me and telling me what goes on. In my experience if you put an actor on the board of directors he starts behaving like a director. I don't have any ambitions to be running the National in five years' time.' He also said that after his initial wariness about joining the NT he had now settled in and thought he would like to have more part in it, but that, 'Personally, I would not want to stick with one group exclusively so I'll move around'.[11] As ever, with McKellen, what he says he will *not* do is the very next thing he does, for on the twenty-first anniversary of the opening of the National Theatre, on 22 October 1984, Sir Peter Hall announced that he was going to have five companies contained within the NT, each producing their own work. Each company would perform, during one year, three plays in each of the auditoria – the Lyttleton, the Olivier and the

Cottesloe. He was to have overall authority and run one group; the director Richard Eyre was to run another with the writer David Hare; Peter Wood would run the third, and Bill Bryden the fourth. The fifth group would be run by McKellen with Edward Petherbridge. (There was also an experimental group to encourage new writing and acting talent in the Old Vic Annexe, lent by Ed Mirvish.) Inevitably, the press thought that the McKellen/Petherbridge company was a new Actors' Company in a different guise, especially as the two men said that part of their policy was to tour as much as possible.

McKellen had been quite adamant that he would not run the company without Petherbridge's help. He said: ' . . . When I first arrived I said to Peter Hall that I was going to be very nosey about the way the National Theatre is run and perhaps be critical of it. I felt I had to warn him that I'd be prepared to speak up. And I think that it was as a result of that attitude that he said this company which we are now forming was going and was I up to running it? I said that I would only do it if Edward could work with me on it. So although I was first asked to do it, I would not have taken it on if he'd not been able to come in on it with me.'[12] The company was not to be run on such democratic lines as the Actors' Company either. Though everyone gets equal billing on the posters – this is normal NT practice – and has to understudy, the actors are not all paid the same. McKellen was reputed to be earning £25,000 a year, though, for once, he has not publicly stated his earnings, while 'spear-carriers' at the National get about the Equity minimum and performance fees, which totals less than the national average of about £174 a week for men. McKellen feels that the system at the NT is somewhat unfair as many actors play there for 'perhaps a tenth of their going rate' having certain assumptions about their prospects and are often disappointed. In all his pronouncements about actors being badly paid in subsidized companies he forgets that these companies offer regular work for a specific amount of time, while in the commercial theatre the run of the play is not guaranteed and much of a star actor's salary comes from a percentage of the take.

Before the McKellen/Petherbridge Group could form, McKellen had *Coriolanus* to rehearse and open. Again he tried to find a modern parallel for the part – 'Muhammed Ali at his height may get near it, but Coriolanus is fighting not on behalf of himself, as an athlete tends to do, but on behalf of his society, his city, and the country he had lived in. I see that side of him as being admirable . . . So I must encourage the audience to see Coriolanus as admirable.'[13] Another aspect, that of Coriolanus's arrogance was based on the tennis star, John McEnroe.[14]

He discovered that the part needed immense physical stamina and energy so he prepared for it with more than usual intensity. He gave up smoking, drank only a little wine and stopped eating red meat. He also underwent a punishing course of physical training at Dreas Reyneke's Studio. This remarkable man who has a small exercise room where the atmosphere, according to Maria Aitken, is 'half cocktail party, half church',[15] believes in each client finding his/her own ideal. 'Each body has a point where it finds its own ideal and that is what I help with. People ... go to their psychiatrists for their minds but they come to me to keep in contact with their bodies.'[16] No slacking is allowed and McKellen went regularly before rehearsals to strengthen himself. Coriolanus is an exhausting part physically, the actor is rarely off-stage, never sits down and is continually fighting or running – and all this in the vast Olivier auditorium where entrances and exits were made through the audience. Backstage it was the same. Before dressing, his 'wounds' were stuck on and Kensington Gore (stage blood) was painted on his body. Then he had to constantly change costume: from his own white suit with a lush camel coat slung around his shoulders, to ceremonial robes, then to strip down almost naked, and for some scenes again daubed with quantities of Kensington Gore. He had always wanted to play the part[17] but he hints in the piece he wrote for *Drama* that not all was well: 'Here we are three weeks before the first night and I do not know what exactly will emerge. Often the things one imagines are the keynotes of a performance are overlooked in favour of an aspect that everyone has taken for granted. But certainly, you cannot fairly play the part without going for the characteristics of nobility, pride or disdain.'[18] Further on he declares, 'I do not want to distort the picture at all but there is much to be said in favour of Coriolanus in that his imagination is extremely limited, so are his talents and abilities, and he probably has not got a very big brain for a start! Certainly he has far too little experience of the world and he is dragged away from his soldiering, at which he is supreme, into a public world of politics for which he is totally unsuited at the *very* point at which the old order of Rome, in which he was trained by his mother and by the patricians, is breaking down ...' A central relationship in the play is that between Coriolanus and Volumnia, his mother. For this part he was determined to get Irene Worth, the great actress who divides her time between Broadway and the English stage. Ms Worth had been with the NT before, playing in *Oedipus*, and she has won innumerable awards both here and in the States. 'He has great energy,' she said. 'He was determined to get me for the part and he did. And I was longing to play

Volumnia!' And the acting between the two of them was wonderfully moving. 'He has dazzling intelligence,' Ms Worth went on, 'I adore him. He has angelic sweetness, too, and it is mysterious how he gets it, but he does get his own way. I was interested to observe how he and Peter [Hall] would work together but Ian takes criticism from a director even if he doesn't always see eye to eye with him. He is very resilient that way. His very, very, very concentrated will sustains him ... sustains him in life ... sustains him in his work.'

Rehearsals can always be difficult, especially when two great talents are involved, working for another great talent, but Irene Worth found McKellen, 'a dream to work with, very supportive. He is generous, not selfish and is extremely understanding of other people's difficulties.' The two built up an enormous trust in each other, 'so much so,' Ms Worth went on 'that we were able to improvize in performance. We had mutual confidence in each other's discipline and quickness and that kept our scenes dangerous and exciting and gave us freedom. In fact, I enjoyed it so much that I stayed on longer than I had intended. I adored working with him.'[19]

This concentration and energy between the two showed in performance for the critics were admiring. Irving Wardle commented in *The Times* (17 December 1984) ' ... it is at its most thrilling in the scenes with Volumnia, the source of his dream and the audience for whom he is playing it. There is nothing in the least martial about Irene Worth's Volumnia ... Nor does she raise her voice at her son's rebellion: all she does is to turn her back on him, and slowly restore her approval once she has reduced him to a gauche, guilty adolescent with mouth stupidly agape.

'The supplication scene, equipped with perfectly timed false exits, and low-registered vocal resources, I have never previously heard from this actress, is as spell-binding a demonstration of emotional blackmail as I have ever seen. At the end of it, McKellen's hand snakes out to take hers. There follows an immensely prolonged pause, packed with racing thoughts and emotional reversals, which McKellen finally breaks with the line 'O Mother, what have you done?', delivered in a tone of pure horror. A great partnership!'

The production did not live up to this partnership, however. It was a strange mixture of old and modern, the senators' robes being worn over business suits; the women in timeless dresses; McKellen, as already said, changing from stylish Bond Street to primitive; Greg Hicks, who played the part in which McKellen made his name in Nottingham, as Tullus Audifius wearing black leather and stripping to nakedness also.

Most disturbing of all was that members of the audience (paying £2 for the privilege) sat on the stage and became part of the Roman rabble, directed by members of the company on stage. One saw ladies with Hermès bags and Gucci shoes; exhibitionist girls determined to be looked at; awkward men in tweed jackets, open-necked shirts and sandals; middle-aged couples not sure what they were doing, plus enthusiastic members of amateur dramatic societies relishing their chance of appearing on the stage of the National, all clapping and shouting rather self-consciously for Coriolanus's banishment. It was really distracting, to say the least, from the main, serious intent of the play. Benedict Nightingale wrote, 'Myself, I've seen more suddenness and ponderosity in the throng at a bring-and-buy sale than at the National Theatre last Saturday ...'[20] And McKellen's performance as Coriolanus was not to be counted among the critics as one of his greatest. To continue with Benedict Nightingale:

'Early in *Coriolanus* one of the Roman generals exotically claims that he's as good at telling the sound of the title-character's "tongue from every meaner man" as shepherds are at distinguishing thunder from tabors. One knows what he means, because the tongue in question belongs to Ian McKellen and has just been heard transforming the simple sentence "Come I too late?" into "Caahm Ai too laiyate?". And so it goes on, insistently displaying its dissatisfaction with vowels as they are used by patricians and plebians, not to mention the average citizen and theatre-goer of 1984. At the point of death the word "boy" becomes a weird gurgling wail of "booyaahayaaee". In fact, there are times when one feels that Mr McKellen's tongue has invented a new tongue, or at least a new regional accent: a blend of melodic throb and euphonius whinny, mainly to be found on upmarket stages in and out of the metropolis. There's Welsh, there's Somerset, there's Yorkshire, there's Ulster, and now there's McKellen.'

He then goes on to say that McKellen is undoubtedly a major actor ... and his 'Coriolanus is in many ways a fine, intense performance' but some twenty-two lines of fine criticism later comes to the conclusion that 'until McKellen gets style and content, manner and matter, consistently in sync., that present eminence of his will, I fear, never become pre-eminence'.[21]

As usual, McKellen continued to work on the part – the performance that he gave towards the end of the run had been refined and simplified, and, seeing it again, the shock of the unrealized production was not so great and could be ignored, and more concentration given to what had become a fine performance. McKellen was awarded the *Evening*

Standard Drama Award for the Best Performance by an Actor for 1984 and the play was chosen to go to Greece for the Common Market's first Cultural Capital of Europe Festival in 1985.[22] Here the company played in the six thousand seat Herod Atticus amphitheatre, achieving full houses for both performances.[23] It was a fit end for a heroic performance, to play it in a heroic place.

THE MCKELLEN/PETHERBRIDGE COMPANY

While he was rehearsing *Coriolanus* and playing the part along with *Wild Honey*, McKellen and Petherbridge were setting up their own group within the National Theatre. The original plans had to be modified as the National Theatre grant was not as much as had been hoped for, the company being cut to seventeen actors/actresses, and plans for the Cottesloe were abandoned for the time being, as that theatre closed for a short time. McKellen had already faced up to the fact that artistic decisions were governed in the final instant by financial ones – he had served on the Arts Council Drama Committee for several years and he told Anthony Holden, 'Those years on the Arts Council taught me just how little one can do about it. In the end, all the decisions – mostly about money – are made by faceless grey men who neither know nor much care what they're doing.

'What clout I can wield is best used here, at a place like this, as an actor. If I say OK, I'd like to take this show on tour, then it's much more likely to happen than if I brought it up at an Arts Council committee meeting.'[24]

The way he and Petherbridge started working was different from the way they had set up the Actors' Company. This time instead of choosing actors first and then having endless discussions on plays they asked Philip Prowse the renowned designer and director from the Glasgow Citizens' Theatre, who McKellen thought had been neglected, to direct the first play. Next actors were chosen and asked to join the company. As Sheila Hancock writes in her autobiography, it was not easy to find a company that would be able to encompass all the styles needed for the diverse range of plays chosen. Everyone was looking for something different. McKellen wanted people who were language-orientated. Tom Stoppard (who was directing one of his own plays) needed people who would fulfil his inner vision of what his characters looked like, while Philip Prowse wanted people who would look good in his costumes. Hancock says that the company was the oddest that she had ever worked with and in consequent memories she substantiates this opinion.

'I was very touched to be asked, really very touched,' Robert Eddison says. 'It was so kind of Ian, but they only suggested one small part and had not fixed the other plays, and I had other plans so I declined. It was nice of Ian though.'[25] Greg Hicks, who had played with McKellen in *Coriolanus* was someone from within the existing company who accepted, and Eleanor Bron, who was at Cambridge at the same time as McKellen, was also asked to join. 'I sat thunderstruck,' she said when asked, as she thought that she would never be asked to work at the National. She agreed though she expected to feel crushed by the structure, 'but to my surprise, I actually feel supported'.[26] Another, somewhat surprising choice, maybe, was Roy Kinnear, though he had been with the RSC and the National before and had been part of the pioneering work done by Joan Littlewood at her Theatre Workshop. He enjoyed the meetings that McKellen and Petherbridge held for actors that wanted to attend. 'I love these meetings,' he said, 'we all chip in but, of course, there ain't such a thing as democracy in the theatre. The theatre is a dictatorship and it has to be. In the end an actor's always doing what the director wants. And you've got to have someone you can blame. But it's nice to have the *semblance* of democracy.' Sheila Hancock, experienced both as an actress and a director said, 'The fact that I'm here, directing and understudying and playing a small part, tells you something about Edward and Ian's charm.'[27] Petherbridge and McKellen decided that they would play in all three plays to be presented, McKellen saying, 'We can't sit in an office and phone down to see how it's all going. We have to be down there too doing it. We're workers and bosses at the same time.'[28]

The Duchess of Malfi was the play that Prowse eventually chose and it was to be performed in the Lyttleton Theatre. He had been much praised for his production at Greenwich for Webster's other play *The White Devil*. For its Olivier Theatre Production the group chose to do a double bill of Sheridan's *The Critic*, with McKellen as Puff and Sheila Hancock directing and *The Real Inspector Hound*, with the playwright Tom Stoppard directing. McKellen had directed the latter years ago at Leicester with Derek Jacobi. McKellen praised his three directors: 'We were chairmen really on the decisions that were taken. But the commitment of the directors involved to the idea of the actors' company is wonderful and it should not come as a surprise. Philip Prowse has been devoted for many a long year to a corporate company at the Glasgow Citizens'. Sheila Hancock has run a small-scale touring company herself [for the RSC] and Tom Stoppard is not an ivory tower writer but a

gregarious person, liking and used to working with companies.'[30] The
reason for choosing these directors was that it was thought they would
challenge the actors in different ways to perform exciting work.[31]

The choice of *The Duchess of Malfi* might seem to have been an ideal
one for McKellen (he was to play Bosola) with its strange, high-romantic,
not to say flamboyant style. But, in the event, according to Petherbridge,
the company found the verse difficult to deal with: 'During rehearsals
Philip has been careful to steer us away from the melodramatic. The
style we have been wrestling with is that of speech and how you heighten
it without falling into "poetic delivery" ... and I can tell you that with
old Webster it's a knotty problem too. And as for "high acting", well
Ian and I are just trying to create a company where it's possible for
individual performances and ensemble to go together.'[32]

Philip Prowse conceives of a play in visual terms first and then makes
it sound like it looks. He admits that he doesn't fit into the mainstream
of the theatre and his strong, rather frightening visual conceptions can
sometimes seem stark and unfriendly, but always exciting: he is the
master of a *coup de theatre*, there being a coolness in his work which
joins with dramatic effects, both scenic and in acting, that can bring
audiences a *frisson* that is pure theatre. He says that he is 'rather at
odds with the English theatre because my interests and enthusiasms are
not those of my contemporaries or theatre people who're a bit younger –
I'm nearly fifty'.[29] He conceived the play as being aristocratic, very
Catholic, redolent with sin and redemption and imbued with a sense of
Death (who indeed became a silent character in the play).

Prowse, also, was to prove a difficult director, not one in tune with
McKellen's idea that actors should contribute and complain. Speaking
at a two-day seminar for *The Duchess of Malfi* McKellen said that
Prowse was a director 'who is capable of admitting publicly that he is
not in the least interested in actors' opinions and would as soon work
with marionettes'. Prowse had no truck with actors' attempts to understand the characters' psychology and he especially disapproves of them
appealing to the audiences' sympathies. He was, it seems, also displeased
when making a visit to a performance, after the play had been running,
he found that the actors had changed their readings.[33] He also told
McKellen at one rehearsal that he couldn't act![34] According to Sheila
Hancock in *Ramblings of An Actress* the company were disconcerted
by Prowse's method of working. He told them 'Oh, ducky, I hate all
that RSC acting – it's too poetic, too expressive. I don't want sub-text.'
And she goes on to say that it was difficult to fall in with his tendency
to describe the finished product rather than being helped to achieve it.

Malfi was a very stylized production and McKellen seemed somewhat uneasy as Bosola, who is the villain of the play, a macabre, Iago-like figure, whose outrage at his treatment in life acts as a catalyst among the high-born nobility and princes of the Church amongst whom he finds himself. Critics remarked on the poor speaking, even inaudibility of the cast[35] and while admiring of what was termed 'The Glasgow Style' they thought that it was wilful for a Jacobean play. Michael Ratcliffe in the *Observer* (7 July 1985) thought the style was both 'hypertense and austere' while several critics pointed out that the politics of this intensely political play had been ignored. (Prowse says that he is not interested in politics[36].) The critical reception was definitely cool. It was equally cool of McKellen's Bosola. Francis King in *The Sunday Telegraph* said, 'As one would expect, Ian McKellen has many superb moments as Bosola, but one never feels that he has approached near to the enigma of the character'. Robert Hewison in the *Sunday Times* wrote, 'Ian McKellen, however, as Bosola, holds back the histrionics, and even begins by pretending to be an intellectual by wearing reading glasses. He knows he has the best part, and fills it without any need of overflowing.'

The group had presented its first play, but it could not be classed as a success, though the *New York Times* said it was 'stunning' and Michael Coveney in the *Financial Times* thought that it was, 'a truly magnificent presentation of one of the greatest plays in the language'. It *was* stunning visually, but the coolness seemed to inhibit the actors, who were at their best when thoroughly stylized (Jonathan Hyde caught the style perfectly) and McKellen seemed a little subdued in a part in which, given full reign, he could have dominated. In the programme for *The Duchess of Malfi*, McKellen and Petherbridge issued a signed statement of intent:

In the decade since Laurence Olivier retired from the National Theatre at the Old Vic, British theatres have been ruled not by actors but by directors. Coincidentally, over the same period, there has been a total decline in the numbers of acting companies working together for longer periods. Those regional theatres, where actors of our generation learned our business, cannot nowadays afford to retain such companies. Even in this theatre, there is no pattern of prolonged contracts such as are available to actors working in the national theatres of Europe. British actors are in danger of becoming mere casual employees.

We are delighted to accept Peter Hall's invitation to organize the company of seventeen whose first production is *The Duchess of Malfi*. The same actors, with their stage-management of four, will all work on *The Real Inspector*

Hound and *The Critic* (opening together on 12 September in the Olivier Theatre) and will advise us on the choice of our third production (opening in the Cottesloe late in 1985). Neither of us will direct these plays. Instead we have asked Philip Prowse, Tom Stoppard, Sheila Hancock and Mike Alfreds, knowing that their versatility and experience will make exceptional demands on our acting. We hope that our identity as a company may in turn support and influence them.

Under this there was a picture of the seventeen actors and the legend, 'Every member of the group will be understudying.'

The next production was the double bill of *The Critic* with McKellen as Puff and *The Real Inspector Hound* with Roy Kinnear and Pether-bridge as the two critics, the major parts. Again the critics were dis-paraging, thinking that *Hound* was the wrong choice for the Olivier and as for *The Critic* Michael Ratcliffe in *The Observer* (15 September 1985) exclaimed: ' . . . to stage *The Critic* in the Olivier Theatre shows a masochism bordering on the perverse. It is almost certain that Sher-idan's last comedy is much funnier to read than to see . . .' – a judgement with which anyone who has seen the Old Vic production with Olivier at the New Theatre (now the Albery) would profoundly disagree. He went on to say, 'Here again is an experienced company giving less value to the structural consonants than melodious vowels, slurring and plumming their way through sentences so that, even when the words themselves are clear, their meaning is often not.

'Petherbridge and McKellen are themselves among the worst offenders, although in *The Critic* Petherbridge does a very funny turn as the mute Lord Burghley, agonized epitome of statesmanship, while McKellen's irresistibly enchanted innocent, drifting vocally between Stage Ireland and Central Lancs, ensures that Mr Puff's energies and optimism give the piece what energy it has.'

John Peter in the *Sunday Times* wrote 'Mr Puff, the self-admiring dramatist, is played by Ian McKellen with relentless, arch bumptiousness and a bizarre north-country accent, like a cross between Gracie Fields and Frankie Howerd: it isn't always easy to tell him apart from the characters in his play.'

The last play put on by the group was Chekhov's *The Cherry Orchard* in the re-opened Cottesloe, which proved to be a resounding success with critics and audiences, judged one of the best productions to be done at the National for some time. Again, McKellen was acting in a small theatre, which he has always said he prefers. Irving Wardle in *The Times* said that it was the most passionate performance of the play he had ever seen, praising all the cast and saying of McKellen's Lopakhin, 'a figure sometimes given to laughing and bending his knees at his own boorish jokes, but otherwise a totally sympathetic person; in whom the harsh memories of the old landowners have done nothing to cloud his feelings towards their descendants'. Michael Ratcliffe in *The Observer* said that this performance was his most completely successful at the National, rating it even above *Wild Honey* though, having seen the performance twice, he commented on how differently McKellen played the part the second time. He attributed this to Mike Alfred's method of direction, a method which calls for the cast to improvise during performances, while not actually changing the inner shape of the play. This obviously suits McKellen, for, as we have seen, he likes keeping a performance alive during a run by improvisation.

Certainly the night I saw it in mid-January 1986 the performances had lost any subtlety they might have had, the cast grossly caricaturing their parts, leaping around the stage, falling off chairs and generally hamming it up. But McKellen did play the part with a great deal of warmth, but lacking the *weight* of the man. Although the audience, and the house was packed with people standing, the applause was only respectful and the cast took but two calls. Perhaps I was unlucky and saw it on a bad night, but if McKellen's theory that a small group playing in small theatres produces the best acting and direction, this was not a night that proved it. And Mike Alfreds also felt this, as according to Sheila Hancock after seeing one performance he sent the following note to the company saying 'You have made your contribution to Deadly Theatre. Would you please return to Lively Theatre. Please all think and prepare before all performances. You can't just go on ...'

In February 1986 the group presented *Not About Heroes* Stephen MacDonald's play about Siegfried Sassoon in the Cottesloe, with the author as Siegfried Sassoon and Simon Dutton, one of the young actors in the group as Wilfred Owen.

Also in February 1986 the double bill of *Inspector Hound* and *The Critic* was presented in Paris, representing Britain at Le Théâtre de l'Europe and in March *The Cherry Orchard* went to Aberdeen. In May the double bill and *Malfi* was taken to Chicago for the International Theater Festival, finishing McKellen's contract with the National Theatre. The group will have then completed a year of work which – if not great and outstanding – has, at least, been intensely interesting. It has introduced new directors to the National, ones which perhaps would not have otherwise had an invitation to work there. Although the work has not been as successful as McKellen's admirers had hoped for, he has once again proved himself to be a good leader of a company and has put himself at service to the company, rather than, Wolfit-style, dominated a weak company. For this he is to be praised. Writing in the programme for *The Cherry Orchard* the group says:

> Our original aim was to present at the National Theatre a versatile company of seventeen challenged by a repertoire of varied plays and distinctive directors. We have been rewarded by full and enthusiastic audiences.

One would have hoped that this group could have continued working together but in May 1986 it was disbanded, and another group was formed to replace it under Jonathan Lynn.

AFTER THE NATIONAL

Immediately after leaving the National Theatre, McKellen consented to appear in a production of *Wild Honey* in the USA. It was to be substantially the same as that in which he appeared at the National and it opened in Los Angeles to good reviews but, unfortunately, it flopped in New York and because the overheads were so high, the management decided to pull it out of the theatre after a short run. McKellen did not find favour with the critics: they found him mannered, technically brilliant, but lacking heart. McKellen had let his house for a reputed £10,000 for the year so he decided to take his one-man show around the States. It was changing, for he was learning to have more rapport with his audience, drawing them in by asking questions – 'How many plays did Shakespeare write? Call them out. Anybody know of a happy marriage in Shakespeare?' The spiel surrounding the actual extracts from Shakespeare became highly romantic and not entirely accurate, but it made for a good evening.

'He really turned me on to Shakespeare,' Lee Armitage told me. 'Until then I didn't like it a bit.' Lee, a schoolgirl, got to know McKellen and when he heard she was bringing her younger brother Chris to see him as a birthday treat, he called Chris onto the stage and got the whole audience to wish him a 'Happy Birthday!' *Acting Shakespeare* was performed two hundred times and the television version is used as a teaching aid. But in spite of the success of the one-man show he came back disillusioned with America telling the *Evening Standard*, 27 November 1987, 'I am now clear I would not want to do a play on Broadway again'.

When he returned he discovered that a young actor who had appeared in *Coriolanus* with him had died of Aids. McKellen then offered to give more performances of *Acting Shakespeare* for nothing if a theatre could be found. Jeffrey Archer made his newly acquired Playhouse available and McKellen played a sell-out season raising over half-a-million pounds for the London Lighthouse Hospice and other Aids charities. He also campaigned against the notorious Clause 28 which forbad the promoting of homosexuality. Originally intended to stop the extolling of homosexuality in schools, the Clause was so badly drafted that it could mean that the writers and actors involved in any book or play which entailed any description of homosexuality could be prosecuted. The government refused to amend the Clause, saying that it would be tested in the Courts. He organized and acted in a benefit performance of *Bent*, also for Aids charities.

The next campaign in which McKellen was involved was that to save the Rose Theatre. During excavations in Southwark, remains of the original Elizabethan Rose Theatre were found and anxious to preserve these for future generations McKellen, along with other distinguished actors such as Dame Judi Dench, Dame Peggy Ashcroft, Vanessa Redgrave and Tim Piggot-Smith, held a vigil on the site and organized a campaign to 'Save the Rose'. Unfortunately the courts upheld the rights of the developers, who, nonetheless modified their plans for the building to be put on the site, saying that they would eventually allow the public in to see what was left of this historic place.

At this time – summer 1989 – McKellen was appearing in a strange play, by Alan Ayckbourn, at the Vaudeville Theatre. Called *Henceforward* it was a typically bitter Ayckbourn play in which McKellen played a surly genius but it was the play more than the actors that received attention in the notices, though McKellen played in it for over six months together with Jane Asher. He had also appeared as Jack Profumo, the Minister at the centre of a sex scandal in the sixties, wearing a bald head and giving what was generally acknowledged to be an average performance. In the late summer of 1989 he played a manic Adolf Hitler in *Countdown to War* presented by Granada television. For this performance which he claimed was authentic, McKellen watched archive films to make sure that his mannerisms were the same as the Fuhrer's.

BACK WITH THE RSC

In February 1989 McKellen was seen with his head together with Trevor Nunn, ex-Artistic Director of the RSC at Joe Allan's, the late-night restaurant. What they were discussing was their return to the RSC. Nunn had spent several years in the commercial theatre directing musicals and opera, including a spell-binding *Porgy and Bess* at Glyndbourne with the Jamaican singer, Willard White. He conceived the idea of casting White as Othello and McKellen as Iago. The production was to be the last at The Other Place and then to transfer, with the support of Eddie Kulukundis, to the Young Vic. The run was to last five weeks at Stratford and eight weeks in London only and was sold out immediately. It was to be the most memorable and distinguished production of 1989.

The set was simple and the men's costumes reminiscent of the American Civil War. The women – the brilliant Imogen Stubbs as Desdemona and Zoe Wannamaker, equally brilliant, playing a disillusioned, plaintive Emilia – wore vaguely Edwardian costumes in low-key colours. What was remarkable about the production was the feeling that Othello and his soldiers were on campaign, with little luxury, under orders to fight. The tension was high. Willard White, whom McKellen described as 'being so very athletic, very beautiful and attractive' (*The Observer*, 20 August 1989) has a magnificent presence on stage and, playing one of the most difficult of Shakespeare's heroes as his first speaking part, was a personality to be reckoned with. But it was McKellen, always stimulated by forceful acting around him, who turned in the most compelling performance. As he showed when playing Face in *The Alchemist*, he is astute at playing chameleon characters, a characteristic that Nunn said 'made him a wonderful person for Iago as he has the ability to slip into another personality'. His Iago was very much of the barrack-room, a soldier to his fussy finger tips, forever straightening his blanket, wiping used glasses, putting brandy in the basin of wine which he prepares for the drinking scene. There was one magic moment when he realized that he had indeed caught everyone in his trap and, slowly, very slowly, his face went sodden, a look he used again right at the end when he refused to say why he had done what he had.

Michael Billington in *The Guardian*, 26 August, wrote: 'with his ramrod back, swinging arms and clipped Northern consonants, Mr McKellen is the absolute embodiment of the professional soldier; every detail is correct down to the little baccy-tin for half-smoked cheroots ... (he) relishes his role as the camp entertainer ... he is an old sweat warped and corroded by fantasies of power and by a destructive jealousy far greater than Othello's. Mr McKellen not only makes you understand Iago: he also induces a compassion for this pitiable creature ... This is great acting.'

Yes, great acting. But again of a heartless character, and again we see only too well how the effects are obtained. McKellen showed once more that he has all the technical gifts, but lacks the art that conceals art. But, having said that, it was a gifted, towering performance which won an *Evening Standard* award for Best Actor.

McKellen

'The joy's gone out of the job: even the acting,' so said McKellen in *The South Bank Show*, which was a diary of his life, shown on 20 October 1985. He has certainly found his work at the National exhausting. He told Sarah Gristwood of *Ms London*: 'I can't see beyond this treadmill of work. I am usually in the office by 9.30, and if I've got a performance I don't finish until eleven. Then, while I was rehearsing the double bill, there was also some learning to be done. It's daft. No way to carry on. If you're not used to it, making decisions that affect other people's lives is much, much more worrying than making decisions about your own life. It's exhausting – and then you have to forget all that, and go on stage.'[1]

Well, it is an exhausting life, but is it any more exhausting than, say, that of the big businessman or the politician? Take the life of a cabinet minister: decisions that affect millions of lives, not just twenty or so members of an acting company; 'performances' in the House of Commons and speeches outside. But, say actors, acting is very exhausting, with hours of concentration on stage. Yes, indeed, but a West End actor will only be doing that for less than twenty-five hours a week after rehearsal period is over. It is true, that in the subsidized theatre, actors play at night and rehearse during the day, but often, leading players only give three or four performances a week. Or, to take another branch of the theatre, ballet dancers have a gruelling day: one-and-a-half hours in class; rehearsals; fantastic memories to keep a whole range of parts in their heads. Yet the best of them – Rudolf Nureyev in Paris, Marcia Haydee in Stuttgart, Peter Schaufuss with the English National Ballet and Anthony Dowell at the Royal Ballet – manage over a hundred dancers, a large repertoire *and* dance themselves. It can be done.

McKellen says that he is interested in being 'the best'. He told *The Observer*, 'Everything I've done in my career has been about becoming *the best*, and *best* is being better than you were last time, and stretched as far as you can make it'.[2] Having said that he must expect to be judged by his own high standards and, I think, he would not wish it otherwise. So is McKellen the best?

'We seem to throw up three great actors at a time,' says Duncan Weldon, 'Olivier, Richardson, Gielgud: Burton, Neville, O'Toole: and now McKellen, Jacobi and Hopkins, though there is also Alan Bates and Albert Finney.'[3] Many people would also add Alan Howard. So how does McKellen compare?

Burton, O'Toole and Neville were the bright meteors of the previous generation, Burton of course, is dead: Neville has retreated from the British scene, whilst O'Toole survives, swooping from triumph to disaster and back again with a charming insouciance – yet he has 'star' written all over him, even his disasters being worse than other people's! Gielgud, Richardson and Olivier come from a different world, one where there was no state subsidy as a safety-net at the start of their careers. They were professionals who had no guiding paternalism to help and nourish their talents, though, of course, it must be admitted that Gielgud did come from a distinguished stage family which had some useful connections. These were only useful at the beginning, thereafter he made his own way, often risking his own money to get a production together, and several times he ran his own company, most notably at the Haymarket Theatre in 1944 where he played in *Love for Love, The Duchess of Malfi* and his last *Hamlet*. Peggy Ashcroft, Leslie Banks, Max Adrian and a very young Rosalie Crutchley were in his company. Richardson was a star of British films and the stage, well-established by the time he was McKellen's age. He and Olivier ran, with John Burrell, the Old Vic Theatre Company at the New Theatre from 1944 onwards, playing lead parts in *Peer Gynt, Arms and the Man,* a definitive Falstaff and a Cyrano de Bergerac that still haunts the memory. As for Olivier, the actor to whom McKellen is compared the most, his career was so dazzling that it is difficult to understand how one man could have achieved so much. Recognized in the pre-war West End and the Old Vic he became a Hollywood star with credits such as *Wuthering Heights, Rebecca* and *Lady Hamilton*. After serving in the Fleet Air Arm, he produced the film *Henry V* and directed and starred in it. Then came those legendary New Theatre seasons where he first played *Richard III, Arms and the Man,* that tremendous double bill of *Oedipus* and *The Critic, Uncle Vanya* and *King Lear* and he led the company on an exhausting tour of Australia and New Zealand. At the same time he directed other plays and in 1950 set up his own company at the St James's Theatre, playing in Christopher Fry's play *Venus Observed,* Caesar in Shaw's *Caesar and Cleopatra* and Antony in Shakespeare's play. In 1953 he directed and played in Terence Rattigan's *The Sleeping Prince*. He also produced, directed and starred in the film of *Hamlet*, played memorably in *Carrie* and was MacHeath in Peter Brook's film of *The Beggar's Opera*. All this time he was struggling with a difficult marriage. Olivier was a giant, touched with more energy than any human being has a right to have!

It is interesting to note that McKellen had a picture of Ashcroft, Gielgud and Richardson in his dressing-room; 'national treasures' he calls them. He admitted that he plays Gielgud's recording of *Ages of Man* every time he undertakes a Shakespeare part 'because there is so much to learn from it ... the rapidity with which he delivers the lines. The agility with which the poet's mind and the character's mind are revealed!' Another record he plays a lot is *Under Milk Wood*, calling Richard Burton's voice 'beautiful'.[4]

But, as I have said, things are different in the theatre today. The RSC and the NT and other subsidized theatres mean that actors no longer have to risk their own money to appear in parts they wish to play. Someone of McKellen's stature can be reasonably sure that one or other of the theatres will be delighted to present him in a classic role that he wishes to play – as can Jacobi, Hopkins or Alan Howard. So how does he stand within his own generation? 'No one,' several people, including Richard Cottrell and Bob Chetwyn, said to me, 'has played so many classic parts as McKellen, really great parts.' And, at first, this seems true. His range of Shakespeare parts, the standard by which serious actors have to be judged in England, is immense: Richard II; Hamlet; Romeo; Leontes; Macbeth; Coriolanus; all leads, all tremendous in length and energy required. Add to that Face in *The Alchemist* and impressive roles in Russian drama – Platonov in *Wild Honey* and Andrei in *The Three Sisters*. But what of Jacobi? Not so much Shakespeare, of course – a distinguished Hamlet, a magical Benedict in *Much Ado*, and in 1989 he played Richard II and Richard III with his own company at the Phoenix Theatre and he has played *Peer Gynt* and Cyrano de Bergerac as well as his brilliant leads in several television series, which made him an international star. Alan Howard has played the most Shakespearean parts – *all* the Kings, besides Hamlet and Antony. McKellen's record, though amongst the best, is not unique among his peers.

Is he then a star? Or is such a term irrelevant today? Being a star need not, necessarily, have anything to do with being a great actor. There are, of course, great actors who are great stars, but stardom is something apart from acting ability. There are stars who are personality actors, that is they always act themselves. Kenneth More was the epitome of the personality star. An actor has to be willing to take opportunities that will lead to stardom, but it is not always conferred. 'The play, the actor and the time all have to be right,' says Elspeth Cochrane. 'No one can really explain it, it just happens.'[5] 'I don't think he is ruthless enough to become a star,' says John Andrew.[6] Certainly he wasn't prepared to sit around Hollywood waiting to see what happened,[7] though he was extraordinarily tired. If stardom doesn't happen to you in a play, and you don't like the 'waiting to be discovered' boredom, then TV is the only way to acquire stardom. Felicity Kendal says that a good TV series 'puts you five rungs up the ladder'[8] – as *The Good Life* did for her and Penelope Keith. Again, this has never happened for McKellen. It did for Derek Jacobi in *I, Claudius* and Anthony Hopkins became well-known throughout the country as Pierre in *War and Peace*. McKellen is aware of this himself, he told Michael Billington: 'Compared to some actors of my generation I'm not in those terms [being a star] very successful: think of Alan Bates or John Hurt or Derek Jacobi. I've got the capacity to get work in the English Theatre. But I don't have international status.'[9] He realizes that he has missed his chance in films, 'I never tire of saying that I'd like to find out how movies work, how to be good in them. But I'm now forty-six and I am under no illusion that the time to make your name in movies is really in your early thirties – as Tony Hopkins did, as Jonathan Pryce is doing ... If you are in demand as a theatre actor it's not that easy suddenly to pick up the offer of a film. And giving a year to make a series is a big decision for me to make. In that time, I could have been in three plays. Actors who manage to do both (stage and screen) are very, very rare indeed ...'[10] But he is also capable of saying: 'Besides, I have no desire to be a token British actor in Hollywood. And I've never had any ambition to be a film star. But if you're an actor, not to have been involved in the great art discovery of the century is ludicrous, even if you live in England, where there's no film industry to speak of ...'[11]

There are actors who make a great success in all media – both Glenda Jackson and Alan Bates manage it. Is there some reluctance in McKellen to alternate between stage and screen as other actors do? Does he really want to be a star, in fact? He certainly is starry-conscious – he loves stars, he loved working with Meryl Streep in *Plenty* finding her 'delightful' and the whole thing 'a delightful experience'.[12] As a friend told *The Observer*, popular success on film is 'the one area he hasn't cracked. I think it might irk him a bit. He'd really like to be Robert Redford.' Let us admit that McKellen hasn't become a star in the international sense. Is he a star of the theatre?

There are various definitions of what a star is in the theatre. *Someone who can recite the Alphabet/Telephone Directory and still keep an audience enthralled* is one description. Well, I'm not aware that McKellen has ever recited just the alphabet on stage, but he has certainly recited part of a telephone directory in his recital *Words, Words, Words* and the audience enjoyed that! *Someone who can fill the seats in a theatre no matter what the play is*, is a commercial definition given by Duncan Weldon. As we have seen Ian couldn't do that with *Cowardice* and of his other ventures in the West End, only *Richard II* and *Bent* brought people in; though *Henceforward* by Alan Ayckbourn had a respectable run in 1989/90. 'You can put Penny Keith's name up in any play and she'll fill a theatre for six months at least,' says Weldon.[13] Keith also risks her own money to present plays. *Someone who enters the stage and all eyes immediately focus on him*. Well, McKellen can enter a stage and be quite unobtrusive, if the part demands it. He lets the writer decide whether he should be dominant at that point or not. He can and does make the spectacular entrance, as in *Richard II* and *Wild Honey*, but he can be effacing as in *Macbeth* where all the actors entered at once to sit round the circle and one did not realize that McKellen was there. Peter Hall does not hesitate to call him a star – 'which, for me, is an actor who can be downstage with his back to the audience, in the dark, and still be the centre of attention'.[14]

McKellen has a quality that is indefinable, he is a charismatic actor, but he has not yet attained an instant recognition factor that is the *sine qua non* of stardom. One could, I imagine, walk down the street with him without anyone asking him for an autograph, which wouldn't happen with many a lesser actor who happens to have caught the public imagination. For this is exactly what he has not yet done. Stars form part of our fantasy life, we like them to be more glamorous, more fantastic, almost untouchable, so that we can dream about touching them. We can even dream about making love to them. Noel Coward, surely a star of stars, said that when he appeared on stage he had to make every member of the audience, men and women, want to go to bed with him. As yet, McKellen doesn't do that, though he has looks, plenty of charm, and knows how to ingratiate himself with an audience.

He is still a master of make-up, as Alan Dent noted so long ago, though nowadays he uses very little, perhaps shading to alter his cheekbones or to enlarge his eyes. More often than not he uses his own hair, keeping gel on his dressing-room table to style it (along with Johnson's Baby powder and a jar of honey from which he eats spoonfuls, sometimes actually drinking it before he goes on stage). 'If he does have a wig,' says Bob Peck, 'he makes it so much part of himself that you wouldn't know it was a wig.'[15] There is nothing on the technical side of his business that he doesn't work on and try to perfect.

It is perhaps a matter of character, and of upbringing. He is a Cavalier at heart, but one that has had a Roundhead upbringing. Lancashire piety and socialism, an inbred feeling that other people matter as much if not more than oneself and frugal standards are all part of his nature. 'He thinks he ought to have champagne in his dressing-room,' says Bob Chetwyn, 'but he can't quite bring himself to be that extravagant, so he has Veuve de Vernay.'[16] Though he does give champagne as gifts to people. He drives a very modest car – a recent acquisition, he always had a motor-bike – and has always lived in the shabbier parts of London. His first house was in Camberwell, paid for with money carefully put into building societies,[17] and he now lives in Narrow Street, overlooking the Thames with David and Debbie Owen as neighbours. Not Mayfair, or Kensington: not Hampstead or 'a little place in the country'. The house has three storeys, but is quite small. 'It is elegant, spare, stripped-wood Victorian. The only real flourishes are a lightning-blue front door and a terra-cotta bust of Shakespeare which squats on his riverside balcony.'[18]

His friends attest to his generosity. 'I remember,' says Bridget Turner, 'going to a wedding with another actress and Ian, and we had to stay overnight. When we two girls went to pay our bill we found that Ian had paid it.'[19] Sara Kestelman says that he is very supportive and he keeps in touch even if either she or he are on tour. 'He writes the most beautiful letters, beautifully expressed. And he can always help you with love if you are down.'[20] He is generous, too, in rehearsal: 'I remember when we were doing Richard,' reminisces Richard Cottrell, 'he went over and over again doing a small scene with Bagot and Bushey and Green – doing this way and that way to help release them and to get it right. He was wonderful like that.' Yet this expansiveness can be pulled back; if he thinks that anyone is intruding on private territory he will retire into himself and become impenetrable.

Although he is an innate showman and has plenty of charm – indeed, some people think that 'he flogs the charm too much' and that he is 'all actor. It's his passion, it's his life'[21] – he is also endearingly modest. His saying that he has to pull himself up to Judi Dench's level is indicative of this, and, once when I met him in a dressing-room and overwhelmed him with praise, he backed out of the door and didn't come in until I'd shut up.

'He dresses like a schoolboy', a friend who wishes to be anonymous said, and that criticism it true. You rarely see him in a suit – if he does put one on it looks as if it has been bought 'to allow' as children's clothes are, and the tie is never quite tied properly. He affects, like most actors, casual clothes, but his always look quite well-worn and rarely look as if they are designer, status symbol clothes. At Covent Garden, where he will sit in company seats in the Grand Tier, he will wear a Madras jacket with white cotton trousers. He wears schoolboy V-necked pullovers for interviews and used to wear flowered shirts when they were in fashion. Though he takes an interest in clothes he does, indeed, look as if he has unwillingly flung them on.

He is also frugal about holidays. 'He goes on walking holidays,' Elspeth Cochrane said, 'and he always writes you long letters when he is on them. He likes reading and does that widely and as much as his busy life lets him.'[22] In a profession which is always very secretive about what it is paid, Ian will usually say – there were several references to his earnings in the *South Bank Show* – and he always seems haunted by the fact that he hasn't been paid enough. As we have seen, he has, with the exception of his first job at the Belgrade, always got well above the national average. And now, when he is being paid the equivalent of a managing director of a medium-sized company he still went to Canada during his two-week break to do his One-Man Show 'and earn some more money'.

Rewards in the acting profession can be immense. If he were in the West End, McKellen's basic weekly wage would be double that he would get at the National, and he would get a good percentage of the 'take' as well, which could triple his money. 'I live on my voice-overs for commercials, and keep a wife and children on them, too,' an actor, of considerably less status than McKellen, told me. McKellen doesn't do this, though it is a lucrative part of show business, for besides the initial quite generous fee there is a royalty for each repeat. Some stars ask as much as twenty-thousand pounds for an 'appearance' in a commercial – Glenda Jackson once got three times that amount (which she gave to charity). Television can also be a lucrative source of income, Joan Collins, for example, getting nearly twice what McKellen gets in a year for just one episode of *Dynasty*. But McKellen prefers to do classic work and chooses what he does with discrimination, so the rewards are not, in money terms, as high as he would perhaps like. 'He could – he *should* – be earning two hundred thousand a year,' an actor told me.

It is perhaps understandable in a precarious profession that money is important to him, but, as he has been outstandingly successful in working continuously, it is part of the dichotomy in his character that he should be so concerned about it.

His character has a great divide in it. This can be seen in all his actions. The puritan North Countryman wars with the romantic actor; the generous friend wars with the frugal private person; the giving leading-man who helps lesser actors in his company wars with the self-centred star who is impatient with himself or any lack of professionalism. 'He expects everyone to do his or her job properly,' says Clare Fox.[23] He does his own superbly well, but can sometimes leave fellow players agape on stage. 'I remember once,' says Margery Mason, 'I suddenly found him mopping and mowing in the floor when I least expected it. That really left me with egg on my face.'[24] Other actors, such as Irene Worth, welcome this. Although he can, and does, improvize on the stage and always works at a part throughout a run, he is, as he admits, a very technical actor and proud of it. The feeling, the passion is always tempered by technique. He told Robert Cushman that he is 'a very technical actor indeed. When I come to a performance, there's nothing I do that I'm not aware of. Most nights that I'm on stage I do something, consciously or unconsciously, that I've never done before.' And in the same interview in 1978 he said, 'It's only very recently that I've had the courage to forget the technical side and think about the spiritual side. Not think about it, just let it happen.'[25]

To just let it happen is, perhaps, one of the hardest things for anyone who is at all intellectual to achieve. That McKellen is one of the most intelligent actors around is not in doubt. That he understands and can analyse a text meticulously with an intellectual director is also not in doubt. But how intelligent is he? Would he be considered intelligent in the outside world? Intelligence in the theatre is not necessarily needed, many gifted actors are not intellectuals, and though the greatest actors and actresses have intelligence, it is of a more usual non-intellectual kind. They are intelligent about people, not necessarily about texts. 'Acting is *instinct*,' Margery Mason says, 'instinct and observation.'[26] In reading some forty interviews which McKellen has given over the years, and reading pieces he has written himself (he says that he writes slowly and laboriously), I am often struck by a vividness of phrase or an immediate communication of emotion or thought. But on more careful reading I find the thought not carried through to its logical conclusion and the final effect is more of a clever undergraduate than a fine thinker. Take his undoubtedly sincere belief that the provinces should have good theatre. It is a worthy ideal, one that stems from his socialistic background, something about which he feels passionately, yet never once, has he, in public at least, actually committed himself to working out why this doesn't happen and how it could happen.

Today's audiences are very sophisticated, trained by television to expect a very high standard of entertainment. Even popular television has exceptional excellence of design, clothes, presentation. Audiences therefore expect this in the theatre. Gone are the days when a Donald Wolfit would draw in audiences all round the country by the magnetism of his personal performances, which were shown against abysmal sets, tatty costumes and a poor back-up cast. If in the space of one week-end one can see Makarova, McKellen, a first-rate thriller-series, a glossy soap opera like *Dynasty* and a Dickens serial on the TV, it is going to take a really powerful production and a very prestigious group of actors to entice people to a theatre. People like stars, and they can see them regularly on television. The RSC can take out non-starry tours, because the company itself is a star and confers its own prestige on anything it does, even its rare failures have quality! To send round a company of stars costs money, as indeed McKellen and Petherbridge found with the Actors' Company. Even then, when they were young and happy to live out of suitcases for a moderate wage, they found it difficult to sustain the Company, and now, with costs ever-spiralling and actors wanting even more money it would be impossibly hard to achieve. McKellen would undoubtedly reply that it is the duty of governments to subsidize this kind of work. But is it? While Governments should, and do, have the ability to be patrons, they have to consider the whole picture. They quite often decide that to impose more taxes for what is one of many interests they have to support would be wrong. They may feel there are many more worthy claims on what is, after all, everyone's money. Business patronage can be sought, but again, no actor has a right to it, over and above any other section of the community. Actors choose to be actors, as writers choose to be writers, and writers have few safety-nets of subsidy to support them.

Anyway, do actors want to work exclusively for a company? McKellen obviously enjoys being with a supportive group and does much to support his actors. But many actors prefer the varied life. One quite well-known leading man (who doesn't want to be named) said to me, 'I can earn more money in a year by doing several bit parts on television: a good twelve-week tour and one or two good engagements in places like Leicester and Watford with a chance of a West End transfer, than I could doing medium parts with the RSC or the National – and have more variety of work too.'

Do audiences always want to see the same dozen or so actors playing contrasting parts, often, just because they are the only parts available, and ones to which they may not really be suited? Even with a talented group of really chameleon actors this happens. But a group cannot take on one actor just for one play – economics won't allow it. On none of these questions has McKellen ever expressed an opinion in public. Many people in the Arts, seem to think that governments exist only to support the Arts, and forget that government money is *ours*, everyone's money, and that many people resent the Arts having money at all.

Another point to consider is whether company productions are always better than *ad hoc* ones. Admittedly the standard of productions in companies like the National or RSC is very high, but there are productions that are put together commercially that are just as good, and which survive changing casts.

How does McKellen see his job as an actor? That he is attached to the theatre and thinks that it is pre-eminent is obvious. He told Roberta Plutzik: 'I get enormous satisfaction out of the theatre. I agree with most actors that that's where, in the end, we belong. It's the most testing place ... On stage, the actor's job is to communicate the playwright's words and intentions to the audience. It's an enormous responsibility and takes a great deal of effort ... There's no doubt about it that actors, and other artists, are more obsessive than people in most other jobs. You have to delve into yourself in a way that you don't always have to do in other jobs. You cannot just turn up and do it, at least not while you're rehearsing or preparing. There is an intensity of concern and concentration to have the whole body and maybe memory at the service of a particular line or whatever is being delved into.

'At such times, an actor is extremely vulnerable, that's why actors call each other "darling" and "love", they couldn't work if they didn't feel surrounded by friends. That's why we make friends so easily in our work. If they are going to laugh at the risks we take or be critical of them or talk about them afterwards in an uncaring way, we wouldn't survive. We need trust and love in order to make ourselves vulnerable in our work. If that delicate process gets intruded upon, or is going badly, then the actor is likely not to have the resources to do anything more than scream like a child.'[27] And in a burst of enthusiasm he said to Anthony Holden: 'I don't look upon acting as a profession. I hate that word. Acting is a business. Show Business. God, how I love that phrase!'[28] On the negative side, he admits that, 'I'm not an innovator or leader, not in the sense of discovering a style or being *avant garde*.' Over and over again he says that an actor's job is to open out and show the audiences strong emotions. This is what, perhaps, he does best of all; becomes vulnerable, opens out and blasts a charge of emotion into the audience.

McKellen's reputation in this country rests on five brilliant performances: *Richard* II; Face in *The Alchemist*; Platonov in *Wild Honey*; the definitive Macbeth, and his meticulous, pitiless Iago. There are four other parts, in lesser plays, in which he gave superb performances: The Burglar in *Too True to be Good*; The Marquis of Keith; Bernick in *Pillars of the Community* and Max in *Bent*. Add to that an interesting Edward II, Hamlet, Coriolanus and Romeo, all of which were controversial, but then all great actors stir up controversy.

Let us concentrate on the five great classic roles – Richard, Face, Platonov, Macbeth and Iago. Three tragedies and two farces. Is there any common denominator between them? I think there is. All five men are isolated, heartless, even: all are playing a part, even Macbeth, unable to distinguish between reality and illusion. They all assume different characters for different people and none show any tenderness.

'Ian is really a superb character actor,' Jack Lynn told me,[29] 'and no one is better than he in a farce which has to be played with technique and without much heart.' With this I would agree. McKellen, with the exception of the one scene in *Bent*, shows very little tenderness on stage – sex, yes, but not tenderness. Look at the way he *devours* Judi Dench's face in *Macbeth*. The hunger of sex, not the tenderness of love. His Romeo failed ultimately because of this lack of tenderness, only apparent when he held the dead body of Juliet in his arms. He totally mis-said 'My Gracious silence' in *Coriolanus*, surely one of the loveliest lines from a man to a woman in Shakespeare, though he gave Wendy Morgan a very sexy kiss sometime afterwards. I asked an actress who had worked with him about this and she was reluctant to discuss it, but said, 'You cannot act what is not in your physical nature.'

McKellen talks about vulnerability, but this is a different quality – he can and does display vulnerability very often, changing suddenly into a small boy. But he doesn't radiate the tenderness of sex to women members of the audience and this puts a whole lot of parts out of his range. One wonders what his Othello, for instance, would be like. In interviews he speaks of playing Othello[30] as though he, too, had some doubt about it.

I have not considered his Saleiri for I did not see it. Jack Lynn, Bridget Turner and Richard Cottrell all assured me that it was brilliant and certainly the New York critics and the British one who saw it all agree. It was again, a character who was acting, not being himself. 'He is full of tricks,' another actress said to me, 'not instinctive. A technical actor. He doesn't ultimately show his real feelings.'

After Richard II, McKellen was considered a coming star, the bright, blazing young talent of his generation, making his claim before Jacobi or Bates, before Howard or Hopkins. But somehow it hasn't happened – yet. 'When I meet him, I sense a feeling of disappointment. He is a disappointed man,' an actor said to me. Maybe his wish to work so much in the provinces – a selfless and kind though, in my opinion, muddled wish – mitigated against this. Maybe he isn't ruthless enough? Maybe he tries to do too much and doesn't concentrate exclusively on being a star? He does seem to shudder away from the idea sometimes. Or maybe it is just his nature. There are certain artists, writers, actors, and above all poets who when they are young are very tender and perceptive, but unfortunately they do not develop as they grow older.

The great critic James Agate gave in his Diaries a list of things needed to become a great actor. The entry for 12 September 1941 reads:

Greatness in acting requires a combination of things not all of which are under the artist's control. Enough height and not too much; beauty, or if not beauty, then power to suggest it; brains and the ability to conceal them; physical health and the system of an ox; indomitable spirit and natural grit; the flair for the right opportunity; luck or the knack of turning bad luck to account; a ruthless capacity to trample on competing talents; *a complete lack of interest in the drama except in so far as it provided the actor with striking parts*. In addition to all this the great player, male or female, must possess that indefinable something which makes the ordinary man abase himself without knowing why.

How does McKellen measure up to this list? There are two which he seems to lack: he actually likes working with comparable talents and does everything to nurture them rather than trample on them; and he has a vivid, informed knowledge of the drama and has often taken subordinate parts.

McKellen, like Salieri, realizes that he hasn't yet touched the heights that his promise led us to expect – he hasn't in Benedict Nightingale's words slipped from eminence to pre-eminence. He foresees the future like Olivier and Gielgud, as always acting; perhaps doing more cameo parts in films or television. But what he really longs for 'above all would be to have a big popular success here. A Broadway hit like *Amadeus* comes, if you're lucky, once in a lifetime. I'd love something on that scale here at home. Perhaps a part like Olivier made out of *The Entertainer*.'[31]

Let us hope that it happens, for it would be wonderful for us all if that blazing talent really turned into a bright and beautiful comet. He has the undoubted talent, looks, voice, everything, plus stamina and intelligence. He is a wonderful actor to watch, even his mistakes are interesting, and if his performances do not always get critical acclaim there is no one, I think, who would deny his greatness (even if they don't actually *like* his acting).

Though Gielgud and Olivier are considered great now, they too had their share of dreadful notices when younger. If one aims high, then one is judged by the highest standards. McKellen would not wish otherwise for as he has said, it is all about being the best. Among the best he certainly is, and soon he could be the very best. Then the British theatre, already enriched greatly by him, will again give a pre-eminent actor to the world. Ian McKellen is an actor to his finger-tips, and like Coriolanus has already been crowned with oak leaves. Let's hope that the laurel leaves will now come.

Appendix

PRINCIPAL PARTS PLAYED BY IAN MCKELLEN AS A PROFESSIONAL ACTOR

THE BELGRADE THEATRE, COVENTRY 1961–2

A Man for All Seasons	Son Roper
When We Are Married	Fred Dyson
You Never Can Tell	Philip
Black Coffee	Tredwell
Celebration	Stan Dyson
End of Conflict	Mason
Mr Pickwick	Mr Snodgrass
Toad of Toad Hall	Chief Weasel
The Seagull	Konstantin
The Bride Comes Back	Joe Tilney
Much Ado About Nothing	Claudio
Happy Returns (Revue)	
Ten Little Niggers	
Irregular Verb to Love	
Semi-Detached	Tom
Noah	Shem

MAY 1963

The Big Contract	Robin Green

IPSWICH 1962–3

The Gazebo	Elliott Nash
Caste	
The Big Killing	
The Amorous Prawn	
The Keep	
David Copperfield	David
Aladdin	Chinese Policeman
How Dare We!	

Henry V   Henry
Luther
Arsenic and Old Lace
Long Day's Journey Into Night
I, John Brown
Salad Days
The Corn is Green   Evans
All In Good Time   Bridegroom

NOTTINGHAM 1963–4
Coriolanus   Aufidius
The Life In My Hands   John
The Bashful Genius   Winifred Hutchins
The Mayor of Zalamea   The Captain – Don Alvaro
Saturday Night and Sunday Morning   Arthur Seaton
Sir Thomas More   More

DUKE OF YORK'S 1964
A Scent of Flowers   Gogo (Godfrey)

NATIONAL THEATRE – LONDON AND CHICHESTER 1965
Much Ado About Nothing   Claudio (London only)
Armstrong's Last Goodnight   Protestant Evangelist
Trelawney of the Wells   Captain de Foenix

HAMPSTEAD THEN WEST END (ST MARTIN'S) 1965–6
A Lily in Little India   Alvin

ROYAL COURT 1966
Their Very Own and Golden City   Andrew Cobham

MERMAID 1966
O'Flaherty, V.C.   O'Flaherty
The Man of Destiny   Napoleon Bonaparte

OXFORD, LONDON (FORTUNE THEATRE) AND NEW YORK (HENRY MILLER) 1966–7
The Promise   Leonidik

LONDON (LYRIC THEATRE) 1968
White Liars   Tom
Black Comedy   Harold Gorringe

LIVERPOOL PLAYHOUSE MAY 1969
The Bacchae   Pentheus

PROSPECT THEATRE COMPANY: NOVEMBER 1968 TOUR
Richard II   Richard II

EDINBURGH FESTIVAL 1969 AND TOUR: MERMAID
THEATRE AND PICCADILLY THEATRE, LONDON
1969/70
Richard II   Richard II
Edward II   Edward II

TOUR, BOTH ENGLAND AND EUROPE: CAMBRIDGE
THEATRE, LONDON 1971
Hamlet   Hamlet

THEATRE UPSTAIRS 1970
Billy's Last Stand   Darkly

CAMBRIDGE THEATRE COMPANY: CAMBRIDGE AND
TOUR 1970
The Recruiting Officer   Captain Plume
Chips With Everything   Corporal Hill

CRUCIBLE THEATRE, SHEFFIELD 1971
Swan Song   Svetlovidov

ACTORS' COMPANY: CAMBRIDGE AND TOUR
INCLUDING EDINBURGH FESTIVAL 1972
Ruling the Roost   Page-boy
'Tis Pity She's a Whore   Giovanni
The Three Arrows   Prince Yoremitsu

EDINBURGH FESTIVAL AND TOUR 1973
The Wood Demon   Michael
The Way of the World   Footman

SHAW THEATRE
Knots

NEW YORK, BROOKLYN ACADEMY
King Lear   Edgar
plus *'Tis Pity, Way of the World* and
Knots

WIMBLEDON THEATRE 1974
Same repertoire as New York

YOUNG VIC 1975
Ashes   Colin

ROYAL SHAKESPEARE COMPANY: EDINBURGH FESTIVAL 1974 TOUR AND LONDON (ALDWYCH)
Dr Faustus   Faustus

LONDON (ALDWYCH) 1974-5
The Marquis of Keith   The Marquis
King John   The Bastard
Too True To Be Good   Aubrey Bagot
  (transferred to Globe)

STRATFORD-UPON-AVON NEWCASTLE AND LONDON 1976/7
Romeo and Juliet   Romeo
The Winter's Tale   Leontes (not transferred)
Macbeth   Macbeth (The Other Place, Main Theatre, Warehouse and Young Vic)

The Alchemist   Face (TOP and Aldwych)
Pillars of the Community   Bernick (Aldwych only)
Days of the Commune   Langevin (Aldwych only)
Every Good Boy Deserves A Favour   Alex

RSC TOUR 1978
Twelfth Night   Sir Toby Belch
The Three Sisters   Andrei

LONDON, ROYAL COURT, TRANSFERRING CRITERION 1979
Bent   Max

NEW YORK, BROADHURST
Amadeus   Salieri

LONDON, AMBASSADORS AND TOUR 1983
Cowardice   Boy

HAMPSTEAD
The Short List   Terry

NATIONAL THEATRE 1984-6
Venice Preserv'd   Pierre
Wild Honey   Platonov
Coriolanus   Coriolanus

Duchess of Malfi	Bosola
The Real Inspector Hound	Inspector Hound
The Critic	Mr Puff
The Cherry Orchard	Lopakhin

RSC 1989
Othello   Iago

Notes

CHAPTER ONE

1 Letter from Mesnes High School, formerly Wigan Grammar School
2 *People* Ed. Susan Hill, Pub. Chatto and Windus
3 Robert Cushman: *Observer Magazine*, 29 January 1978
4 Letter from Mesnes High School, formerly Wigan Grammar School
5 Elspeth Cochrane in interview with author 1985
6 *Sunday Times* Colour Supplement 2 January 1977
7 *Sunday Times* Colour Supplement 2 January 1977
8 *Sunday Times* Colour Supplement 2 January 1977
9 Mrs E. Parkinson in letter to author
10 *The Observer* 16 December 1984
11 Elspeth Cochrane in interview with author
12 Mrs E. Parkinson in letter to author
13 *The Times* 9 October 1976
14 Donald Torkell in conversation with author
15 Mrs E. Parkinson in letter to author
16 *The Boltonian* – the school magazine of Bolton School
17 *Daily Mirror* 7 October 1969
18 *The Boltonian*
19 *The Observer* 16 December 1984
20 *Bolton Evening News* 22 August 1961
21 *The Boltonian*
22 *The Boltonian*
23 *The Boltonian*
24 *The Boltonian*
25 *Sunday Telegraph Magazine* 14 January 1982
26 *She* April 1982
27 *People* Ed. Susan Hill, Pub. Chatto and Windus
28 *The Boltonian*
29 *The Boltonian*
30 Interview with author
31 *The Times* 9 October 1976

32 *People* Ed. Susan Hill, Pub. Chatto and Windus
33 *People* Ed. Susan Hill, Pub. Chatto and Windus
34 *The Times* 9 October 1976
35 *The Times* 9 October 1976
36 *People* Ed. Susan Hill, Pub. Chatto and Windus
37 *Woman and Home* May 1984
38 *TV Times* 17 August 1972
39 Interview with author
40 Interview with author
41 *Sunday Times* Colour Supplement 2 January 1977
42 *Sunday Telegraph Magazine* 14 February 1982

CHAPTER TWO

 1 J. Andrew in interview with author
 2 *The Times* 9 June 1981: John Heilpern
 3 Pat Garratt interview: *Woman's Journal*
 4 Clive Swift in interview with author, 1985
 5 *My Cambridge* by Eleanor Bron, Pub. Robson Books
 6 Clive Swift in interview with author, 1985
 7 *The Observer* 18 December 1984
 8 *Sir Peter Hall's Diaries*, Pub. Hamish Hamilton
 9 *Sir Peter Hall's Diaries*, Pub. Hamish Hamilton
10 *The Common Pursuit* by F. R. Leavis, p. 174, Pub. Chatto and Windus
11 'Word of Mouth': *The South Bank Show*, London Weekend TV 16
     December 1979
12 *New York Times*, 27 September 1981
13 J. Andrew in interview with author 1985
14 Clive Swift in interview with author 1985
15 *Playing Shakespeare* by John Barton, Preface by Trevor Nunn, Pub.
     Methuen
16 *The Guardian* 3 August 1977
17 J. Andrew in interview with author
18 Dr Richard Bainbridge in interview with author 1985
19 *The Observer* Magazine 29 January 1978 in interview with Robert
     Cushman
20 *The Observer* Magazine 29 January 1978 in interview with Robert
     Cushman
21 Richard Cottrell in interview with author 1985
22 *People* Ed. Susan Hill, Pub. Chatto and Windus
23 Clive Swift in interview with author 1985
24 *News Chronicle* 11 March 1959
25 *The Daily Telegraph* 11 March 1959
26 *Sunday Telegraph Magazine* 14 February 1982
27 Richard Cottrell in interview with author 1985

28 *The Times* 9 October 1976
29 *The Times* 9 March 1960
30 Marlowe Society's Archives
31 Richard Cottrell in letter to author 1985
32 Clive Swift in interview with author 1985
33 Clive Swift in interview with author 1985
34 J. Andrew in interview with author 1985
35 Interview with Michael Owen, *Evening Standard* 3 March 1978
36 *People* Ed. Susan Hill, Pub. Chatto and Windus
37 J. Andrew in interview with author 1985
38 Clive Swift in interview with author
39 Trevor Peacock in interview with author

CHAPTER THREE

1 *Time Out* 26 July 1984
 2 *Woman and Home* May 1984
 3 *People* Ed. Susan Hill, Pub. Chatto and Windus
 4 *People* Ed. Susan Hill, Pub. Chatto and Windus
 5 *Nuneaton Evening Tribune* 6 September 1961
 6 Elspeth Cochrane in interview with author 1985
 7 Bridget Turner in interview with author 1985
 8 Elspeth Cochrane in interview with author 1985
 9 Elspeth Cochrane in interview with author 1985
10 Philip Grout in interview with author 1984
11 Robert Chetwyn in interview with author 1985
12 Robert Chetwyn in interview with author 1985
13 Robert Chetwyn in interview with author 1985
14 Robert Chetwyn in interview with author 1985
15 Robert Chetwyn in interview with author 1985
16 *Playing Shakespeare*, p. 185, by John Barton
17 *East Anglian Times*
18 *East Anglian Times*
19 Robert Chetwyn in interview with author 1985
20 Elspeth Cochrane in interview with author 1985
21 *East Anglian Times*
22 Robert Chetwyn in interview with author 1985
23 *People* Ed. Susan Hill, Pub. Chatto and Windus
24 Clare Fox in interview with author 1985

CHAPTER FOUR

1 Clive Swift in interview with author 1985
 2 *People* Ed. Susan Hill, Pub. Chatto and Windus
 3 Elspeth Cochrane in interview with author 1985

4 *The Guardian*, interview with Catherine Stott, 10 February 1969
5 *People* Ed. Susan Hill, Pub. Chatto and Windus
6 *People* Ed. Susan Hill, Pub. Chatto and Windus
7 Programme – Nottingham Playhouse
8 *People* Ed. Susan Hill, Pub. Chatto and Windus
9 *People* Ed. Susan Hill, Pub. Chatto and Windus
10 *People* Ed. Susan Hill, Pub. Chatto and Windus
11 Emrys Bryson, *Nottingham Post*
12 Emrys Bryson, *Nottingham Post*
13 Emrys Bryson, *Nottingham Post*
14 Interview with Peter Ustinov by Ann Leslie in the *Daily Express*
15 Elspeth Cochrane in interview with author 1985
16 Interview with Elspeth Cochrane in letter to author
17 Emrys Bryson in *Nottingham Post*
18 Elspeth Cochrane in interview with author 1985
19 Elspeth Cochrane in interview with author 1985
20 The *Guardian*, interview with Catherine Stott 10 February 1969
21 McKellen, talk on Radio Forth 1984
22 Elspeth Cochrane in interview with author 1985
23 *The Times*, interview with Edward Petherbridge by John Higgins, 3 July 1985
24 Talk with Radio Forth 1984
25 *The Times* 23 November 1965
26 *Plays and Players* March 1966
27 *Plays and Players*
28 Interview with author 1979
29 *Who's Who in the Theatre*
30 *Oxford Mail* and *Times* Group papers
31 *Judi Dench* (p. 54) by Gerald Jacobs, Pub. Weidenfeld and Nicolson
32 *Judi Dench* (p. 54) by Gerald Jacobs, Pub. Weidenfeld and Nicolson
33 *New York Times* 27 September 1981
34 *Sunday Times* 25 February 1968

CHAPTER FIVE

1 *The Times* Saturday Review 30 August 1964
2 Richard Cottrell in interview with author 1985
3 Interview with author
4 Interview with author
5 Richard Cottrell in interview with author 1985
6 *The Times Educational Supplement*: interview with Peter Ansorge, 16 June 1972
7 Richard Cottrell in interview with author 1985
8 Toby Robertson in interview with author 1985
9 *The Times* 5 November 1968

10 Richard Cottrell in interview with author 1985
11 Elspeth Cochrane in interview with author 1985
12 Clive Swift in interview with author 1985
13 Interview with Catherine Stott, *The Guardian* 10 February 1969
14 Interview with Catherine Stott, *The Guardian* 10 February 1969
15 Interview with Michael Owen, *Evening Standard* August 1972
16 Toby Robertson in interview with author 1985
17 Toby Robertson in interview with author 1985
18 Toby Robertson in interview with author 1985
19 Toby Robertson in interview with author 1985
20 Sara Kestelman in interview with author 1985
21 Elspeth Cochrane in interview with author 1985
22 *The Times* 30 August 1969
23 Bill Beresford in interview with author
24 *Sunday Times* 31 August 1969
25 Toby Robertson in interview with author 1985
26 Bridget Turner in interview with author 1985
27 Robert Chetwyn in interview with author 1985
28 Bridget Turner in interview with author 1985
29 Clare Fox in interview with author 1985
30 Interview with Michael Owen, *Evening Standard* 1969
31 Eddie Kulukundis in interview with author 1985
32 *Playing Shakespeare* by John Barton, Pub. Methuen
33 Toby Robertson in interview with author 1985
34 *Playing Shakespeare* by John Barton, Pub. Methuen
35 Robert Eddison in interview with author 1985
36 Interview with Robert Cushman, *Observer Magazine* 29 January 1978
37 Interview with Rosemarie Wittman 17 October 1970
38 Trevor Peacock in interview with author 1985
39 Trevor Peacock in interview with author 1985
40 *Cambridge Evening News* 26 October 1970
41 *Cambridge Evening News* 9 October 1970
42 Interview with Catherine Stott, *The Guardian* 10 February 1969
43 Toby Robertson in interview with author 1985
44 Robert Chetwyn in interview with author 1985
45 Toby Robertson in interview with author 1985
46 Robert Chetwyn in interview with author 1985
47 Robert Chetwyn in interview with author 1985
48 Robert Chetwyn in interview with author 1985
49 Robert Chetwyn in interview with author 1985
50 Interview with Patrick Wymark, *The Times* 29 March 1971
51 Interview with Patrick Wymark, *The Times* 29 March 1971
52 *Nottingham Evening Post* 1971
53 *The Guardian* 25 March 1971
54 *The Times* 16 April 1971

55 Elspeth Cochrane in interview with author 1985
56 Jack Lynn in interview with author 1985
57 Eddie Kulukundis in interview with author 1985
58 Elspeth Cochrane in interview with author 1985
59 Tim Pigott-Smith in interview with author 1985
60 Tim Pigott-Smith in interview with author 1985
61 Robert Chetwyn in interview with author 1985
62 Tim Pigott-Smith in interview with author 1985
63 Tim Pigott-Smith in interview with author 1985
64 Robert Chetwyn in interview with author 1985
65 *Sunday Times* 8 August 1971
66 *No Turn Unstoned* Ed. Diana Rigg
67 British Council Archives

CHAPTER SIX

1 *Sunday Times* 27 August 1972
2 *The Times Educational Supplement* 16 June 1972
3 Richard Cottrell in interview with author 1985
4 *The Guardian* 1 September 1972
5 Margery Mason in interview with author 1985
6 Richard Cottrell in interview with author 1985
7 Robert Eddison in interview with author 1985
8 Richard Cottrell in interview with author 1985
9 William MacDonald in interview with author 1985
10 Richard Cottrell in interview with author 1985
11 Letter to author 1985
12 Margery Mason in interview with author 1985
13 Robert Eddison in interview with author 1985
14 Margery Mason in interview with author 1985
15 Margery Mason in interview with author 1985
16 Margery Mason in interview with author 1985
17 *New York Times* 15 February 1974
18 Robert Eddison in interview with author 1985
19 Margery Mason in interview with author 1985
20 Clare Fox in interview with author 1985
21 Clare Fox in interview with author 1985
22 *Evening Standard* 13 September 1972
23 Ronald Eyre in interview with author 1985
24 Robert Eddison in interview with author 1985
25 Margery Mason in interview with author 1985
26 Robert Eddison in interview with author 1985
27 Margery Mason in interview with author 1985

CHAPTER SEVEN

1 Interview with Tom Sutcliffe, *The Guardian* 14 December 1977
2 Interview with Roberta Plutzik, *She*, April 1982
3 Interview with Tom Sutcliffe, *The Guardian* 14 December 1977
4 Interview with Caryl Brahms, *The Guardian* 26 January 1975
5 *Harpers and Queen* April 1977
6 *The Times* 9 October 1976
7 *The Times* 9 October 1976
8 Sara Kestelman in interview with author 1985
9 *Judi Dench* by Gerald Jacob, Pub. Weidenfeld and Nicolson
10 Sara Kestelman in interview with author 1985
11 Ronald Eyre in interview with author 1985
12 Sara Kestelman in interview with author 1985
13 Ronald Eyre in interview with author 1985
14 Sara Kestelman in interview with author 1985
15 Sara Kestelman in interview with author 1985
16 Telephone conversation with author 1985
17 *The Times* 9 October 1976
18 In interview with Tom Sutcliffe, *The Guardian* 14 December 1977
19 In interview with Tom Sutcliffe, *The Guardian* 14 December 1977
20 'Word of Mouth', *South Bank Show*
21 Eddie Kulukundis in interview with author 1985
22 In interview with Tom Sutcliffe, *The Guardian* 14 December 1977
23 *The Times* 1976
24 Donald Sinden in interview with author 1977
25 *Playing Shakespeare* by John Barton, Pub. Methuen
26 *Playing Shakespeare* by John Barton, Pub. Methuen
27 Interview with John Walker *The Observer* 21 March 1976
28 Sara Kestelman in interview with author 1985
29 John Andrew in interview with author 1985
30 *Daily Telegraph* 2 April 1976
31 Interview with author 1979
32 Interview with John Heilpern, *The Times* 9 June 1981
33 *Shakespeare Superscribe*, Pub. Penguin/Capital Radio
34 *Daily Mail*
35 British Council Archives
36 In interview with Alix Coleman, *TV Times* 30 October 1982
37 *The Times* 9 October 1976
38 RSC Archives
39 *Diaries, Sir Peter Hall,* p. 314, Pub. Hamish Hamilton
40 *The Times* 9 October 1976
41 Bob Peck in interview with author 1985
42 *Judi Dench* by Gerald Jacobs, Pub. Weidenfeld and Nicolson
43 Bob Peck in interview with author 1985

44 *Judi Dench* by Gerald Jacobs, Pub. Weidenfeld and Nicolson
45 Bob Peck in interview with author 1985
46 *Judi Dench* by Gerald Jacobs, Pub. Weidenfeld and Nicolson
47 *South Bank Show*: October 1985
48 *Shakespeare Superscribe*, Pub. Penguin/Capital Radio
49 *Shakespeare Superscribe,* Pub. Penguin/Capital Radio
50 Interview with author
51 Judi Dench in interview with author
52 Ronald Eyre in interview with author 1985
53 Bob Peck in interview with author 1985
54 Bob Peck in interview with author 1985
55 Tim Pigott-Smith in interview with author 1985
56 Sara Kestelman in interview with author 1985
57 *The Guardian*
58 Interview with Michael Owen, *Evening Standard* 3 March 1978
59 Interview with Michael Owen, *Evening Standard* 3 March 1978
60 Interview with Michael Owen, *Evening Standard* 3 March 1978

CHAPTER EIGHT

1 Interview with Michael Owen, *Evening Standard* 3 March 1978
2 Interview with Michael Owen, *Evening Standard* 3 March 1978
3 Richard Cottrell in interview with author 1985
4 Bob Peck in interview with author 1985
5 RSC Archives 1978
6 Feature by Victoria Radin, *The Observer* 10 September 1978
7 Feature by Victoria Radin, *The Observer* 10 September 1978
8 Feature by Victoria Radin, *The Observer* 10 September 1978
9 Feature by Heather Neill, *The Times Educational Supplement* 6 October 1978
10 Feature by Heather Neill, *The Times Educational Supplement* 6 October 1978
11 *Peterborough Evening Times*
12 *Peterborough Evening Times*
13 *Peterborough Evening Times*
14 *Peterborough Evening Times*
15 Feature by Heather Neill, *The Times Educational Supplement* 6 October 1978
16 Feature by Heather Neill, *The Times Educational Supplement* 6 October 1978
17 *Financial Times*
18 Interview with Sheridan Morley, *The Times* 12 June 1978
19 Interview with Sheridan Morley, *The Times* 12 June 1978
20 *New York Times* 27 September 1981
21 Interview with author

CHAPTER NINE

1 Clive Swift in interview with author 1985
2 Bill Wilkerson in interview with author 1977
3 Jack Lynn in interview with author
4 Robert Chetwyn in interview with author 1985
5 Eddie Kulukundis in interview with author 1985
6 Clare Fox in interview with author 1985
7 Eddie Kulukundis in interview with author 1985
8 Jack Lynn in interview with author
9 Interview with author
10 Clare Fox in interview with author 1979
11 John Andrew in interview with author 1985
12 Tim Pigott-Smith in interview with author 1985
13 *Evening Standard* 1980
14 *Sunday Times* 27 July 1980
15 *Sunday Times* 27 July 1980
16 Robert Cottrell in interview with author 1985
17 Gerald Pollinger in interview with author 1985
18 Interview with Charles Spencer, *Evening Standard* 6 June 1980
19 Interview with Charles Spencer, *Evening Standard* 6 June 1985
20 Interview with Charles Spencer, *Evening Standard* 6 June 1985
21 *New York Times* October 1980
22 Interview with Charles Spencer, *Evening Standard* 6 June 1985
23 Interview with John Heilpern, *The Times* 9 June 1981
24 Richard Cottrell in interview with author 1985
25 Jack Lynn in interview with author 1985
26 Bridget Turner in interview with author 1985
27 Interview with John Heilpern, *The Times* 9 June 1985
28 Richard Cottrell in interview with author 1985
29 *New York Times* 27 September 1981
30 Interview with John Heilpern, *The Times* 9 June 1985
31 *Evening Standard* 13 February 1981
32 *New York Times* 24 April 1981
33 *New York Times* 27 April 1985
34 Press Association
35 Interview with Nicholas de Jongh, *The Guardian* 4 August 1983
36 Interview with Nicholas de Jongh in *The Guardian* 4 August 1983
37 Interview with John Heilpern, *The Times* 9 June 1981
38 Interview with Nicholas de Jongh, *The Guardian* 4 August 1983

CHAPTER TEN

1 James Fenton in *Darling, You Were Marvellous!*
2 Feature by Michael Billington in *Drama* magazine 1983

3 British Council Archives
4 British Council Archives
5 British Council Archives
6 British Council Archives
7 British Council Archives
8 British Council Archives
9 British Council Archives
10 British Council Archives
11 Feature by Michael Billington in *Drama* magazine 1983
12 British Council Archives
13 *Daily Express* 28 October 1982, by James Murray
14 Interview with Alix Coleman in *TV Times* October 1982
15 Interview with Alix Coleman in *TV Times* October 1982
16 Interview with Alix Coleman in *TV Times* October 1982
17 Interview with Alix Coleman in *TV Times* October 1982
18 Duncan Weldon in interview with author 1985
19 Interview with Nicholas de Jongh in *The Guardian* 4 August 1983
20 Duncan Weldon in interview with author 1985

CHAPTER ELEVEN

1 Interview with Anthony Holden, *Sunday Express Magazine* 16 December 1984
2 Talk on Radio Forth
3 The South Bank Show, October 1985
4 The South Bank Show, October 1985
5 *Drama* magazine 1984/4
6 *Drama* magazine 1984/4
7 *Drama* magazine 1984/4
8 *The South Bank Show*, October 1985
9 *The South Bank Show*, October 1985
10 *The South Bank Show*, October 1985
11 Interview with Michael Owen, 30 March 1984
12 Interview with Peter Roberts, *Plays and Players* June 1985
13 *Drama* magazine 1985
14 *TV Times* 19 October 1985
15 Maria Aitken in interview with author 1984
16 In interview with Alexandra Shulman in the *Sunday Times* 1 July 1984
17 *Drama* magazine 1985
18 *Drama* magazine 1985
19 Irene Worth in telephone conversation with author 1985
20 Benedict Nightingale, *New Statesman* 20 December 1984
21 Benedict Nightingale, *New Statesman* 20 December 1984
22 *The Sunday Times* 22 September 1985
23 National Theatre Press Release 29 July 1985

24 Interview with Anthony Holden, *Sunday Express Magazine* 16 December 1984
25 Robert Eddison in interview with author 1985
26 Feature with Janet Watts in *The Observer* 30 June 1985
27 Feature by Janet Watts in *The Observer* 30 June 1985
28 Feature by Janet Watts in *The Observer* 30 June 1985
29 Interview with Nicholas de Jongh in *The Guardian* 5 July 1985
30 Interview with Peter Roberts, *Plays and Players* June 1985
31 Interview with Peter Roberts, *Plays and Players* June 1985
32 Interview with John Higgins, *The Times* 3 July 1985
33 Heather Neill in *The Times Educational Supplement* October 1985
34 *The South Bank Show*, October 1985
35 Michael Ratcliffe, *The Observer* 7 July 1985
36 Interview with Nicholas de Jongh in *The Guardian* 5 July 1985

CHAPTER TWELVE

1 Sarah Gristwood in *Ms London* 12 September 1985
2 *The Observer* 16 December 1984
3 Duncan Weldon in interview with author
4 *The Observer* 16 December 1974
5 Elspeth Cochrane in interview with author 1985
6 John Andrew in interview with author 1985
7 In interview with Roberta Plutzik, *She* April 1982
8 Felicity Kendal in interview with author 1978
9 Interview with Michael Billington, *Sunday Telegraph Magazine* 14 February 1982
10 In interview with Sarah Gristwood, *Ms London* 12 September 1985
11 In interview with Roberta Plutzik in *She* April 1982
12 *The South Bank Show*, October 1985
13 Duncan Weldon in interview with author 1985
14 *The Observer* 16 December 1984
15 Bob Peck in interview with author 1985
16 Robert Chetwyn in interview with author 1985
17 Robert Chetwyn in interview with author 1985
18 Interview with Michael Billington, *Sunday Telegraph Magazine* 14 February 1982
19 Bridget Turner in interview with author 1985
20 Sara Kestelman in interview with author 1985
21 *The Observer* 16 December 1985
22 Elspeth Cochrane in interview with author 1985
23 Clare Fox in interview with author 1985
24 Margery Mason in interview with author 1985
25 Interview with Robert Cushman, *The Observer Magazine* 29 January 1978
26 Margery Mason in interview with author 1985

27 In interview with Roberta Plutzik, *She* April 1982
28 In interview with Anthony Holden, *Sunday Express Magazine* 16 December
    1984
29 In interview with Jack Lynn
30 In interview with Anthony Holden, *Sunday Express Magazine* 16 December
    1985
31 In interview with Anthony Holden, *Sunday Express Magazine* 16 December
    1984

Bibliography

An Actor in his Times John Gielgud (Sidgwick and Jackson, 1979)
The Common Pursuit F. R. Leavis (Chatto and Windus, 1952)
Diaries, Sir Peter Hall Ed. John Goodwin (Hamish Hamilton, 1983)
Ego James Agate, Ed. Tim Beaumont (Harrap, 1976)
The Garrick Year Margaret Drabble (Weidenfeld and Nicolson, 1964)
Judi Dench Gerald Jacobs (Weidenfeld and Nicolson, 1985)
Laurence Olivier John Cottrell (Weidenfeld and Nicolson, 1975)
My Cambridge Ed. Ronald Hayman (Robson Books, 1977)
No Turn Unstoned Diana Rigg (Elm Tree Books, 1982)
Playing Shakespeare John Barton (Methuen with Channel Four, 1984)
The Royal Shakespeare Company David Addenbrooke (Kimber, 1974)
Shakespeare in the Theatre Richard David (C.U.P., 1978)
You Were Marvellous James Fenton (Jonathan Cape, 1983)
Ramblings of An Actress Sheila Hancock (Arrow Books, 1989)

Index